JOHN SEVIER

*The University of North Carolina Press, Chapel Hill, N. C.;
Baker and Taylor Company, New York; Oxford University
Press, London; Maruzen-Kabushiki-Kaisha, Tokyo; Edward
Evans & Sons, Ltd., Shanghai; D. B. Centen's Wetenschappelijke
Boekhandel, Amsterdam.*

From a portrait by Charles Wilson Peale in the possession of the Tennessee Historical Society and reproduced by their courtesy.

JOHN SEVIER

JOHN SEVIER

PIONEER OF THE OLD SOUTHWEST

BY

CARL S. DRIVER, Ph.D.

*Assistant Professor of History
in Vanderbilt University*

CHAPEL HILL
THE UNIVERSITY OF NORTH CAROLINA PRESS
1932

COPYRIGHT, 1932, BY
THE UNIVERSITY OF NORTH CAROLINA PRESS

PRINTED IN THE UNITED STATES OF AMERICA BY EDWARDS & BROUGHTON
COMPANY, RALEIGH, N. C.; BOUND BY L. H. JENKINS, INC., RICHMOND, VA.

TO
LEOTA

PREFACE

THIS STUDY of John Sevier is an attempt to explain the events in his colorful and checkered career and to examine older and romantic traditions in the light of more recent historical findings. He was frontiersman, Indian fighter, land speculator, state senator, congressman, only governor of the State of Franklin, and first governor of Tennessee. This powerful figure in the Old Southwest has lived in history as one of its heroes, but few attempts have been made to discover if the glamor and romance which surround his name have had a real or an idealized character as their source. The author has attempted to contribute something of reality to the estimate of a very real and human person.

Half forgetful of the early days, students for the most part have interpreted Tennessee history in the light of a dominating figure or an epic struggle—Andrew Jackson or the Civil War. Sevier has been looked upon as a leader of minor importance in the history of the state. Historians are now attempting to reconstruct the early history of the commonwealth which he helped to found and to protect. He furnished a vital energy and a determinative influence in the life and times of the Old Southwest and of Tennessee. His methods were no better and no worse than those of others in commanding positions during that era of individualism and expansion. He showed remarkable ability as a military leader of frontiersmen against the savages and the English, an ability which made possible his speculative ventures in the acquisition of land. When he is cast upon the background of the frontier and its restless pioneers, he assumes a position of some dignity and importance above others of his time and section. This study attempts to sketch his silhouette upon the shadowy canvas of that age of conquest.

PREFACE

I desire to express my appreciation for their kindness and aid to the officials in charge of the following libraries and manuscript collections: Vanderbilt University Library, Library of the State of Tennessee, and the Tennessee Historical Society Library, Nashville, Tennessee; Lawson McGhee Library, Knoxville, Tennessee; Manuscript Division, Library of Congress, and the State Department Archives, Washington, D. C.; Draper Collection, Wisconsin Historical Society, Madison, Wisconsin; and the Massachusetts Historical Society, Boston, Massachusetts.

I feel a deep sense of gratitude for the aid which has been given me by my friends in the preparation of this work. Dr. Frank L. Owsley, of Vanderbilt University, first interested me in Sevier. He generously gave of his time, directing and criticizing this study during my research and writing. Dr. Walter L. Fleming, of Vanderbilt University, proposed valuable suggestions as to organization and arrangement of material. Professor Irby R. Hudson, of Vanderbilt University, and Dr. A. P. Whitaker, of Cornell University, read the manuscript and offered many helpful criticisms. Dr. W. C. Binkley, of Vanderbilt University, and Judge John H. DeWitt, of Nashville, Tennessee, gave encouragement and suggestions concerning its publication. My wife, Dr. Leota S. Driver, has been my constant companion and critic in research and composition. She read the manuscript and proof, made the index, and gave invaluable criticisms without which the work could not have been completed. Mr. Edd W. Parks, of Vanderbilt University, also read the proof and contributed greatly to the improvement of the volume. Its failings result from my inability to incorporate successfully the suggestions of these friends.

CARL S. DRIVER

Vanderbilt University
July 23, 1932

TABLE OF CONTENTS

Chapter		Page
	PREFACE	vii
I.	FROM SHENANDOAH TO WATAUGA	1
II.	"'CHUCKY JACK," SCOURGE OF THE CHEROKEES	16
III.	KING'S MOUNTAIN	39
IV.	A FRONTIER LAND GAMBLER	61
V.	GOVERNOR OF FRANKLIN	79
VI.	IN CONGRESS AND IN THE TERRITORY	99
VII.	FIRST GOVERNOR OF TENNESSEE	117
VIII.	HONESTY OR FRAUD?	145
IX.	THE SEVIER-JACKSON FEUD	168
X.	GOVERNOR AND "WAR HAWK"	190
XI.	PIONEERING PAST	211
	BIBLIOGRAPHY	219
	INDEX	227

JOHN SEVIER

CHAPTER I

FROM SHENANDOAH TO WATAUGA

JOHN SEVIER was a product of the frontier, a pioneer of the most aggressive type. The society in which he lived moved with a restless surge toward the untamed and unsettled West. The current drew him into the Old Southwest, where he soon proved himself to be a virile leader of frontiersmen. With his arrival in the Holston settlements, there began one of the most romantic careers in the conquest of the West. Daring and impetuous, magnetic and powerful, he came to represent the heroic life of the border. His life was thrilling in many respects, but its romance accompanied the hard and often cruel elements present in the westward advance of civilization. Sevier was a pioneer and a leader of pioneers in a time which required perseverance and vision as well as sternness of character and singleness of purpose. He became Tennessee's first hero.

The West fascinated Sevier. He felt its romance, which perpetually intrigued young Americans. It was a land where all ills were remedied and where men were free and untrammeled by restrictive conventions. It symbolized opportunity. Like many young men in the newly settled regions, he listened to stories of the fantastic wonders to be seen in unclaimed lands beyond the rim of civilization. Strange narratives of ever present dangers regaled his mind. Exultation of spirit in the face of danger caught his restive imagination and strengthened his determination to experience the thrill of subduing the untamed. He felt the lure which had enticed men since the first settlers touched the coast of the new world—the West, and again, the West. To men of the tidewater, the hand of fortune seemed to beckon from the piedmont; to those of the piedmont, it called from the mountains. When they reached that wall, they sought out its breaks and sighted the river valleys and wide plains beyond.

Men moved into the West for various reasons. The call of adventure led some to leave the ease and opulence of a stable society and to strike out boldly into the interior. They were interested in taking part in the fearless conquest that was being waged against the savage. Tales of blood and cruelty attracted instead of repelled them, and they desired to participate in the deeds of valor. Other independent spirits chafed under the paternalism of the ruling classes in the East. They saw in the freedom of the frontier a release from a tutelage which irked and irritated. The restrictions and expenses of government bore heavily upon them. They could not see the benefits of a system which they supported but in the operations of which they could not participate. Men, too, sought the oblivion which might be found on the fringe of civilization. Sorrow as well as crime was left behind and forgotten. Debts could be evaded, and the toils of the law, sidestepped. The poor man could become financially independent. The trader passed freely across the borderland, gaining a rich profit from the exchange of cheap trinkets, firearms, and firewater for valuable furs.

None of these adventurers really pushed the line of civilization from the Alleghenies to the Mississippi. They played their part in presenting the gilded picture to the potential pioneer. Upon no one of them, nor all of them combined, could the West depend for stability and consolidation. *Land* constituted the fundamental consideration in the westward movement of settlers. Possession of an estate guaranteed social and economic independence. The availability of land determined the progress of the frontier. The reports which came to the substantial citizen in the established areas caused him to see the possibilities of acquiring land easily and cheaply. Accounts told him that the unclaimed soil was fertile and that the greatest difficulty to claiming it lay in subduing the savage. The method of acquisition did not deter him, for an estate could be had by title for the asking or without title for the taking. Pioneers thought that Providence had placed within their reach these limitless areas of unimproved soil. The natives were insensible to its worth and made no efficient use of the fertile acres nominally in their possession. Why should not the savage make way for civilization?

The seaboard offered precedents for such an attitude. There, wealth centered in land. Great tracts had been granted to individuals, and the influential men of any colony were those who held the largest portions of the most productive sections. The possession of an estate carried with it a commanding position in government. Consequently, the ideal to which every enterprising man aspired was that of the country gentleman who possessed a large tract of land.

The average individual, such as Sevier, could not realize this ideal. The choice land of the settled regions had already been appropriated; only the unproductive and undesirable remained. The fertile river bottoms were no longer open to any settler unless he could pay dearly for them. Even then he resented reimbursing their owner with a substantial profit for something which had been given by a benevolent government. He looked forward to the time when he might move to the free lands of the West and there establish himself upon somewhat the same conditions enjoyed by the envied neighbor. The venture meant sacrifice and strife, but these had always been the price of property to the pioneer. The steady movement into the back country of individuals motivated by such ideals steadily advanced the frontier and conquered the West.

Beyond the limits of established society, the settler found himself released from many of the restraints which formerly held him. After he had braved the rough life for a time, he became careless of its dangers. He then disposed of his improved lands for a consideration and moved on into the interior to repeat the process. Bold, hardy, and independent, he feared neither beast nor savage. He was dauntless, rude of speech, frank, and hospitable. Although he was an individualist, necessity forced him to coöperate with his neighbors. Common perils bound him to his friends. He formed the advance guard which moved to the frontier and waited for civilization to overtake him.

All characteristics of the pioneers blended in the personality of John Sevier. He was settler and speculator, adventurer and trader, Indian fighter and law-maker. He moved into the West with the frontier and participated in the various activities of the border. His whole life was connected with the development of the West, and he died in its service.

Sevier descended from French-English stock. His grandfather emigrated from France to England, probably because of religious persecution.[1] It seems that the original family name was Xavier, but when this immigrant renounced his allegiance to France, he anglicized his name

---

[1] There is no direct evidence that he was a descendant of the family of Francis Xavier. It is entirely possible that he was, but this family connection is purely an inference. Cf. F. M. Turner, *Life of General John Sevier*, p. 12.

to Sevier. Tradition intimates that this French grandfather married a Miss Smith of London. Two of their children, Valentine and William, ran away from home when young and came to America. They landed at Baltimore, probably about 1740, and Valentine, father of John Sevier, pushed into the interior. He settled in the Shenandoah Valley of Virginia on Smith's Creek in what was then Augusta, now Rockingham County, where he married a Miss Joanna Goade. Here he adopted the usual methods of acquiring a fortune upon the frontier. He became a farmer, trader, and merchant. By 1753 he owned a tavern and had a substantial trade in furs and rum with the Indians and the settlers.[2]

In 1740 the Shenandoah Valley was a part of the frontier. Settlement had begun there about eight years earlier, near the present town of Winchester.[3] Indians remained in the Valley until 1754, but in that year they suddenly disappeared from this fertile region, leaving the whites in complete possession.[4] The savages had appeared peaceable enough prior to that time, but when they crossed the Alleghenies ahead of the ever advancing settlements, their peaceable manners left them, and for a period of ten or twelve years following their departure they visited depredations upon the Valley settlers. The last great outrage in the Valley occurred in 1766,[5] after which time the settlers lived in peace, protected by the great wall of mountains to the west.

---

[2] "Moravian Diaries," *Virginia Magazine of History and Biography* (1904), pp. 144-47.

[3] Samuel Kercheval, *History of the Valley of Virginia*, p. 31.

[4] *Ibid.*, p. 49.

[5] *Ibid.*, p. 103; Jos. A. Waddell, *Annals of Augusta County, Virginia*, p. 129, n. The author of the *Annals* questions this date, feeling "quite sure that it is not correct. Bouquet concluded a treaty with the Indians in November, 1764, and it is not probable that the massacre mentioned was perpetrated nearly two years afterwards during a time of peace. Most likely it occurred in August, 1764."

Valentine Sevier also interested himself in the acquisition of land and became something of a speculator. The county records of the region show that he sold different tracts of real estate during this period.[6] His membership in a company of militia in 1742 indicates that he interested himself in military affairs.[7] Little is known of his life in the Shenandoah Valley. A record remains of a sale of all his moveable property in 1763 to a man in Augusta County. By that time he had moved into Frederick County.[8] It is probable that he invested in lands in Frederick and sold his moveable property when he moved to that county from Augusta. He is reputed to have been an inveterate gambler and drinker, always in easy circumstances but never wealthy.

It is supposed that John Sevier's birthplace was located about six miles southwest of the present site of New Market, a town which he founded in his young manhood.[9] He was born on September 23, 1745,[10] the oldest of a family of seven children, five boys and two girls. Early in his life his father moved for a time to Fredericksburg because of Indian troubles, and while there John attended school a part of the time. When the family returned to the Valley, he entered a school in Staunton. A story re-

---

[6] J. W. Wayland, *History of Rockingham County Virginia*, p. 349.

[7] "Militia Companies in Augusta County in 1742," *Virginia Magazine of History and Biography*, VIII, 280.

[8] Wayland, *op. cit.*, p. 429.

[9] *Ibid.*

[10] This is the supposed date of his birth. It is taken from the Draper Manuscripts, Draper's Notes, XXX, 351-64, and is an account derived from Sevier's son, George W. Sevier, in an interview dated Feb. 16, 1844. There are two letters from G. W. Sevier to Dr. Draper, Feb. 9, 1839, and Apr. 28, 1841, in regard to John Sevier. The first one mentions no date; the last one states that he had no knowledge of the year or month of his father's birth, but it states that he was the oldest of the family. Evidently some sort of evidence had been examined between the time the letters were written and the time of the interview.

mains of how two sisters saved his life when he fell into a mill-race near that place. After leaving school he entered his father's store and later became a partner in the business. This probably occurred in 1763.[11]

At the age of sixteen he married Sarah Hawkins, a young lady near his own age and of a very respectable family. He settled in the Long Meadows and devoted his time to farming. Later he moved to the present site of New Market where he purchased a tract of land which he laid off in town lots and sold. He erected a tavern and continued his occupations of farming and merchandising.[12] He gave three acres of land to the Baptists upon which to build a church, and at the present time it is still in the possession of that denomination. The historians of Tennesseee have asserted that Governor Dunmore granted him a captain's commission in the militia during his young manhood in Virginia.[13] If the commission came to him during his life in that state, he had impressed the people of the Valley with his qualities of leadership and courage at a very early age.[14]

About 1770 he removed from New Market to Millerstown in Frederick County within the limits of the present county of Shenandoah. Woodstock is supposed to have been the village which the settlers called Millerstown in

---

[11] Draper MSS, Draper's Notes, XXX, 351-64.

[12] It is said that some of the logs from this original tavern are at present in the walls of one of the old hotels in the village. This information was given me by Adam Turner, an antiquarian of Rockingham County, Virginia.

[13] J. G. M. Ramsey, *Annals of Tennessee*, p. 108; John Haywood, *Civil and Political History of the State of Tennessee*, p. 62.

[14] Draper MSS, Draper's Notes, XXXII, 140 f. This is Draper's report of an interview with Major James Sevier, son of John Sevier. Major Sevier reported that his father had been out on several scouts near "the close of the old French War"; George W. Sevier, in Draper's Notes, XXX, 351-64, reported that the commission must have been issued after his removal to the Holston region.

those days.[15] Dunmore County (now Shenandoah) separated from Frederick in 1772, and, if Sevier held a commission in the state militia, he most probably received it during his residence there.[16]

Very little information can be obtained concerning his life in the Shenandoah Valley. The frontier, however, trained him for his career of advancing civilization to the west. Farming interested him, as it interested other pioneers, but he came to look upon land as a commodity to be bought and sold, not merely to be purchased and improved as a place of permanent residence. He moved from place to place, which indicates that he engaged in a limited amount of speculation in soil. He continued the business of merchant and trader as well, occupations which he inherited from his father. Some of the children of his large family were born before his emigration to the southwest. His life, so far as is known, passed as pleasantly and as congenially as might be expected under the difficult and adverse conditions of pioneer existence. He found delight and recreation in hunting and in the rough sports in which the settlers indulged. What success he realized from his business is entirely unknown. His father never became wealthy because of habits of drinking and gambling, but there is no indication that young Sevier acquired the weaknesses of his parent to an intemperate degree.[17]

Just what specific motives caused the Sevier family to leave the fertile Valley of Virginia and to emigrate to the southwest remain obscure. Up to this time the family had shown an unsettled and roving disposition. As merchants, traders, and farmers, they were ready and willing to move from place to place if there appeared to be an advantage in the change. There is no indication that the father and his sons had financial reverses of any kind which would have

---

[15] Wayland, *op. cit.*, p. 348.   [16] Ramsey, *op. cit.*, p. 108.
[17] Draper MSS, Draper's Notes, XXX, 351-64.

made them desirous of selling out and moving to a region where they might find cheap lands. In 1765 several transactions in land were recorded which might have had a bearing upon the question. On May 10 of that year Valentine Sevier sold to his son John 378 acres of land on Smith's Creek in Frederick County. The next day John Sevier and his wife mortgaged the same tract to two men of King George County.[18] Whether financial pressure was brought to bear upon the family by 1772 is purely conjectural. If Sevier really received a commission in the state militia, this fact would show that he stood well in the community and would eliminate the possibility that social conditions necessitated the move. By this time the Valley was settling up rapidly, but not so rapidly that it would have been necessary for the family to make the long journey to Watauga in order to find suitable lands. The Indians had ceased to give serious trouble, and it seemed evident that the Valley was destined for a peaceful development.

On the other hand, it is certain that reports concerning the land to the southwest circulated in the Valley. The geographical conditions of the Appalachian region made it a highway of the westward movement.[19] Communication between the two sections encountered no more serious obstacles than were to be found within the Valley itself. The settlers who moved into the Watauga region thought they still lived within the confines of the state of Virginia and under the jurisdiction of laws with which they had become familiar.[20] The members of this trading, farming, and speculating family naturally turned their eyes in

---

[18] Wayland, *op. cit.*, p. 349.

[19] E. C. Semple, *American History and Its Geographic Conditions*, p. 56.

[20] Ramsey, *op. cit.*, p. 135: Petition of the inhabitants of Washington District, etc., ". . . many of your petitioners settled on the lands of the Wataugah, &c., expecting to be within the Virginia line."

the direction of the cheap lands on the Watauga, and this may be accepted as at least one of the most probable reasons for the transfer to the border settlements. The Seviers constituted one of many families which moved west with the frontier, willing to pay the price in hardship for the profits which lured them into the wilds.

John Sevier and his brother Valentine probably made several trips to the Watauga settlements before the family emigrated. It was reported that they went out in the years of 1771 and 1772,[21] and it is likely that Valentine settled upon the Holston in the latter year.[22] In the late autumn of 1773 John Sevier, with his family, his father and mother, and the families of his brothers, moved to the southwest and settled on the north side of the Holston in the Keywood settlement.[23] Three years later John moved his family to the Watauga, near the present location of Elizabethton.

The Watauga Association drew up its constitution in 1771, and John Sevier is mentioned as being one of the commissioners elected by the people and also a member of the first court established to maintain order in the settlement.[24] At first thought there appears to be some mistake here: If Sevier did not move to the settlement until 1773, how was it possible for him to have been named as a commissioner and a member of the court in an Association formed two years earlier? The date of the removal of the family to the Holston may be rather definitely fixed, not only from the accounts given by Sevier's sons, but also from the record of a deed made by Valentine and Joanna Sevier to Michael and David Holsinger for land on Long

---

[21] Draper MSS, Draper's Notes, XXXII, 140 f.
[22] *Ibid.*, XXX, 351-58.
[23] *Ibid.*, XXXII, 140 f. This is James Sevier's account. He was about nine years of age when this trip was made, and his account is accepted by others of his family.
[24] Ramsey, *op. cit.*, pp. 106-7.

Meadows. This deed was made on August 15, 1773.[25] It most probably represented a sale of land just prior to the departure for the southwest. James Sevier, John's oldest son, stated that they arrived in the Holston settlement on Christmas Day, 1773.[26] In view of these facts, 1773 may be accepted as the year of the removal to the West. This need not be accepted, however, as positive proof that Sevier had not been elected to official positions under the Association in 1771. It would appear reasonable to suppose that he had visited the region before he definitely decided to emigrate, and his son George stated that his uncle Valentine moved to the Holston in 1772.[27] If these reports are true, as they seem to be, neither the date of the removal nor the election to office before that date need be looked upon as inaccurate, for it is entirely probable that Sevier had already obtained possession of the land to which he later moved and that he had remained there for a time during the year in which the Association was formed. The frontier had developed his qualities of leadership, and the people of the new settlement desired to have the most capable of their citizens in control of affairs. His election to these official positions leads to the acceptance of the report that he had held a captain's commission from Lord Dunmore while in Frederick County. The people believed they were still in Virginia, and the acquisition of Captain Sevier proved an important one to the community. On Sevier's part, this preferment may have added weight to the influences which caused him definitely to decide to bring his family.

The move to the southwestern frontier at once placed him in a position of power and influence. Two years after his removal he aided in the negotiation of a treaty which

---

[25] Wayland, *op. cit.*, p. 9.
[26] Draper MSS, Draper's Notes, XXXII, 140 f.
[27] *Ibid.*, XXX, 351-58.

resulted in some of the most important cessions of land made by the Indians up to that time. On March 19, 1775, Charles Robertson leased from the Cherokees a large tract of land in the valleys of the Holston, Watauga, and New rivers.[28] The settlers expected the lease to be indefinite in its duration, in reality a purchase, for no pioneer feared that he would be forced to relinquish land obtained in any manner from the savages after it had been improved to any degree. Robertson made the lease for the Association, and Sevier, among others, signed the deed. A month or two later Sevier received a patent for some of the land included within the bounds of this area. At the time they obtained the lease, Jacob Brown, under similar conditions, purchased two tracts of land lying on the Nolachucky River.[29] These purchases were made a few days after those of Richard Henderson on behalf of the Transylvania Company, which had opened the Kentucky country for settlement, and the combined acquisitions presented a boundless opportunity to pioneers and speculators. Sevier had no connection with the Transylvania Company, but he was greatly interested in the Watauga region. The frontiersmen owed much to Henderson and his company for providing the opportunity to treat with the Indians under circumstances most favorable for success.

These leases were made in violation of English regulations published in the Proclamation of 1763.[30] No private citizen possessed legal authority to purchase land from the Indians. The Watauga citizens had previously held their lands beyond the line designated by the officials of the Crown by reason of an agreement with the Cherokees which had no permanency, and of course they wished to

---

[28] Ramsey, *op. cit.*, pp. 119-20; A. Henderson, *The Conquest of the Old Southwest*, p. 224.

[29] Ramsey, *op. cit.*, p. 121. [30] Henderson, *op. cit.*, p. 201.

perfect their title to the land already held and to acquire the right to extend their holdings. It seems certain that they were influenced in this course by the Henderson project, which they were induced to believe in accord with English law; that is, Judge Henderson believed that, in spite of the regulations of the British government, a purchase would stand the test of legality.[31] Actually, the legality is open to question, for Henderson based his judgment upon a private opinion of certain English judges, and not upon a case appearing in court. The American Revolution effectually prevented any attempt to test the authority under which they obtained the concessions, and in the end the states confirmed the claims of the settlers.

In his capacity as commissioner of the Watauga Association Sevier, together with the other members, signed a petition on behalf of the western settlers asking that the district west of the mountains be incorporated into the state of North Carolina.[32] The petition stated that the area had been left out of the state of Virginia when the line between the two states had been extended.[33] The North

---

[31] *Ibid.*, p. 202, n. 137.

[32] Ramsey, *op. cit.*, p. 134: "The document appears to be in the handwriting of one of the signers, John Sevier, and is probably his own production."

[33] This misunderstanding of the location of the boundary was possibly accentuated by the temporary provision adopted after the Treaty of Lochabar, when the Holston River was made the line until the true line should be ascertained according to the original charter. See *State Records of North Carolina* (hereafter cited as *SRNC*), XIV, 314: A resolution was passed by the Virginia House of Delegates, June 15, 1779, in which it was proposed to the state of North Carolina that an act be passed by the latter state making provision for the protection of the inhabitants of Virginia who had taken up lands which had fallen to North Carolina, and that North Carolina should give these settlers preëmption claims. ". . . This proposition is made to the Assembly of North Carolina because, upon running the Cherokee boundary subsequent to the treaty of Lochaber, it was agreed that a due west course from Sleep rock to the intersection of the Holston river, and

Carolina legislature granted their request, and representatives of this western district, which they named Washington, participated in the Provincial Congress of North Carolina which met at Halifax in November, 1776. Sevier, John Haile, and Charles Robertson served as delegates from the frontier.[34]

Sevier had risen rapidly from the time of his removal to the Holston. His personal characteristics made him popular with his friends and neighbors, and his success in office was due to his good sense, his affability, and his devotion to the public welfare. Flattering estimates of his personal traits have been rendered by those who knew him. Haywood said that he "was endowed by nature with those rare qualities which make the possessor in all places and with all people an object of attention and a depository of their confidence—qualities which cannot be learned, and which cannot be kept from observation."[35] Ramsey painted a vivid picture of him: "He was fluent, colloquial, and gallant—frolicsome, generous and convivial—well informed, rather than well read. Of books he knew little. Men, he had studied well and accurately. Oral communications had been the source of his mental culture and his knowledge. He was impulsive, but his impulses were high and honorable. . . . He was without pride—if that feeling is not one of the ingredients that constitute a laudable

---

down the same, should be a temporary Boundary until the Line should be ascertained according to charter which sanctified the Settlement of the country under the jurisdiction of this State, and because it may prevent the strife and contention that may otherwise ensue." The Treaty of Lochabar was drawn up Dec. 12, 1770. For the line provided by this treaty, see *Va. Mag. Hist. & Biog.*, IX, 362; also Henderson, *op. cit.*, pp. 192-93.

[34] *Colonial Records of North Carolina*, X, 951: "Mr. John Sevier, one of the members from Watauga Settlement and Washington District, appeared, subscribed the Test, and took his seat in Congress." Also see Ramsey, *op. cit.*, p. 139.

[35] *Op. cit.*, p. 61.

ambition—for he was ambitious—not of anything low or ignorable; he was ambitious of fame, character, distinction and achievement."[36] Many other eulogies have been heaped upon the man who thus began his interesting career among the southwestern pioneers.

It is certain that the new friends whom he had made upon the border held him in high esteem. The year 1776 became one of the turning points in his career. It marked his entry into state politics. The first Indian war of any importance in which he took part began in that year. The Revolutionary struggles were crystallizing. His adopted country had become a part of North Carolina. The final mark of distinction opened to him the door of opportunity through which he became the idol of the Southwest. The Congress at Halifax promoted him to the office of lieutenant colonel of Washington District.[37] Sevier may have attracted the pioneers by his brilliant personality, and he may have commanded their respect by his devotion to the public good, but his military prowess blazed the path by which he trod into their hearts and became their hero. It was a feeling common to the frontier —the protector who shielded them from the savage became their ideal.

---

[36] *Op. cit.*, pp. 108-9.   [37] *SRNC*, X, 998.

CHAPTER II

'CHUCKY JACK, SCOURGE OF THE CHEROKEES

SEVIER'S career as an Indian fighter in the Southwest began in 1776. The uprising there resulted from the Revolutionary troubles which started in the early part of the year, and it is probable that Sevier's participation in quelling it, though negligible, had some influence in securing for him the commission of lieutenant colonel of Washington District. The organization of a regiment for the western settlements became necessary on account of the Indian hostilities.

Before this time the settlers on the Watauga and Holston rivers had enjoyed comparative quiet from Indian attacks. But with the actual resistance of the colonies to the mother country, the frontiersmen believed that the English government had adopted the policy of using the Indians as allies in the attempt to maintain its power in America. They clearly understood the resentment of the savages against them because of their desire for Indian lands. The British had sought to limit western expansion. Now the pioneers believed that English agents were attempting to induce the savages to destroy the settlements. By limiting the western movement, the British government had protected the Indians, but the colonists had nevertheless continued to advance into the West.[1] They were now convinced that British emissaries, while posing

---

[1] Ramsey, *op. cit.*, p. 109. This gives Cameron's attempt to drive the Watauga settlers from the Indian lands.

as protectors of the Indians, had persuaded the savages to exterminate the aggressive settlers.[2] The indignation of the Wataugans became very bitter when this idea circulated among them. Colonel Arthur Campbell of Virginia was reported to have referred to it as an "infernal malignity" which had been "reserved to be exhibited to the world in the reign of George III."[3]

The hatred of the settlers was directed particularly against Stuart and Cameron, the British Indian agents in the South. The frontiersmen believed that these men had planned attacks against the colonists of Georgia, South Carolina, North Carolina, and Virginia, with the fixed intention of driving them from the Indian territory.[4] They feared that an English army would land upon the coast of West Florida, pass through the Creek and Chickasaw country, and with the Indians as allies strike a devastating blow against the settlements.[5] Letters which were supposed to have been written by Stuart to those whom he thought sympathetic to the British cause were circulated among the settlers. It was explained that friends of the settlers had given warning, and in this manner the scheme had leaked out.

The English agents, contrary to this belief, had not only not attempted to instigate the Indians against the settlers in 1776 but in reality had sought to prevent the savages from making the attack. Zealous patriots in the Revolutionary cause had used the credulity of the westerners as a means to increase their opposition to the mother country.[6] But the settlers accepted the informa-

---

[2] *SRNC*, X, 763-85. This is a report of Stuart concerning his and Cameron's relations with the Indians.   [3] Haywood, *op. cit.*, p. 60.

[4] A. V. Goodpasture, "Indian Wars and Warriors," *Tennessee Historical Magazine* (hereafter cited as *THM*), IV, 28.

[5] *SRNC*, X, 606-7.

[6] Philip M. Hamer, "John Stuart's Indian Policy During the Early Months of the American Revolution," *Mississippi Valley Historical*

tion as true, and it produced the intended effect. Their hatred of the British became greatly intensified when they believed that these agents were inciting hordes of bloodthirsty savages to kill them and destroy their property.

Other information came from traders who knew that the Indians were preparing to go on the warpath.[7] Nancy Ward, an Indian woman friendly to the whites, gave definite advices of these preparations to traders who relayed the news to leaders in the settlements.[8] Immediately the people fled to the forts and called to the state governments for aid. The frontiersmen instantly recognized the danger and adopted plans to defeat the movement at its inception. The Indians depended upon secrecy and surprise, but the settlers forestalled them by leaving their farms and taking refuge behind adequate defenses. Some casualties occurred, but the pioneers suffered no serious losses.

The state governments adopted a method of drastic punishment of the hostile Indians. Each of the states affected sent forces to retaliate and drive out the savages. Colonel Christian led an army of two thousand men from Virginia. General Rutherford commanded about the same number from North Carolina, while Colonel Williamson led another of equal strength from South Carolina. A strong force was mobilized in Georgia under Colonel McBury and led to the frontier.[9] These armies marched into the western country and proceeded to lay waste the Indian villages with a devastation which forever broke

---

Review, XVII (December, 1930), 351-66; Philip M. Hamer, "The Wataugans and the Cherokee Indians in 1776," *East Tennessee Historical Society's Publications*, No. 3 (January, 1931), pp. 108-25.

[7] *Ibid.*, p. 149.

[8] Haywood, *op. cit.*, p. 60; Goodpasture, *op. cit.*, p. 28.

[9] W. R. Garrett and A. V. Goodpasture, *History of Tennessee*, pp. 61-62.

the effective offensive strength of the Indians. From this time forward the whites of the Southwest always assumed the offensive in Indian wars. They burned village after village and destroyed large stores of provisions. These forces visited a terrible vengeance upon the savage.[10] The treaties of Dewitt's Corner and Long Island brought the war to an end in July, 1777.[11]

During most of this warfare, Sevier lived in the fort at Watauga. It appears that the western settlers left the punishment of the Indians to the military forces sent out by the states, while they remained behind the defenses protecting their families and property. A fort was located generally as near the center of the settlement as possible. This position made it convenient for the inhabitants to remain within its protection when any signs indicated the presence of Indians in the neighborhood. In the Watauga fort the families of Sevier and his associates, Robertson, Carter, Greer, and others found refuge. The defense rested in the hands of James Robertson, and Sevier acted as one of his most energetic supporters. An incident occurred during an attack upon this fort which has often been cited as the beginning of a romance between Sevier and the woman who later became his second wife. Catherine Sherrill was surprised by an Indian attack while milking a cow outside the walls of the fort. The defenders of the fort hurriedly closed the gates and locked her out. She ran to the palisades and, aided by Sevier, climbed to safety. Just why this incident should have been magnified by some writers is unaccountable except upon the ground that tradition may be easily expanded. One of Sevier's sons mentioned the incident but did not

---

[10] Ramsey, *op. cit.*, pp. 152-57, gives an excellent account of this retaliation.

[11] For a copy of this treaty of Long Island and an explanation of the events connected with it, see Haywood, *op. cit.*, pp. 501-14.

connect it at all with the marriage of his mother and father, and another son made no mention of it.[12]

While the militia retaliated against the Indians, Sevier and his colleagues represented the western settlements in the Halifax Congress. As this convention met late in the autumn, the representatives of Watauga and Washington District had left their homes in comparative safety. This accounts partly for the fact that Sevier played a negligible rôle in the fighting. He would have been most interested, possibly, in the expedition led by Colonel Christian against the Overhill Towns, but no record remains that he engaged in any offensive operations at this time. He received his appointment as lieutenant colonel during the time of the campaign. The organization of the Washington regiment indicated that the people of the West planned to engage in their own defense and expected to protect themselves without depending upon the military forces east of the mountains. It formed one feature of the general plan of organization made necessary by the Revolutionary disturbances. John Carter received appointment as colonel of the regiment, and under his direction Sevier resumed his military activities.

When the victors negotiated the Treaty of Long Island, which brought this early Indian war to an end in 1776, the whites regretted the absence of one of the most influential chiefs, Dragging Canoe. They felt that his absence indicated the lack of a desire for peace with the colonists by his group of Indians.[13] This suspicion proved correct. The followers of the disaffected chiefs of the Cherokees withdrew from those who had agreed to make peace with the whites and to give up their lands.

---

[12] Draper MSS, Draper's Notes, XXX, 351 f; XXXII, 140 f. Theodore Roosevelt, *The Winning of the West*, I, 292, gives the popular version of this incident. [13] Haywood, *op. cit.*, pp. 506, 512.

Dragging Canoe and his followers entered into communication with Governor Hamilton at Detroit and promised to aid the British in the reduction of the frontiers. He collected a band of about a thousand warriors from the Cherokees and other tribes who were influenced to oppose the advance of the whites into Indian territory. This band, known as the Chickamaugas, ranged from Georgia to Pennsylvania.[14] The success of Colonel George Rogers Clark against Vincennes and Kaskaskia led Hamilton to push his preparations against the pioneers. A supply of goods worth $125,000 was collected at Chickamauga for distribution to these Indians. The capture of Hamilton by Clark released these marauders from the influence and direction of the British governor, and they then turned against the Holston settlements.

An expedition was organized against them under the command of Colonel Evan Shelby, and he applied a policy of destruction of their towns and goods so as to put an end to their raids. This force destroyed eleven of their towns and burned twenty thousand bushels of corn, together with the stores of provisions and goods provided by the British. The invaders brought back with them one hundred and fifty horses, a large number of cattle, and a great quantity of deerskins, all of which they sold at public auction.[15] The success of this expedition constituted one factor in the failure of the British to form the Indians of the Northwest and of the Southwest into a coalition against the colonies.

Sevier did not take part in this expedition.[16] In the

---

[14] *Ibid.*, p. 72.   [15] *Ibid.*

[16] James Sevier said that his father and Colonel Carter were probably serving in the North Carolina legislature at the time of Shelby's expedition. Draper MSS, Draper's Notes, XXXII, 140 f. There is no mention, however, of their names in the lists of members of either House of the Assembly in the session beginning May 3, 1779. Washington

early part of the year 1780 he probably saw some service in scouting against the Indians along the Holston and Tennessee rivers. At the head of a small body of ten or twenty men he went into the Indian territory and watched for signs of an approaching enemy. He also kept an eye on the Tories, who began to forment trouble in the western settlements about this time. Their activities among the pioneers will be reviewed in connection with the rising of the frontiersmen against the British.

Increased activity among the groups of settlers on the outposts filled the years from 1776 to 1781. They continued the work of improving their lands and increasing their holdings. The threat of the British came first from the west and the south, and it appeared that the possessions of the frontiersmen might be wrested from them by a savage foe. Then the forces of disaffection began to work from within, and it seemed that anarchy would result. Another threat followed, this time from the east. Rapid immigration added to the uncertainty, for it was difficult to distinguish between friend and foe among the newcomers. Out of this chaotic condition Sevier emerged as a leader of the military forces of the district. He did not take a prominent part in either of the important campaigns against the Indians prior to 1780. His work lay principally in the field of organization and in the protection of the homes and families of those actually living on the frontier. As has been said, in the early years of the warfare the infant settlements depended upon the

---

County was not represented. *SRNC*, XIII, 735, 784. Major John Sevier reported to Dr. Draper that "In '79 Colo Sevier and John Carter were elected to the Legislature; but so troublesome were the Tories that they did not dare leave their families and the country, and did not attend—'79 was a troublesome Tory year on the Western Waters." Draper's Notes, XXXII, 222. This appears to establish the fact that Sevier and Carter were elected but did not serve.

military forces of the states for protection. Without the prompt help from these states the line of settlement would have been swept back across the mountains. The growth of the West progressed so rapidly that by 1780 it was possible for the pioneers, who had been weak only a few years earlier, to repay this debt in full measure. They defeated the British forces which had overrun the Carolinas and threatened the settlements from those states.

In the spring of 1780 Sevier departed from the Holston. It is uncertain whether he moved directly to the Nolachucky or whether he lived several years on Little Limestone. It is possible that he went first to the Nolachucky, then moved to Little Limestone, and finally, about 1783 settled permanently on the Nolachucky.[17] He had mills on Little Limestone and continued his occupation as merchant and farmer. On the bank of the Nolachucky River he built his homestead—he called it a plantation—and named it Plum Grove. He occupied this residence during most of his Cherokee wars, and because of its location the Indians gave him the name of " 'Chucky Jack." The residence was not "forted," but its owner built a house which provided a certain amount of protection—the doors were braced and portholes were cut—and furnished a temporary defense in case of emergency. He also served as clerk of the county court, having been appointed in 1778 at the organization of Washington County.[18]

---

[17] Draper's MSS, Draper's Notes, XXXII, 140 f. On the authority of James Sevier, his father moved to the south bank of the " 'Chucky" in '78, then moved to Limestone Creek in the spring of '80, and in the fall of '83 he moved back to the bank of " 'Chucky." Draper's Notes, XXX, 351 f; Draper MSS, 11DD168.

[18] Ramsey, *op. cit.*, p. 181; "Records of Washington County," *American Historical Magazine* (hereafter cited *AHM*), V, *passim*. Sevier was also a member of the Assembly which drew up the law opening the land office in 1777. See *SRNC*, XII, 265.

His success in any line seems to have been determined by his genial good nature and by his ability to make loyal friends. He was a natural leader of men. The stern discipline of military life did not make a martinet of him. He gave his commands as to equals, and, because these orders appealed to his men as being wise and practical, they gave unquestioned obedience. This loyalty of his friends formed one of the outstanding features of his success throughout his whole career. Military leadership did not draw him apart from his fellows, and the spirit of real democracy, so prominent a characteristic of the frontier, loomed especially large in John Sevier. His interests linked him inextricably with those of his neighbors —he had ambition, but this ambition did not embrace the nation, it remained local to the end. The surest path to public esteem lay in military leadership, and Sevier always wished to be at the head of the militia.

The Battle of King's Mountain carried Sevier forward in the public estimation to such a degree that it is necessary to add a more detailed study of that event in a separate chapter. In the absence of the settlers on this campaign another Indian uprising began, possibly induced by the knowledge that the frontiers lacked the necessary protection. The soldiers returned just in time. Sevier ordered the Washington County troops to be mustered for an expedition against the offending Cherokees. Without waiting for this muster to be completed, he started out with one hundred and seventy men and marched to intercept the invaders. The first skirmish occurred at Long Creek and ended in an Indian retreat.[19] This campaign was the first in which Sevier had complete charge and the first that he conducted without other aid than that from his own county. His activity on this occasion

---

[19] Garrett and Goodpasture, *op. cit.,* p. 87.

met with some criticism, however, though not from the neighbors whom he led. Some thought that he should have waited for reinforcements, which were advancing from Virginia under Colonel Arthur Campbell. This criticism came from the adherents of Joseph Martin, the North Carolina Indian agent. They complained that this move was a rash one because it apprised the Indians of the approach of the army before the force arrived at a position where it could act efficiently. Sevier, never very solicitous of the rights of the Indians, quite frequently came into conflict with those appointed to care for the interests of the natives.[20]

Sevier pushed on into the Indian country with his small force to meet the Cherokees before they crossed the French Broad River and overtook the Indian force at Boyd's Creek, a small tributary of the French Broad. He sent a small party of men ahead to locate the Indians and to decoy them to Sevier's force. This ruse was successful.

---

[20] Draper MSS, 3XX4: Account of Wm. Martin to Dr. Draper: ". . . Col. Sevier of Washington went on, of his own accord, with some three or four hundred men, several days before the army—met with a party of Indians—had a little fight—killed a few, and retired some distance waiting for the main army. This was complained of at the time not only as an unauthorized move, but as apprising the Indians of their approach, before the army was in a situation to act efficiently. It was thought that the motive of Sevier was to get glory to himself. He and my father did not agree. The former was at the head of the party that was continually intruding on the rights of the Indians—which often provoked hostilities, and which, in a great measure, paralyzed the efforts of the other to preserve peace, as was his office. And I believe that all the outbreaks of the Cherokees after Christian's campaign of 1776 might be traced to the invasion of the whites. . . ."

This is an admirable statement of the viewpoint of the Indians and of the agents who were appointed to look after Indian affairs. While it was made by one who was personally at enmity with Sevier, it gives the correct attitude of Sevier toward the savages. The reference to the battle of Boyd's Creek as "a little fight" is a patent attempt to minimize Sevier's popularity and shows that the prejudices of the father were shared by the son.

The plan of battle divided the forces into three divisions under the immediate command of Sevier, Major Jesse Walton, and Major Jonathan Tipton. Sevier commanded the center, Walton the right wing, and Tipton the left. The two wings expected to swing in a sort of enveloping movement and to attempt to encircle the Indians. This maneuver succeeded except for one detail which resulted in the escape of many of the Indians. Tipton did not get into position and did not maintain his advance, which allowed a space to remain uncovered through which the Indians fled.[21] The savages lost twenty-eight or thirty killed, while the whites suffered no casualties, only one man being slightly wounded. Sevier, acting as commander, carried out his project with precision and energy. He is reported to have been one of the party in the advance which decoyed the Indians into the ambuscade of the whites. An Indian in a tree attempted to shoot him; he escaped another by running him down with his horse. A bullet grazed his head cutting off part of his cue. The army returned to an island in the French Broad River and awaited the advance of Colonel Campbell.

That officer consumed several weeks in coming up with his forces. The provisions of the little company under Sevier became exhausted, and the men foraged for game, but they were unsuccessful and had to live upon haws. They finally found a lean cow and a calf which helped out somewhat. Colonel Campbell reached the island several weeks after the battle. They resumed their advance and marched upon Chota Town, one of the chief villages of the Cherokees. There they found plenty of provisions, but the town had been hurriedly abandoned by the Indians.

---

[21] Draper MSS, Draper's Notes, XXXII, 140 f; *ibid.*, XXX, 351; Ramsey, *op. cit.*, pp. 262-64; Haywood, *op. cit.*, pp. 74-75. Haywood places the battle in 1779, but evidently he was incorrect as to the date.

From this place as a base, they moved against the towns along the Tennessee River, among them being Tellico and Hiwasse. They destroyed all these towns and extended the policy of desolation to the Chickamauga strongholds. The army applied the torch to each in turn, destroyed provisions and ruthlessly devastated Indian property. The force returned to Chota, where representatives of the Indians made peace with the whites.[22] Upon the return of the white forces, they found settlers erecting cabins in the wake of the army as far in the Indian country as the French Broad River. There is no reason to suppose that Sevier, with his sensitiveness in regard to the soil, had not noticed the fertile and attractive lands in the region visited by the soldiers.

Stealthy hostilities of the Indians caused another expedition under Sevier to march against them early in the spring of 1781. With something over a hundred men he advanced against the Middle Settlements of the Cherokees. This company killed fifty warriors, captured many women and children, and burned fifteen or twenty other towns with all food supplies. The settlers lost one man killed and had one wounded.[23] During the summer of that year Sevier led about the same number of men in another raid. He visited the Cherokee settlements on Indian Creek with the same sort of punishment meted out to the Middle Settlements. In an engagement fought at War Ford, his forces again routed the Indians.

Immediately after these expeditions, Sevier and Shelby received a call from General Greene for aid against Cornwallis.[24] Sevier raised two hundred mounted men for

---
[22] Draper MSS, Draper's Notes, XXXII, 140 f; Ramsey, *op. cit.*, pp. 266-67.

[23] Haywood, *op. cit.*, pp. 111-12; Ramsey, *op. cit.*, pp. 268-69; Draper MSS, Draper's Notes, XXXII, 140 f.

[24] Draper MSS, Draper's Notes, XXXII, 140 f.

this purpose, crossed the mountains, and joined forces with Marion. Colonel Shelby also joined this army. They took part in the capture of Monk's Corner, which fell through a stratagem employed by Shelby. After the evacuation of Charleston, the forces from the frontier returned to their homes.

In 1782 Sevier and a body of about two hundred men entered upon another campaign of the same nature as those of the previous year. Their raid extended into Georgia on the Coosa and Estenaula rivers. A comparatively long period of peace followed this invasion, during which the settlers occupied themselves with the problem of their relation to the state of North Carolina and with the organization of their own government of Franklin.[25]

The Hiwasse campaign of 1786 was the next important expedition for Sevier. With one hundred and sixty mounted men, he crossed the Unaka Mountain to Hiwasse, where he destroyed the Valley Towns. Spies brought news of locating a large Indian trail leading toward the mountain. John Watts, a daring and cunning chief, led the savages. This leader was destined to have an important influence in the affairs of the Cherokee Nation from this time forward, and in many instances he communicated with Sevier concerning Indian affairs. This warrior attempted to lead the settlers into an ambuscade, but Sevier ascertained that at least a thousand warriors composed the band, and so he prudently retreated.

The government of North Carolina attempted to placate the Indians at the expense of the western settlers. This furnished one of the primary causes for the attempt at self-government made by the western counties. The State of Franklin resulted from the dissatisfaction of the

---

[25] Ramsey, *op. cit.*, pp. 272-73.

frontiersmen at measures taken by the state and represented an interesting separatist movement of the West, which will be discussed in a separate chapter.

After Sevier served his term as the only governor of this separatist movement, he found himself, at the end of its operation, the leader of a group of citizens not at all satisfied with the subjection of their interests to those of the state. With him at their head, they turned against the Indians in spite of the attempts of General Martin to dissuade them from attacking the savages. Indian atrocities in 1788 aroused the citizens, and they thirsted for revenge. It appeared that Sevier acted as one of the leaders in stirring up this resentment against the Cherokees. The United States Indian superintendent, Richard Winn, reported to Secretary Knox that he had received a report from the Cherokees regarding the movement. This communication stated that Sevier at the head of a party of Franklinites had come over and destroyed several of their towns and killed about thirty of the Indians, causing them to flee to the Lower Towns. It also mentioned the fact that the whites were encroaching upon the Indian lands.[26] Sevier addressed a gathering on the French Broad just before the expedition, and is reported to have said he had information that the Assembly of North Carolina had thrown the people of that section on their own defense and that, as the Cherokees had refused to sell their lands, they (the settlers) had no other recourse but to take it with the sword, killing the warriors and capturing their women and children, destroying their provisions and compelling them to give up their lands.[27] A certain Bellew attempted to engage an interpreter to bring about, in a private manner, a lease or purchase of

---

[26] Richard Winn to Secretary Knox, Aug. 5, 1788, *American State Papers, V, Indian Affairs*, I, 28. (Hereafter cited as *ASPIA*.)

[27] Deposition of Anthony Forman, Jan. 26, 1789, *SRNC*, XXII, 1007.

land from the Cherokees. According to this interpreter, Bellew reported that he had been employed by Sevier, David Rose, and Joseph Martin.[28] Bellew also persuaded the Indians that they should not attend certain conferences with the United States commissioners because the latter were only trying to get their lands. Joseph Martin complained to Patrick Henry that Bellew, "a man of Infamous character who is set on by Mr. Savier," had collected a few of the fugitive Cherokees and by underhand means had "Got a Deed or lease from the Indians for Great part of their country."[29] Martin also had conceived the idea that Sevier was "Trying hard to be appointed superintendent, and has several friends in North Carolina assembled who have wrote in favor of him to Congress, they are thro him to share part of that Valuable Purchase you have lately made."[30] These reports cast a different light upon the motives of Sevier in initiating this enterprise as well as the earlier ones. Sevier needed little urging to depart for the Indian country at the head of a dissatisfied group of citizens bent upon driving the savages from choice lands.

This expedition occurred at a very opportune time for Sevier. The Franklin government had just collapsed. A feud between Sevier and Tipton, resulting from the Franklin movement, which will be discussed in another chapter, had ended shortly before this time in a fiasco for the Sevier partisans. The North Carolina government had just then issued a warrant for the erstwhile Franklin governor. Something of a startling character seemed necessary to restore to the ex-governor of this sporadic state

---

[28] *North Carolina Historical Commission Publications. Steele Papers*, I, 52-54.

[29] Joseph Martin to Patrick Henry, July 23, 1789, *Publications of Southwestern Historical Association*, VI, 28-29.

[30] Martin to Henry, Jan. 18, 1790, *ibid.*, pp. 30-32.

the popularity which had been diminished by his leadership in a lost cause. Naturally, as Haywood related, he "was himself again; elastic, brave, energetic, daring and patriotic. At the head of a body of mounted riflemen he was at once upon the frontier to guard and protect its most defenseless points."[31]

An atrocity occurred on this expedition which his enemies used to his disadvantage. In the outrages which the Indians committed, a family of eleven persons by the name of Kirk had been practically wiped out. In the campaign several Indians were captured. During an absence of Sevier from camp, Kirk's son, who had escaped the massacre, took revenge upon the prisoners by tomahawking them in cold blood. Sevier was charged with complicity in the crime because he did not punish Kirk for the deed.[32]

This expedition had far-reaching consequences. Richard Winn, the Indian superintendent, wrote also to Governor Johnston of North Carolina in regard to the uprising,[33] giving reasons for the movement. The Governor appeared to be very much disturbed by the affair.[34] The situation had its serious aspects. There were

[31] Ramsey, *op. cit.,* p. 415.
[32] Haywood, *op. cit.,* pp. 195-96.
[33] *SRNC,* XXI, 523-24: "A party of men have lately met on French Broad and called themselves a Convention of the people and have passed several Resolves, one of which is to raise a number of men by subscription and to be commanded by Col. Sevier, saying that North Carolina refused to aid the people over the Mountains, and in consequence of the Assemblies not making any allowance to the people that went against Chickamawga. . . ."
[34] *SRNC,* XXI, 536-37. Gov. Johnston to the Indian Agent: "Sevier, from the state of his conduct set forth in your letter appears to be incorrigible, and I fear we shall have no peace in your quarter till he is proceeded against to the last extremity. It is a pity that any of the ignorant deluded people should suffer with him. . . . They can be considered in no other light but that of free Booters and Robbers and unless they refrain . . . they will be looked upon as enemies of Mankind in general and treated accordingly."

some fifteen hundred families living south of the French Broad River at this time in defiance of the laws of North Carolina and of the United States regulations in regard to the Indian line.[35] They lived openly upon the Indian lands, and they had determined to remain. The agents of the United States were attempting at the time to make a treaty with the Creeks by which lands might be added to Georgia. This fresh outbreak against the red men brought these negotiations to a halt.[36] Congress passed resolutions regarding the affair and forwarded copies of them, together with evidences of hostilities, to Governor Johnston of North Carolina. The arrest of Sevier had been ordered previous to the time of the protests,[37] but on account of the Franklin troubles.

Before the end of the next year the whole affair appeared to have blown over. Sevier capitalized the success of the expedition and the renewed popularity occasioned by it. Washington County elected him to represent its people in the state Senate, and he took his place in that body on November 7, 1789.[38] The Senate appointed him to the committee on Indian affairs, and he took an active part in the proceedings of that house during the session. On December 5 of the same year he appeared in the rôle of prosecutor in an investigation into the affairs of General Joseph Martin, Indian agent for the state.[39]

The question of the official position of Sevier in the militia came before the Assembly on December 22, 1789.

---

[35] *SRNC*, XXI, 501.

[36] *SRNC*, XXI, 497: Hugh Williamson to Gov. Johnston, Sept. 6, 1788: ". . . the conduct of Mr. Sevier was not only fatal to their hopes, but perfectly alarming to the states of South Carolina and Virginia, each of them might suffer by a general Indian War." The delegates in Congress from these states had raised their protest against the movement.

[37] *SRNC*, XXI, 490-93.   [38] *Ibid.*, pp. 584-85.

[39] *Ibid.*, p. 659.

Sevier had been issued his commission as brigadier general in November, 1784.[40] His adherence to the Franklin movement had precluded his acceptance of the duties of that office. Now, when the question came before the Assembly, it had to decide whether he was or was not a general in the state militia. That body "Resolved, That it is the sense of the General Assembly that John Sevier is the Brigadier-General of the District of Washington and ought to be obeyed as such according to the date of his commission . . . and that the Governor issue his proclamation requiring all the good people of that district to pay due regard thereto, and govern themselves accordingly."[41] Charles McDowell, a senator, entered a protest against this action because it appeared to remove General Martin from office without any official accusation, it was contrary to the constitution, and it had been introduced at a late hour of the session. This protest was entered upon the Journal and the matter dropped. Evidently Sevier had achieved his object. The Indians had been chastised, and the interests of the settlers and land speculators had been promoted by the expedition. He was not primarily concerned with the affairs of the citizens of Virginia, South Carolina, and Georgia, except in the case of the last named for his interest in Muscle Shoals, which had not been injured.

Sevier's last important campaign against the Cherokees occurred in 1793. The western territory had passed from the control of the state into the hands of the United States government. William Blount, his friend and business associate, had been appointed governor of the territory. Sevier became a member of the legislative council and received a commission as brigadier general of militia.[42]

[40] *Ibid.*, XIX, 468-69.   [41] *Ibid.*, XXI, 725-26.
[42] *Report of American Historical Association*, 1896, Vol. I, 1183, "Public Documents of Early Congresses," Message of the President

THE LIFE OF JOHN SEVIER

Late in 1792 the Indians opened hostilities. The United States government exerted pressure to protect the Indians in their possessions. The western country had developed rapidly. Settlers had poured in, and they had not been particular whether they located within the bounds set for settlement or upon the lands of the Indians. Daniel Smith, secretary of the territory, accurately expressed the frontier viewpoint toward the Indians in a letter to the secretary of state.[43] Since the treaties of New York and Holston, he said, he neither knew nor had heard of any instance in which the Indians had a right to complain of the citizens of the United States—he was confident that they had no right to complain of the citizens of that territory. He said that it would be tedious and disagreeable to enumerate the many barbarous and unprovoked violations of which the Indians had been guilty. The frontier people of the territory deserved praise for the good treatment which they had exhibited toward the savages, relying upon the good faith of the general government to redress their wrongs. That time had now arrived, and the honor and dignity of the government called for redress; the settlers expected it, and it was essential that it be given, or their confidence would be lost with consequences easily conjectured. He explained that the Indians behaved as they did because of their training and because of the influence of the Spaniards. A Mr. Panton,[44] "an instrument in the British war,"

---

transmitting report of Secretary of War Knox relative to the appointment of Brig.-Generals of Militia in the U. S. Territory South of the Ohio, and nominating as such John Sevier and James Robertson. Taken from Senate Executive Journal, 1:75. The Senate Journal was not available.

[43] Daniel Smith to the Secretary of State, Oct. 27, 1792, 7862 *Bureau of Rolls and Library, State Department Archives*. (Hereafter cited as BRL.)

[44] A. P. Whitaker, *The Spanish American Frontier, 1783-1795, passim;* Panton said in 1792 that he had things in readiness so that he could let

acted as a principal instigator of the Spanish policy of arousing the savages. Smith knew that the United States desired peace, but experience had shown that it was not to be had without a war to convince the Indians of the strength of the government: "On these premises a war well directed against the hostile part would be a mercy, as it would check the evil before it becomes too general."

This letter represented the frontier state of mind in regard to the Indians. Less than ten months later, Blount had to face the problem of settlers on the Indian lands. Warrants were being obtained from North Carolina for lands south of the French Broad.[45] These incidents show that the attitude of the citizens of the territory favored aggressions upon the Indian lands. Justice to the Indian meant punishment for his hostilities. They expected the Indian title to be extinguished as quickly as possible.

The hostility toward the savages continued to grow, and it became apparent that the settlers could be restrained very little longer. The policy of the central government attempted to placate the Indians and to prevent war. Blount faced the displeasure of the administration in Philadelphia if he countenanced an attack upon the Indians, and the violent opposition of the people of the territory if he did not take immediate measures to punish the crimes of the savages. The killing of twelve or fifteen Indians by Captain Beard and a party of militiamen illustrated this state of affairs. Some of these Indians were chiefs who had been called for a conference to Hanging Maw's by the agents of the President. Secretary Smith reported that it was out of the

---

loose "as bloody a war as ever the Southern States have experienced." *Ibid.*, p. 168.

[45] Letters between Blount and the secretary of state are preserved in the *State Department Archives*, 7854, 7858, *American Letters*, Vol. 4; 7857 *BRL*.

question to attempt to punish Beard by law at that time.[46] Blount frequently absented himself from the territory during this period, and it is probable that he was partly influenced to do so because of the desire to escape responsibility for any outbreak by the settlers.[47]

Sevier had his headquarters at Ish's Station south of the Holston River when this crisis became acute. When the Indians began an invasion of that part of the territory, he prepared to move upon them. Secretary Smith, acting governor in Blount's absence, ordered troops into service and authorized an expedition against the Indians and their towns. Six or seven hundred men were mustered, and they marched against the towns on the Coosa and Estinaula rivers. They burned several towns on the way; they attacked and destroyed the village of Etowah, but most of the Indians escaped. They devastated the Indian country and broke the resistance in that quarter, after which the army returned to Ish's Station.[48] The campaign had been carried out vigorously and under the usual circumstances. Sevier had applied the method of destruction of provisions and towns which made it impossible for the savages to remain in the vicinity of the settlements.[49]

This campaign ended Sevier's military services against the Indians. The events given in this chapter are those of the outstanding campaigns which he conducted, but he doubtless participated in other lesser expeditions and raids of which the records made no mention.

---

[46] Ramsey, *op. cit.*, p. 577.

[47] Blount was absent for three months in 1791. Smith to secretary of state, Oct. 4, 1791, 7849 *BRL;* same to same, Dec. 9, 1791, *BRL.*

[48] Ramsey, *op. cit.*, pp. 583-88.

[49] See Sevier's *Diary* in S. G. Heiskell, *Andrew Jackson and Early Tennessee History*, II, 513-14, for record which he kept of the movement of the army. Several General Orders were given, a message to the Indians is included, and the progress of the march is recorded.

SCOURGE OF THE CHEROKEES 37

Sevier usually employed a plan of devastation as that best calculated to bring the savages to peaceable manners of living. With a small but well-trained body of men he penetrated into the Indian country and destroyed their villages and supplies. This necessitated a change of location on the part of the tribes in order to secure and preserve their stores of food. It constituted a systematic effort to remove them from their lands, upon which the settlers cast covetous eyes. It is small wonder that the natives nursed an undying hatred for the whites when the latter so ruthlessly expelled them from their hunting grounds. The continued failure of the frontiersmen to abide by treaties and promises and their aggressive seizure of the Indian lands caused perpetual war.

While on these expeditions, Sevier and those whom he led located the most fertile and desirable lands. They became acquainted with the best and most productive areas of the Indian possessions, and, when they had the opportunity, they proceeded to those regions and appropriated the choice sections. The wars were purely wars of aggression on the part of the pioneers. In the warfare Sevier used mounted riflemen, a usual type of soldier upon the frontier. These were hardy settlers, expert with the rifle and at home on horseback. They moved from place to place, with a rapidity which bewildered the Indians and frequently caught them off their guard. The troops made forays into the distant Indian country, struck at the homes of the Indians at the first sign of an outbreak, and destroyed the towns before the warriors could return.

Roosevelt's conclusion that this sort of service brought negligible results is not warranted.[50] It was responsible

---

[50] Roosevelt, *op. cit.*, I, 182 n: "Sevier was neither leader nor participant in any such marvellous feats as Mr. Gilmore describes; on the contrary, the skirmishes in which he may have been engaged were

for the evacuation of the Indian lands. The conditions under which Sevier carried on these campaigns did not require large bodies of troops. A small group of men, striking before the Indians had opportunity to concentrate in any large force, held an immense advantage. The fact that he warred against the villages made such concentration impracticable. By his strategy he forced the Indians to fight the kind of battle in which he was best prepared. It has been said that he participated in thirty-five battles, some of them "hardly contested and decisive."[51] His personal magnetism was contagious, and his discipline voluntary. The soldiers respected him and had confidence in his judgment.

While others may have carried out more spectacular exploits than Sevier, it is doubtful if any leader in the west forced a more systematic and complete evacuation of Indian territory. He continuously exerted military pressure upon the savages for twenty years, and later as governor of Tennessee he carried on a peaceful aggression for nearly twelve years longer. The brilliance of his policy showed itself in its tenacity. The Indians recognized his power with a respect born of fear. No other Tennessean contributed as much to the peace and safety of the old southwestern frontiers as 'Chucky Jack, the Cherokee nemesis.

---

of such small importance that no record remains concerning them. Had Sevier done any such deeds all the colonies would have rung with his exploits, instead of their remaining utterly unknown for a hundred and twenty-five years." This is an entirely gratuitous statement on the part of Roosevelt. While Sevier may not have commanded a large army of troops and made any such spectacular campaign as the conquering of the northwest, his expeditions did not lack importance to the area in which he lived. Absence of source material does not necessarily mean lack of activity or barrenness of results.

[51] Ramsey, *op. cit.*, pp. 588-89.

CHAPTER III

KING'S MOUNTAIN

IN 1780 SEVIER turned from his campaigns against the savages to lend his aid in repelling British invasion. As a continuation of his victories in South Carolina, Major Ferguson threatened to devastate the West as a punishment for its activities in the Whig-Tory strife east of the mountains. His course was suddenly halted at King's Mountain, in a battle which marked the turning of the tide of the Revolution. When an opportunity came, men of the frontier repaid in full measure their debt to the East for its aid during the Indian uprisings of 1776. The militia officers of the western counties led men trained in Indian warfare. In the test with British regulars, they were able to meet and destroy an efficient force commanded by experienced officers. No battle of the war excited such a feeling of confidence in the face of despair as the defeat of Ferguson. It represented the power and determination of a people accustomed to strife and danger. It gave expression to pent-up feelings of hatred and bitterness engendered by real or fancied repressions.

From the beginning, the people of the frontier favored the Revolution because they had felt grievously the restrictive hand of the English government. The foundation for their dissatisfaction centered in its attempt to stay the progress of the settlers into the West. The imperial control asserted itself especially in the limitation which prohibited indefinite westward migration. The Proclamation of 1763 defined the bounds of this movement by establishing a line beyond which settlements might not be made.[1] Although the treaties of Hard Labor[2] and Lochabar[3] modified the Proclamation Line and made a large territory accessible to settlers, restrictions still remained.

In 1775 the Watauga Purchase and the two tracts of land acquired from the Indians by Jacob Brown extended the North Carolina territory.[4] Henderson's Purchase in the same year opened Kentucky to settlement.[5] But all these projects for occupying new lands after 1770 were undertaken by private enterprise, and none of them received the sanction of the British government. The fact that they were independent movements indicated that those interested in westward expansion had become dissatisfied with the imperial control. The British, in the estimation of those connected with these schemes, meant to prohibit any movement into the Indian territory. The natives made no effort to improve the rich lands in their possession, and the fertile soil seemed to beckon to the frontiersmen and to the speculators. Attempts by the British agents to force from their possessions the colonists who had passed beyond the Line encountered resentment and resistance.[6]

The westerner felt no interest in the welfare of the British government. He thought only of the fertile fields

---

[1] C. W. Alvord, *The Mississippi Valley in British Politics*, II, 71.

[2] *SRNC*, VII, 851.

[3] *Va. Mag. Hist. & Biog.* IX, 362.

[4] Ramsey, *op. cit.*, pp. 119-22.

[5] *SRNC*, IX, 1276; C. C. Royce, *The Cherokee Nation of Indians, Fifth Annual Report of the Bureau of Ethnology*, (1883-84), pp. 148-49.

[6] *SRNC*, X, 763-85, for Stuart's report of his and Cameron's transactions with the Indians.

which awaited his occupation. When the government across the sea attempted to force from him that for which he had toiled and fought, he was ready for rebellion. The efforts of the British agents to shield the savages made these representatives appear as the friends and protectors of the Indians and as the enemies of the settlers.

Sevier and his friends never could conceive of the Indian tribes as nations, nor understand the need for governmental protection over hordes of wild men who fought and killed for pastime. They knew no peace with the savage, for he held no treaty sacred nor guaranteed any safety from bitter ferocity. Consequently, the government which protected the Indians must bear the responsibility for their raids and for their murders. In all probability the men of the western waters in general knew little and cared less about the struggle of the seaboard with the mother country. The supposed connivance of the English agents in raids upon them brought these pioneers into the conflict. They hated the British as sincerely as they despised the Indians. From the beginning of the Revolution, most of the conflicts west of the mountains were with the Indians who, so the settlers claimed, were instigated by the English.

But not all residents of the frontier forgot their loyalty to the British government. Although the situation did not approach that which prevailed in the East, Tories operated on the frontier also. Several important cases in the early records of Washington County show the attitude of the authorities towards these loyalists. In August, 1778, the court of that county, for which Sevier served as clerk, ordered Moses Crawford imprisoned for the duration of the war and half of his estate confiscated.[7] He was later released on giving his oath and a bond of

---

[7] "Records of Washington County" *AHM*, V, 351.

ten thousand pounds.[8] At the same session the court ordered Isaac Buller delivered to a Continental officer who should convey him to army headquarters, where he must serve for three years or until the end of the conflict.[9] In February, 1779: "On hearing the facts and considering the testimony of witnesses, It is the opinion of the Court That the defendant be sent to the District Gaol It Apg. To the Court that the said Lewis is a spy or an Officer from Florida out of the English Army."[10] At this same term the court tried ten persons on charges of treason, convicted five of them, ordered their property confiscated, and sent them to the district jail.[11] John Holly was imprisoned in May, 1779, for ill practice in harboring and abetting disorderly persons who were "prejudicial and Inimical to the Common Cause of Liberty and Frequently Disturbing our public Tranquility."[12]

Haywood cites several instances of Tory activity and says that "The Tories upon the waters of the Holston were now as dangerous and as hurtful as the Indians. To watch their motions, as well as those of the Indians, it became necessary to keep up constantly scouting companies of armed men."[13] One, Bradley by name, was killed by such a band. It appears that these troops were called Light Horse Companies and that such groups organized in many of the counties of North Carolina. Their duties included the apprehension of Tories and the return to the army of drafted militiamen who had deserted. In 1780 another Tory by the name of Dykes was captured and hanged. He had formed a plot to kill John Sevier, but his wife gave information of the plot to the Sevier family. Halley, a confederate of Dykes, was captured

---

[8] *Ibid.*, p. 368.
[9] *Ibid.*, p. 351.
[10] *Ibid.*, p. 366.
[11] *Ibid.*, p. 330.
[12] *Ibid.*, p. 373.
[13] Haywood, *op. cit.*, p. 76.

by Robert Sevier, John's son, who led one of the companies, and this group shot both Halley and Bradley at the same time.[14] These men, together with others in the community who aroused suspicion of being sympathetic toward the British, had to submit to the confiscation of their lands.[15]

When the county seized Tory lands, other settlers might enter claims for them upon the same terms as for any unappropriated lands. Sevier and Landon Carter, the entry-taker, filed claims for a good share of these estates. Sevier served as a member of a commission of three appointed by the court to take possession of the confiscated property.[16] This possibly caused the attempt upon the life of Sevier. Whether these men were actually Tories and sympathetic toward the British cannot be ascertained. Sevier certainly knew something of the value and extent of their holdings and proceeded to add to his acquisitions from their possessions.

The situation on the Holston paralleled that in the counties east of the mountains. A further illustration of Tory activity occurred in a section adjoining the frontier. In 1779 such a group lived on the headwaters of the Yadkin in North Carolina and in the adjoining county of Montgomery in Virginia. They meant to destroy the lead mines on New River, to rob the patriot citizens, and finally to join Cornwallis. Colonels Preston and Campbell led their militia against this Tory band and dispersed or captured them in a few weeks. Most of those captured were hanged. The "Tory Trees," according to tradition, formed the scene of one of the hangings by Campbell's men.[17]

---

[14] *Ibid.*
[15] Draper MSS, Draper's Notes, XXX, 351-64.
[16] Ramsey, *op. cit.*, p. 181.
[17] *Va. Mag. Hist. & Biog.*, XXVI, 372, n.

The year 1780 became one of the most trying of the Revolutionary War to the South and indirectly to the West. North Carolina had been selected as the theatre where the British leaders believed they could gain the most success. This movement resulted from the defeat of D'Estaing before Savannah and the subsequent departure of the French fleet from American waters, which left the sea open to the British.[18] Knyphausen remained in command in New York, while Clinton and a force variously estimated[19] at from seven thousand six hundred to eight thousand five hundred men sailed for the South, intending to capture Charleston and use it as a base of operations for the conquest of the Carolinas.

Charleston fell on May 7, and the British deluded themselves by thinking the whole of South Carolina conquered. Clinton turned the southern army over to the command of Cornwallis and returned to New York. The proclamations following the capture of Charleston and the occupation of various posts in the state had brought many Loyalists to the British. Many of them took up arms against the colonists, and others sought the protection of the British in order to save their property.

Clinton and Cornwallis agreed upon the general plan of campaign to be followed in the South before the departure of the former for New York. Clinton directed Cornwallis to advance into North Carolina and General Leslie to move from New York to Virginia. The commander-in-chief designed this movement by Leslie in order to prevent reinforcements leaving Virginia to aid the southern colonial forces.[20] They planned other expeditions to march into the interior, one up the Savannah

---

[18] J. W. Fortescue, *History of the British Army*, III, 305-8.

[19] Cf. *Ibid.* p. 307; F. V. Greene, *The Revolutionary War*, pp. 206-7; and Tarleton, *Campaigns in the Southern Provinces*, p. 3.

[20] *SRNC*, XV, iii, *et seq.*

River in Georgia, another in South Carolina to Ninety-Six, while Cornwallis should cross the Santee River and attempt to strike Buford, who was retreating into North Carolina with arms and provisions.[21]

Lord Cornwallis proceeded to his task and met with uniform success. The defeat of Buford at Rugeley's Mill on May 29, 1780, effectively put an end to the Continental activities in South Carolina and cleared the way for the advance into North Carolina.[22] About the first of June, Cornwallis arrived at Camden. He planned to remain there until the first of September when he expected to leave South Carolina secure and to march into the back part of North Carolina. After conquering that province, he planned to advance to the Chesapeake region and to unite with General Leslie. Together they hoped to gain control of Virginia. The plans of the British commander in the South were embodied in a dispatch[23] to Clinton in June:

> I think that with the force at present under my command (except there should be a considerable Foreign interference) I can leave South Carolina about the beginning of September, with a body of troops into the back part of North Carolina with the greatest probability of reducing that province to its duty; and if this be accomplished, I am of the opinion that (besides the advantage of possessing so valuable a Province) it would prove an effectual Barrier for South Carolina and Georgia, and could be kept, with the assistance of our friends there, by as few troops as would be wanted on the Borders of this Province, if North Carolina should remain in the hands of our enemies.

---

[21] Tarleton, *op. cit.*, p. 27.   [22] Fortescue, *op. cit.*, p. 312.
[23] Cornwalls to Clinton, June 30, 1780, *SRNC*, XV, 249-55; "After having thus fully stated the present situation of the two Carolinas, I shall now take the liberty of giving my opinion with respect to the Practicability and the probable effect of further operations in this quarter, and my own intentions, if not otherwise directed by your Excellency."

Consequently, if your Excellency should continue to think it expedient to employ part of the troops at present in this Province in operations in the Chesapeake, there will be as many to spare as if we did not possess North Carolina. If I am not honored with different directions from your Excellency before that time, I shall take my measures for beginning the execution of the above Plan about the latter end of August or beginning of September.

General Caswell described the situation on the part of the Colonies in a letter to Governor Nash of North Carolina about the end of July: "I have some hopes that our distresses in some measure will be relieved here, especially if I can remain so long as to recruit our Men and Horses, who are much worn down with fatigue. . . . There are very few of the Inhabitants of Anson County who have not taken the oath of Allegiance to the King of Great Britain; most of them are willing to break it and take up Arms against him, saying they were compelled by the British, but come in voluntary to us. Such as were desirous of supporting the British Government are either fled with the British or lye out."[24]

The condition of affairs in both North and South Carolina approached that of civil war. The country swarmed with Tory bands which were opposed by Whig groups under officers in whom the men trusted. Families divided, some going with the British and others with the Whigs. This led to much bitterness and cruelty. Before the coming of the British, the Tories hesitated to declare their allegiance, but when the English forces came into a district the Whig bands remained quiet and kept under cover, while each side carried out confiscations with rapacity. In the summer of 1780 Tory bands operated with more or less success in the North Carolina counties

---

[24] *SRNC*, XV, 11.

of Bladen, Anson, Cumberland, Guilford, and Surry.[25] These counties formed an almost continuous line running in the general direction from southeast to northwest. West of this line the people generally favored the Revolution.[26] As Cornwallis moved up toward the mountains, he encountered more and more opposition. In September he reported that the disloyalty in the country east of the Santee was so great that any person who dared to spread the news of the defeat of Gates at Camden received threats of instant death.[27]

Several incidents illustrated the general bitterness and ferocity of these bands of partisans. At Ramsour's Mill in North Carolina, more than a third of a total of eight hundred combatants, about equally divided, were killed or wounded in an encounter with clubbed muskets.[28] The British ordered an outpost at Cheraw Hill evacuated because of sickness among the men. A group of militia, enrolled under the British Colonel Mills, had camped near the outpost. When they learned of the approach of Gates, they mutinied, seized their own officers and the sick and carried them all prisoners into North Carolina. The incident illuminated the situation for Cornwallis and made him uneasy as to his own position.[29]

On August 16, the battle of Camden was fought. It

---

[25] *Ibid.*, pp. iv-v.
[26] Fortescue, *op. cit.*, pp. 312-13.
[27] *SRNC*, XV, v.
[28] Greene, *op. cit.*, p. 213.
[29] Cornwallis to Clinton, Aug. 6, 1780, *SRNC*, XV, 258-62; "The instant that this [Mill's militia] found that McArthur had left his post and were assured that Gates would come there the next day, they seized their own officers and a hundred sick and carried them all prisoners into North Carolina. . . . The whole country between Pedee and Santee has ever since been in an absolute state of Rebellion; every friend of Government has been carried off and his Plantation destroyed; and detachments of the enemy have appeared on the Santee and threatened our stores and convoys on that river. . . . This unfortunate business, if it should have no worse consequences, will shake the confidence of our Friends in this Province and make our situation very uneasy until we can advance."

proved to be one of the most disastrous to the American cause of all the engagements which took place in the South. After the fall of Charleston, Congress had appointed General Gates as commander of the southern forces. Upon his arrival in the South he disregarded the advice of Baron De Kalb, an experienced soldier who had thoroughly studied the situation and had drawn up a careful and efficient plan of operation.[30] Gates immediately took the offensive and advanced upon Cornwallis. The American loss at Camden, where the two forces met, amounted to about a thousand killed and wounded. The whole organization of the army disintegrated. The militia scattered to their homes, and all effective resistance in the South, save for Sumter's force, appeared to be broken.[31] A few days later Sumter allowed himself to be surprised by Tarleton, and his force was effectively scattered.[32]

The way now seemed open for the invasion of North Carolina. The position of Cornwallis, however, was not so secure as it might appear. He had sickness in his army which incapacitated a great number of men and officers. Sumter, instead of being completely overcome, immediately became active again, and others of like character and energy led partisan bodies in various parts of the South. Elijah Clarke and Francis Marion effectively led groups of this kind and exerted an irritating pressure upon the British loyalists.

In spite of these drawbacks, Cornwallis marched unopposed to Charlotte, North Carolina. Clinton sent General Leslie to the Chesapeake with three thousand men under orders to act at the command of Cornwallis according to the prearranged plans.[33] Thus, the situation must have

---

[30] Greene, *op. cit.*, p. 215.
[31] Fortescue, *op. cit.*, p. 319.   [32] Tarleton, *op. cit.*, pp. 117-19.
[33] *Ibid.*, p. 173.

appeared favorable for the British to complete the conquest of North Carolina and to advance afterward into Virginia.

On the march northward the British threw out flanking parties to disperse the bands of Whig partisans and to rally the Loyalists to the British cause. Cornwallis placed Major Ferguson, a very efficient and well trained officer, in command of a corps and sent him into the back country. Ferguson had seen service in Germany in 1760 and in the Island of St. Vincent against the Caribs.[34] He was an expert rifle shot, and in 1776 he invented a breech-loading rifle which could fire four aimed shots in a minute. In 1777 he came to America with one hundred officers and men who were armed with these new rifles. He formed a corps selected from the various regiments which used his new gun to advantage in the Battle of Brandywine. His command was soon merged into various bodies of light troops, and he received a commission as major in 1779, commanding the Loyalist "American Volunteers,"[35] who were armed also with his new rifle.

Some of the duties which devolved upon Ferguson while in the back country differed from those usually assigned to an officer in the field. He commanded an independent unit and organized and regulated all the Loyalist volunteers. He inspected the quantity of grain and the number of cattle belonging to the inhabitants. An added duty was to perform marriage ceremonies. Cornwallis said that his duty was "more that of a Justice of Peace than of a soldier."[36]

Colonel McDowell, Whig leader of militia, became con-

---

[34] L. C. Draper, *King's Mountain and Its Heroes*, pp. 48-50.

[35] J. W. Wright, "The Rifle in the American Revolution," *American Historical Review* (hereafter cited as *AHR*), XXIX, 296.

[36] Quoted in Draper, *op. cit.*, p. 71.

vinced that Ferguson intended to invade the back country of North Carolina. He sent word to Sevier and Shelby requesting aid from them in meeting this invasion. In response to his message, sent across the mountains in June, Shelby joined McDowell with two hundred mounted riflemen together with a part of Sevier's regiment under Major Robertson. This force engaged in the partisan warfare in western North Carolina until the defeat of Gates at Camden. The most important action in which they took part resulted in the capture of Fort Anderson on Pacolet River. The Tories used this fort as a rendezvous and protection for Captain Patrick Moore, a noted Tory leader of that section who commanded the post.[37]

Shelby then left McDowell and joined Colonel Clarke's force, which was engaged in watching the movements of Ferguson. Clarke had previously made a fierce attack upon the post of Augusta, Georgia, but had been driven back by a British relief force. He had then escaped along the mountains northward.[38] The hope of cutting him off was one of Ferguson's reasons for pushing steadily to the west. Shelby and his force were also in the skirmish at Cedar Spring on August 8.[39] Shelby's account[40] said that they retreated when Ferguson arrived in force, after they had captured twenty soldiers and officers. At Musgrove's Mill, Shelby and Clarke inflicted a signal defeat upon a body of British and Tories and made preparations for an expedition against Ninety-Six. This movement had to be abandoned when they received word of the defeat of Gates at Camden. They then rejoined McDowell and left their prisoners with him. The men from the Holston and the Watauga crossed the mountains to their

---

[37] Cf. *ibid.*, pp. 84-86, and Haywood, *op. cit.*, p. 77.

[38] Draper, *op. cit.*, pp. 199-200.

[39] Allaire's *Diary*, in *ibid.*, p. 503.

[40] Draper, *op. cit.*, p. 99, says that Shelby's account was originally published in Haywood (*op. cit.*, p. 78).

homes, possibly thinking that it was useless to attempt to prevent the reduction of North Carolina at that time with their small numbers.[41]

McDowell's whole army broke up, and he also retreated across the mountains with a few hundred followers. In the pursuit of this force Ferguson advanced as far from his base as Gilbert Town, at least seventy miles from Charlotte. Here he paroled a prisoner, Samuel Phillips, with a message for the officers west of the mountains, saying that if they did not cease their activities he would march over into their country and burn and lay waste that section.[42] Shelby received this message and immediately carried it to Sevier. They determined to raise as large a force as possible, to meet Ferguson and to cripple him so as to prevent his carrying out his threat.[43]

Shortly after the defeat of Gates, Colonel William Campbell of Virginia visited Richmond, and, while there, Governor Jefferson communicated to him something of the plans of the operations against the British in Virginia and the Carolinas. Upon Campbell's return to his home in southwest Virginia, he received the news of Ferguson's advance from Shelby, who had just been with Sevier. Campbell finally decided to join the expedition with his whole force.

It will be seen from the situation described that the movement of the frontiersmen was not so spontaneous as it is usually depicted. Men from the frontier had been taking part in the strife in North and South Carolina for some time previously. The continued aggressions and successes of the British arms caused them to feel that Ferguson would carry out his threat to cross the moun-

---

[41] Cf. Haywood, *op. cit.*, pp. 78-79, and Draper, *op. cit.*, pp. 104-22.
[42] *Official Report* of Shelby, Campbell and Cleveland, *SRNC*, XV, 163.
[43] Haywood, *op. cit.*, pp. 80-81.

tains and devastate their lands. The men from the West who had been engaged in the strife knew of the movements of the enemy and expected the depredations to continue.

The entry-taker of Sullivan County provided a part of the funds for this proposed expedition against Ferguson from the money he had collected by the sale of public lands. He turned over this money to the leaders of the expedition, who used it for the purpose of supplying the troops with the necessary equipment.[44] It is possible that some of the lead used by the pioneers came from a mine on Sevier's land.[45]

The militia rendezvoused at Sycamore Flats on Watauga River, September 25. On the morning of the 26th, they began their march across the mountains. Most of the men were provided with horses, and they advanced rapidly. On the second day of the march they found that two of their number had deserted, and they suspected that these men had gone to report the movement to Ferguson. This incident caused them to alter their line of march and to advance by a more northerly route, with the hope of confusing the enemy by their change of direction.

McDowell united with them on the 29th, and the next day they were joined by Colonels Cleveland and Winston with about three hundred and fifty men. On the night of October 2 they camped about eighteen miles from Gilbert Town where they expected to find the British force. It became evident on the march that discipline might be improved, and the leaders thought that this situation resulted from the lack of a responsible commanding officer. In the evening they met to discuss the problem. They decided to dispatch a messenger to General Gates and to request him to send them a commander.

---

[44] Ramsey, *op. cit.*, p. 226.
[45] Draper MSS, Draper's Notes, XXX, 382.

It is probable that the question of precedence had something to do with the situation. Colonel McDowell was the ranking officer, but he commanded a small force of men and had lost a considerable number after the news of the Camden disaster. Shelby probably originated the move to displace McDowell. He suggested that as all except Campbell were North Carolinians and as that officer had the largest individual force, it was proper that he should lead them until a general officer should arrive. They agreed to this, and McDowell asked that he be the one to carry the message to Gates. Campbell assumed the chief command, apparently to the satisfaction of all concerned.[46]

Ferguson had halted at Brindletown when he received word, on September 30, of the approach of this force, which has been described as "three thousand settlers from the extreme backwoods, rough, half-civilized men whom no labour could tire, and whose rifles seldom missed their mark."[47] He immediately sent word to Cornwallis stating his need for reinforcements. By October 6 he had stationed his force on King's Mountain where he awaited the impending attack.

The King's Mountain range was about sixteen miles long, and the portion upon which the battle was fought lay about a mile and a half south of the North Carolina line. The scene of the engagement was a ridge of about six hundred yards in length and about two hundred and fifty yards from one base to the other. It appeared so narrow on the top "that a man standing on it may be shot from either side," and it rose about sixty feet above the surrounding country.[48]

The Whig forces moved to Green River where they camped the night of the 5th. Here the officers selected the men who should form the attack, and the next day they

---
[46] Draper, *op. cit.*, pp. 165-90.
[47] Fortescue, *op. cit.*, p. 322.
[48] Draper, *op. cit.*, p. 209.

marched to Cowpens. Other partisan groups drifted into the ranks of the men from beyond the mountains. Pouring rain added to their discomfort.[49] Some uncertainty existed as to Ferguson's whereabouts, and it became necessary to obtain information. Sevier's men played an important part in securing it. A girl in a Tory family informed them that the British were encamped on the Mountain. Sevier's troops captured several Tory scouts and forced them to reveal the location of Ferguson's camp,[50] and the same information came from other sources as well. After a night march in the rain and a forenoon passed in discussing plans for the attack, they were ready for the assault upon the British position.

The battle began about two or three o'clock in the afternoon.[51] During the advance upon the Mountain, the officers had formed their plan of attack. Sevier later claimed that Shelby first suggested the tactics adopted.[52] Campbell's and Shelby's regiments formed the center, the former on the right and the latter on the left. The left wing was composed of Williams's and Cleveland's regiments, while the regiments of Sevier and McDowell occupied the right together with a part of Cleveland's men. They executed an enveloping movement, the right of the line crossing the end of the Mountain and the left advancing along the north base. Thus, the first to become engaged were Campbell's and Shelby's regiments since they came into their positions earliest. The arrangements must have been carried out with swiftness, for each group had reached its position in at least fifteen minutes after the attack began.[53]

---

[49] *Ibid.*, pp. 221-30.
[50] Draper MSS, Draper's Notes, XXXII, 503-6.
[51] Allaire's *Diary* in Draper, *op. cit.*, p. 503; *SRNC*, XV, 163.
[52] Sevier to Shelby, Aug. 27, 1812, Draper MSS, 16DD42.
[53] Allaire's *Diary* in Draper, *op. cit.*, p. 503.

The situation appeared favorable to the English, but Ferguson probably repeated the mistake of Braddock in thinking that British tactics were efficient under all conditions. Although not high, the Mountain was not particularly adapted to maneuvering. While on the summit no obstructions hindered, trees covered the sides nearly to the top,[54] forming a natural protection for the frontiersmen who fought in Indian fashion. Ferguson depended upon his regulars to use the bayonet and, presumably, upon his militia to hold the position while the regulars engaged in this work. He rightly assumed that the rebels could not withstand an attack of cold steel, for they gave way before each of three bayonet charges.

But while he charged in one direction with his small body of regulars, the sharpshooters from the frontier directed a deadly fire all along the Mountain. Because of the extreme narrowness of the summit, his regulars found themselves in the desperate position of having to advance while rifle fire picked them off from the rear. The Indian tactics of the westerners admirably fitted the situation. As they advanced behind every possible cover, they directed a withering fire upon the whole of the British line and prevented any attempt to break through. They gave way before the bayonet but returned to the attack as soon as the charge lost its momentum.

Many incidents have been related of particular heroism in the battle. The coolness of the frontiersmen before the bayonet charges of Ferguson's regular troops matched the doggedly brave stand of the British and Tories. It must have been a sharp engagement marked by heroic effort on both sides. More than two hundred and fifty died in the hour and ten minutes of fighting.

It cannot be said that any great amount of scientific skill on either side marked the fight. Ferguson overlooked

---

[54] Draper, *op. cit.*, p. 252.

the vital defects of his position in choosing it. The attacking force simply adopted the method of fighting to which they had become accustomed in their combats with the savages. Colonel Cleveland was reported to have addressed his men before the battle in this manner: "When you are engaged, you are not to wait for any word of command from me. I will show you, by example, how to fight; I can undertake no more. Every man must consider himself an officer, and act from his own judgment."[55] This method of fighting, if not scientific, at least proved effective, for the attackers killed or captured the entire force of Ferguson. The British commander himself was cut down in the midst of the fight while making an attempt to break through and escape.[56] The command then devolved upon Captain DePeyster, and he raised the flag of surrender.[57]

There existed some divergence of opinion as to the numbers engaged on both sides. The official report signed by Campbell, Shelby and Cleveland gave the total number on the American side as 1,780 men. Campbell's regiment of 400, Shelby's of 240 and Sevier's with a like number had gathered at Sycamore Flats. McDowell's refugee militia numbered 160. Colonel Cleveland had joined them at Catawba with 350 militia, and at Cowpens Colonel Williams brought in 400 more. Of this number 900 of the best had been chosen on the day before the battle to pursue Ferguson, and these engaged in the attack. The remainder cared for the weak horses and followed on foot as fast as they could.[58]

The Americans captured the British provision returns for the day which stated that the whole force under

---

[55] *Ibid.*, p. 249.
[56] Ensign Robert Campbell's *Account* (of the battle), *ibid.*, p. 539.
[57] Allaire's *Diary*, *ibid.*, p. 510.
[58] *Official Report* of Shelby, Campbell, and Cleveland, *SRNC*, XV, 163.

Ferguson consisted of 1,125 men.[59] Tarleton tacitly accepted this report as accurate,[60] and it may be taken as approximately correct. The accounts of the numbers given by men on both sides exaggerated the figures to far greater proportions as time elapsed. As for the losses on the American side, reports stated that twenty-eight men were killed and sixty-two wounded. The British loss was given as 225 killed, 163 wounded and 715 taken prisoner. This showed a discrepancy of seventy-nine men from the provision report. There is a possibility that this error came from one of two sources: the list was divided into regulars and Tories, and they may have been confused and some counted in both divisions; the provision returns may not have included the officers, who numbered seventy-seven. The latter supposition seems the more probable.

On the day after the battle the frontier forces began to retire with their prisoners. By Friday, the 13th, they had arrived at Blickerstaff's plantation, about fifty-six miles from the field of battle. Here a court-martial tried such of the Tory prisoners as had been charged with murder and other crimes committed in the partisan warfare of that section. It condemned thirty-two and summarily hanged nine of them, and it possibly would have disposed of the remainder in the same manner had not the commander pardoned them. One of the participants in the battle who was present at the executions reported that Sevier and Shelby desired it to appear that they opposed hanging the men for fear that the Tories might kill them in revenge.[61]

According to Tarleton,[62] this defeat at King's Mountain

---

[59] *Ibid.*   [60] Tarleton, *op. cit.*, p. 168.

[61] Allaire's *Diary*, in Draper, *op. cit.*, p. 511; Campbell's *Account*, *ibid.*, p. 540; Draper MSS, Draper's Notes, XXXII, 503-6.

[62] Tarleton, *op. cit.*, p. 169: "The destruction of Ferguson and his corps marked the period and the extent of the first expedition into

resulted in the immediate withdrawal of the British forces from North Carolina and ended the attempted invasion of the western section of the country. Cornwallis retreated to Winnsboro, South Carolina, ninety miles from Charlotte. It discouraged the Tories in the whole of the back country where the hostility between the two parties assumed greatest bitterness. The news encouraged the militia of North Carolina to rally to the patriots' cause. The loss of an entire corps gave a serious blow to the British, and the partisan bodies became increasingly active.[63]

This battle, however, was a minor engagement. The British commander employed defensive tactics on the field which were unsuited to the occasion. Skilled officers commanded the English force, and temporary fortifications had been erected which proved ineffective. On the American side, it was an action fought by the militia which had learned its art of war from the Indians. It was a fight of individuals, not of a well organized body

---

North Carolina. Added to the depression and fear it communicated to the loyalists upon the borders, and to the southward, the effect of such an important event was sensibly felt by Earl Cornwallis at Charlotte town. The weakness of his army, the extent and poverty of North Carolina, the want of knowledge of his enemies designs, and the total ruin of his militia, presented a gloomy prospect at the commencement of the campaign. . . . He therefore formed a sudden determination to quit Charlotte town and pass the Catawba."

[63] Lord Rawdon to General Clinton, Oct. 29, 1780, *SRNC*, XV, 287-89: "The defeat of Major Ferguson had so dispirited this part of the country and indeed the loyal subjects were so wearied by the long continuance of the campaign that Lt. Col. Cruger (commanding at Ninety-Six) sent information to Earl Cornwallis that the whole district had determined to submit as soon as the rebels should enter it. From these circumstances. . . . Earl Cornwallis has resolved to remain for the present in a position which may secure the Frontiers without separating his force. . . . Earl Cornwallis foresees all the difficulties of a defensive war. Yet his Lordship thinks they cannot be weighed against the dangers which must have attended an obstinate adherence to his former plan."

of troops. The Americans depended almost entirely upon the accuracy of their rifle-fire. The numbers engaged were nearly equal, and no one could charge lack of bravery on the part of the men of either side. The result gave encouragement to the American cause and brought an immediate rally of the militia to the army. These accessions materially aided the Revolution.

In its larger aspects, it cannot be said that the engagement won the War of Independence for the Americans. It contributed its share of the general causes for the failure of the British arms. Distance from the home base; lack of appreciation by the English government of the difficulties to be encountered; poor judgment by the British officers of the temper of the Americans and of the physical obstacles in the colonies; faults of strategy; the diplomatic failure to prevent France from aiding the Americans—these formed far more potent factors in the defeat of the British than this battle and others similar to it. The defeat resulted from blunders by the British rather than from the superiority of the Americans. To say that the American soldier was more efficient and braver than the British contradicts the facts of many encounters of the war.

The Americans showed themselves to be fair marksmen, and they had become accustomed to depend upon accuracy of aim for protection. They had, however, been ill-trained in any sort of movement other than individual efforts executed under the direction of commanders in whom they trusted. Favorable conditions surrounding this engagement counterbalanced the lack of training.

The original plan of Cornwallis's campaign in the South has been described. The Battle of King's Mountain did not prevent him from carrying out, after a time, the original plan arranged between him and Clinton. Leslie was ordered to sail south and join him, and together they advanced into Virginia. If we may suppose that Cornwallis was forced to move into Virginia, it resulted from the efficient strategy of General Greene rather than from the British loss at King's Mountain. This battle may have indirectly influenced Cornwallis's strategy, but it did not provide a determining cause for his plans; neither did the British movement into Virginia form a retreat.

It is impossible to state just how great an influence this event exerted upon the career of Sevier. After it had taken place, he returned to his home and prepared for the campaign which followed against the Cherokees. The estimate of his leadership increased immeasurably in the opinion of his friends on the frontier. His great popularity resulted from his efficient leadership against the Indians and the British. His place in the hearts of his neighbors had been definitely established before King's Mountain, but his participation in this spectacular victory greatly enhanced his prestige as a frontier leader. From this time forward he shared in the glory which surrounded the Revolutionary heroes. He had taken part in the struggle to free the country from the hated oppressions of the British government and had met and helped to defeat some of its finest and most efficient troops. The leaders of the pioneer forces in this battle became well known throughout the states, and Sevier shared this renown with his brother officers. It exalted his reputation at home and marked him as a prominent leader in his section. This engagement introduced him to the country at large and made him a respected character in all parts of the nation.

CHAPTER IV

A FRONTIER LAND GAMBLER

THE TRAITS of the pioneer found expression in the character of John Sevier. Every pioneer was potentially a land speculator. Only a few could acquire vast estates, and those who achieved success in land speculation naturally occupied a prominent place in in the public affairs of the West. The speculator had the opportunity of establishing contact with the mass of immigrants, and by this method he was able to impress his personality upon the newcomer. In return, if he was fair-minded and interested in the development of the country, the public usually supported him in his undertakings. Should he possess attractive human qualities and exert a personal interest in the welfare of those coming into the West, by helping them to acquire homes upon reasonable terms, these new arrivals gladly repaid his efforts with confidence in his integrity. This characteristic represented a vital element in the popularity of such men as Sevier, William Blount, and others who interested themselves in the development of the West.

The frontiersmen soon learned to distinguish among the different types of speculators. Some of these land traders acquired large tracts with the idea of holding the land until they could realize an immense profit at the expense of the immigrant. Others bought and soon sold in order that the country might develop rapidly while they realized a reasonable profit. Some of the speculators lived on the frontier and knew the temper of the settlers. They inspired confidence in those to whom they sold land. They combined their acquisition of wealth with a desire to aid the newcomer in establishing himself. Their activities were open to public inspection, and they did not fear inquiry into their methods, for they confined their operations to practices common on the frontier.

The speculators who lived in the East and invested some of their wealth in western lands soon aroused the contempt of the people in the West. The pioneer realized that the sole object in their minds was personal enrichment at the expense of the westerner. They held their land for an exorbitant price and in this way identified themselves with the wealthy class from whom the pioneer sought to escape. Instead of aiding in the settlement of the country, they were hindrances, in the opinion of the settlers, because they made it impossible for men without means to acquire the best lands. When men of wealth in the East left their homes and actually settled upon the frontier, the pioneers accepted them as friends. In such instances, the speculators subjected themselves to the dangers upon the border and became identified with its common interests. The frontiersmen held no regard for one who profited by the exertions of another or who shunned the treacherous savage.

Sevier represented an unusual combination of these two outstanding types of speculators. He was firmly associated with the West and identified with its activities. Yet he did not scruple to take advantage of the opportunity to unite his projects with land companies from the East. He profited by association with those who had capital to invest in western lands. He did not confine his activities in land dealing, however, entirely to operations directed by corporations. In addition, he acted as a free lance in the game of the west. Partly because of this, he retained the confidence of his neighbors and at the same time reaped the advantages of combination.

The North Carolina Assembly passed a law in 1777 which provided for opening offices to dispose of the lands belonging to the state.[1] Important changes were made in 1783, but the principles established in the earlier year remained the basis upon which the public domain passed into private hands. Its administration rested with the county officials. The significant features of this system, in which speculators were vitally interested, consisted of an *entry* of a claim for certain land, the *warrant* to have it surveyed, the *plots* representing the survey, and the *grant* issued by the state. Around these technicalities revolved the various means employed to acquire an estate.

In the following year, 1778, the Assembly prohibited entries for land beyond the Indian boundary.[2] This act provided only for a temporary limitation, however, and Sevier and his fellow-speculators expected the state to extend its bounds as necessity arose. The primary consideration in passing these laws was to obtain revenue.

Immediately a wave of speculation set in. By 1779 it became necessary to make provision for complaint when grants were obtained secretly "by artful and designing men" for "land to which they have no just title, to the great injury of many of the inhabitants of this State.[3] Complaints against illegal speculation might be made to the governor, who should suspend the execution of the grant and place the facts before the court of the county in which the unscrupulous speculator operated. The practice of speculation became so prevalent, and the Revolutionary troubles had so disorganized affairs, that the legislature closed the land office in 1781 by forbidding entries to be made with any entry-taker.[4]

---

[1] *SRNC*, XXIV, 43-48.
[2] *Ibid.*, pp. 159-61.
[3] *Ibid.*, p. 271.
[4] *Ibid.*, pp. 398-401.

North Carolina used the vast area of unappropriated land in the West to remunerate her Continental officers and soldiers. In 1782 an act passed the legislature setting aside certain amounts for each man who had fought in the Revolution. These amounts ranged from six hundred and forty acres for each private to twelve thousand acres for a brigadier general.[5] The Assembly set aside a large reservation in which it forbade entries to all others except soldiers.[6] In 1783, it created a special office in Nashville for handling these claims and placed Martin Armstrong in charge.[7] The procedure by which the soldier obtained his land differed in some details from the method provided by the first law in 1777.

The Assembly reopened the unsettled western lands to entry in 1783 by creating John Armstrong's land office at Hillsborough. The purchaser then entered his claim with John Armstrong at that place rather than with an entry-taker in the county. This modification of the law of 1777 provided for a centralization of authority under a single officer who had charge of all entries, except those of soldiers, upon lands in the West. Practically no difference in the procedure of obtaining land existed after this change took place except that the price was increased.[8] The warrants issued by John Armstrong came to be known as "supernumeraries."[9] This office remained open for only a year, at the end of which time it was closed and never reopened.[10]

The people of the state generally understood that all entries which had been recorded should be completed, and this necessitated the continuance of the policy of issuing grants even after the land office closed. One of the

---

[5] *Ibid.*, p. 419.
[6] *Ibid.*, p. 480.
[7] *Ibid.*, p. 482.
[8] *Ibid.*, p. 478.
[9] Blount to Secretary of State, Apr. 23, 1792, *BRL*, 7857.
[10] *SRNC*, XXIV, 563-64.

provisions of the final act of cession of the western lands to the United States in 1789 stated that all processes for granting titles which had begun before that time should be completed by the State of North Carolina.[11] The Assembly added amendments to the land laws changing provisions as necessity arose. An important provision made in the year the office closed gave a person full liberty to remove a warrant to land other than that described in the warrant.[12]

In theory these laws created a beautiful system. They were especially well adapted to the purposes of the land speculator. One object of the law of 1777, besides that of providing revenue for the state, intended to prevent single individuals from obtaining large grants. The law of 1783 entirely nullified this intention by raising the limit from six hundred and forty to five thousand acres. A significant omission removed any limit: no provision appeared in any law to restrain a surveyor from making a *union* of several entries in one survey.[13] The limit, therefore, in the amount of land that a person might acquire was determined by his ability to pay the price demanded by the state. As this law meant to provide revenue, the state did not concern itself to any great degree about minor considerations of equity in the disposal of its western lands.

The opportunities for fraud were numerous, and Sevier did not escape charges of sharp practices in connection with his speculative activities. If any entry-taker could be bribed or induced to change the entries in any way, a vast field of operations opened to the speculator who cared to take the risks. Warrants might be forged; the secre-

---

[11] *Ibid.*, XXV, 4-6.   [12] *Ibid.*, XXIV, 682.

[13] This question was settled by the United States Supreme Court in a decision written by Chief Justice John Marshall and delivered Feb. 21, 1815, Polk's Lessee v. Wendel *et al.*, *United States Reports*, III, 665-70.

tary might not investigate doubtful cases or might be connected with a scheme to defraud. The surveyor might be bribed to include more land in the tract than the warrant called for. If a grant once came into the hands of the grantee, no other person could have him ejected unless fraud was proven in court, and this process might require years of litigation and endless expense. Since warrants might be transferred and applied to another tract, a person rarely would carry a case to court when he could acquire other valuable land without additional expense.

The time element also favored the speculator. If he possessed warrants, he might hold them and have them surveyed whenever he wished. They represented the value named on their face. Sevier, together with all the frontiersmen, used them as money in his business transactions. Since the Indian boundary was a temporary affair, the westward progress of the whites was regarded as inevitable. As a reflection of this attitude on the part of the speculators, Governor Martin in 1782 instructed the commissioners whom he had appointed to negotiate a treaty with the Cherokees to ". . . agree upon a western line by which they and you shall be sacredly bounded, which confining and contracting their settlements, they will soon be circumscribed by white Inhabitants and their power reduced to the harmless and inoffensive situation of the Catawbas."[14] The speculator, therefore, expected to locate his warrants upon the choice lands as they opened to settlers.

There was a great amount of indiscriminate dealings in lands upon the frontier. Settlers pushed across the Indian boundary and defied the power of the state to remove them. By 1790, three hundred thousand acres

---

[14] *SRNC*, XVI, 710-11, Gov. Martin to the Cherokee Treaty Commissioners, Sept. 20, 1782.

A FRONTIER LAND GAMBLER 67

had been occupied south of the French Broad River, and three hundred families were living upon those lands without "right or license."[15] Numbers of squatters had not obtained grants for their lands in Washington County.[16] It is to be presumed that they depended upon the provision which gave them preference if they had resided upon the land and had improved it. They reaped crops from their land for nothing under such conditions, and a grant necessitated an outlay of money, which was scarce upon the frontier. If they should be hailed into court, they might pay the price of the grant and receive their title. In either case, they knew that they possessed a valid title, and the attitude of the frontiersmen favored this course of action. The distance of the West from the seat of government, the independence of the frontiersmen, and their contempt of restraint did not favor a correct application of the law. The result was a great confusion in the whole system of distribution of the public lands.

It is impossible to state what amount of land Sevier actually possessed. It is certain that he dealt extensively in the western lands. To make anything like an accurate estimate, it would be necessary to examine the records of many counties in Tennessee. An examination of copies of the grant books of North Carolina furnished the basis for a partial estimate of the land which that state actually granted to him prior to the year 1800.[17]

The first grant recorded is one in which he associated with Richard Caswell, dated November 1, 1786. The tract contained 357½ acres, comprising the whole of an island in the French Broad River: ". . . in Greene County

---

[15] Report of Secretary of State Jefferson to President Washington, transmitted to Congress Nov. 10, 1791. *ASP Public Lands*, I, 22-25.

[16] In the report just cited, it was recorded that there were entries for 746,362 acres, and grants had been issued upon only 214,550 acres.

[17] The Grant Books were copied by Judge Overton, and these copies are now in the *Tennessee State Archives*.

including the Island in French Broad River that the War Path leads through."[18] These same men received a grant jointly for another tract of land "in our county of Greene on the north side of Tennessee River, known by the name of Hackber Bottom."[19] It contained 500 acres and bore the date of April 23, 1787. On November 15 of the same year, they received a third grant for 200 acres "lying and being in our county of Greene on the north side of Tennessee River."[20]

In July, 1788, Sevier received a grant for 1,000 acres "in our Middle District, lying on both sides of Buffaloe River."[21] In the following month another tract was granted him for 2,115 acres "in our Middle District on the South side of Duck River and on both sides of both forks of Rich Creek."[22] Another 1,000-acre grant issued to him on the same day provided for land in the Middle District on the north side of Tennessee River.[23]

By far the greater amounts of land passed into his possession in the year 1795. A grant on August 27 gave him 6,040 acres in Sumner County on the north side of Cumberland River along the Virginia line.[24] On the next day, another grant added a tract of 25,060 acres in Sumner County on Cumberland River touching the Virginia line, joining a survey of Stockley Donelson.[25] The largest tract, granted on November 27, included 32,000 acres adjacent to the 25,060-acre survey.[26] Another grant on the same day conveyed to him 3,000 acres in Greene County on the south side of Nolachucky River along Camp Creek.[27]

---

[18] *North Carolina Grant Book* B, No. 34, p. 175. All the following references to grants are taken from the copies of the *North Carolina Grant Book.*
[19] *Grant Book* C, No. 746, p. 103.
[20] *Ibid.*, No. 569, p. 102.
[21] *Grant Book*, A, No. 8, p. 4.
[22] *Ibid.*, No. 17, p. 9.
[23] *Ibid.*, No. 55, p. 28.
[24] *Ibid.*, No. 229, p. 260.
[25] *Ibid.*, No. 228, p. 260.
[26] *Ibid.*, No. 300, p. 216.
[27] *Grant Book* C, No. 1365, p. 299.

During this period Sevier received grants to himself alone for at least 70,215 acres of land and became the joint owner of 1,057½ acres in addition. A large proportion of these holdings were located on the waters of the Cumberland bordering on the Virginia line. These grants represented the amounts of land for which he actually received the original title. They gave no idea at all of any lands which he may have bought after the title had been obtained by some one else. Neither did they include his holdings on the Holston, Watauga, and Nolachucky rivers, which he had obtained before the opening of the land office in 1777.[28] This summary provides only an uncertain estimate of his speculation in unappropriated lands. Since these grants represent only one phase of his activities along this line, there can be no doubt that he gambled extensively upon the settlement of the West.

Sevier also associated with Landon Carter in land speculation. In 1792 he gave Carter a $200,000 bond in a land transaction. They had procured warrants for 128,000 acres in partnership. The lands had not yet been located, and Carter turned over the warrants to Sevier so that they might be located as "Supernumeries as soon as circumstances will permit."[29] The titles were to be obtained in Sevier's name or in that of "any other person or persons that he may think fit to empower to obtain and receive them on behalf of the parties hereto." When the titles came into his possession, one-half of them were to be made over to Carter after he had deducted the lands due the surveyor and others in payment of fees. Carter evidently wished to keep his name out of any transactions which might take place. It is not known whether the large tracts for which grants had been made to Sevier in 1795

---

[28] These facts could be ascertained only by a minute study of the land records in North Carolina and of the county records in Tennessee.

[29] *AHM*, III, 83-84.

were based upon these warrants which he and Carter held in partnership. It seems evident that those engaged in land speculation on the frontier used almost any sort of means to obtain title to the new lands opened to settlement, and this and other incidents show that Sevier adopted the practices which were common in the West.

Not only did Sevier operate alone and in partnership, but he also united with speculating land companies made up of men from the eastern parts of the country. He manifested a great interest in the Muscle Shoals project.

The first company formed for the promotion of the Muscle Shoals scheme organized in 1783. Men from both East and West had an interest in it. William Blount headed the Company, and other members were Richard Caswell, General Rutherford, John Donelson, Joseph Martin, and John Sevier. These men intended to develop the lands lying in the Great Bend of the Tennessee River, which contained valuable lands for farming and a strategic location for purposes of trade with the Indians.[30]

They did not know at first whether the Bend lay within the bounds of Georgia, South Carolina, or North Carolina. John Donelson and Joseph Martin accomplished the purchase of the land from the Indians. The Company proceeded to establish the southern boundary of North Carolina and found the land in the Bend to be south of the line and within the bounds of Georgia. Blount resigned his seat in Congress and proceeded to Georgia to present the project to the legislature of that state. As a result of his endeavors, the Georgia legislature passed an act which incorporated into a county the lands between the southern boundary of North Carolina and the Tennessee

---

[30] For a thorough discussion of this project, see A. P. Whitaker, "The Muscle Shoals Speculation," *Mississippi Valley Historical Review*, XIII, 365-86.

A FRONTIER LAND GAMBLER 71

River. Seven commissioners were appointed, Sevier being one of the three members of the Company who received appointments. These commissioners organized in July, 1784, appointed militia officers for the new county, which they called Houston, and named officials to regulate the disposal of the lands. Sevier became colonel of the county militia. They also made preparations to open a land office.

Sevier took an active interest in the project. He helped to prepare an expedition which descended the river to ascertain the location and the quality of the land as well as to lay out the boundaries of the county. The situation seemed especially favorable for the planting of a colony, and the Company widely advertised the scheme. In 1785 the Company fitted out an expedition which descended the river to the Great Bend. Reports said that this company consisted of three or four hundred men.[31] They proceeded to open a land office and to issue warrants.[32] Either because of the opposition of the Indians

---

[31] Deposition of James M. Lewis, Apr. 15, 1817, House of Representatives Collection List No. 6, MSS Division, Library of Congress.

[32] Hitherto, this point has not been clear. Whitaker, "The Muscle Shoals Speculation," *loc. cit.*: "The land office was not opened in March, 1785, and the colony was not established. This pause has been attributed by one writer to Indian hostility, an explanation that will not stand in the face of the fact that the Southern Indians committed no hostilities of any consequence until 1785. Altogether it seems much more probable that it was the rise of the state of Franklin that halted the company's enterprise."

In order to obtain land which had been granted by the legislature of Georgia to the commissioners, James Sevier, acting for the heirs of John Sevier, together with representatives of the heirs of the other commissioners, applied to Congress sometime in 1818 for permission to locate these lands from the public lands in other parts of the southwest, as the land in the Bend had all been taken. In support of their claims, they produced a number of affidavits, which gave an account of the expedition which they said took place in 1785. These affidavits are in the MSS Division, House Collection No. 6, Library of Congress.

Deposition of Lewis, cited in Note 31: ". . . proceeded down to the

or because of the Franklin movement, possibly on account of both reasons, the project had to be abandoned at that time.[33]

Sevier opposed the Franklin movement in its early stages probably because he thought it might interfere with the development of Muscle Shoals.[34] He soon saw, however, that the Franklin government would succeed in establishing itself, and then he entered whole-heartedly into its operation. Friends of the Company occupied

---

bent of the Tennessee . . . where they opened an office for Said Land agreeable to Law passed by the Legislature of the State of Georgia—and that the said office was opened in the month of December 1785, Between the twenty & twenty fifth of said month; And issued warrants & . . ."

Deposition of John M. Walker, Dec. 9, 1818: "The company with the Commissioners proceeded down the River until they arrived within the Territorial limits of Georgia, where a Land Office was opened and Warrants were issued for a large quantity of Land. . . ."

Deposition of William Colyar, Dec. 27, 1822: ". . . that they went as far down the tennessee river as the mouth of Chickamaugy creek, That on the north side of the river a few days before Christmas in the same year an office was opened by said Commissioners and entries were made and this deponant obtained a warrant for One thousand acres for which he gave his bond with security. . . ."

Deposition of James Sevier, Feb. 27, 1822: ". . . That they descended the Tennessee as far as the mouth of Chickamaugy Creek and on the North side of the river they opened a land office . . . issued warrants to all that were present, who gave their bond. . . ."

Interrogatories propounded to Zachariah Cox, Jan. 20, 1818: ". . . myself . . . employed to accompany and guard them Down the River—and assist them in their opperations; to what I was informed was the Bend of Tennessee, and which they named the County of Houston lying within the then Charter limits of the State of Georgia where they proceeded to issue Land Warrants. . . . I myself received a Land warrant."

Several of these depositions mention that the Cherokees were cross and surly, and this was one of the reasons that the attempt at settlement was postponed.

[33] Ramsey, *op. cit.*, p. 377.

[34] Whitaker, "The Muscle Shoals Speculation," *loc. cit., passim;* Ramsey, *op. cit.*, p. 291; *SRNC*, XXI, 285-86.

positions of importance in the new state, and it is probable that he thought to use the State of Franklin as a means to advance the interests of the adventurers. Indeed, it was openly stated at the time that the Franklin movement did not contemplate the good of the new "commonwealth" but that it had been created for the benefit of a few "crafty land-jobbers . . . who are aiming at purchasing the great bent of the Tennessee from the Indians, and if not successful that way, to contrive a quarrel and drive the natives . . . out by force."[35]

Georgia's ratification of the United States Constitution checked the progress of the Muscle Shoals venture. The central government then assumed the conduct of Indian affairs, and this change in the control of Indian relations frustrated a joint expedition that Georgia and the State of Franklin had planned against the Creeks. The failure of the infant state added to the discomfiture of the Company, and Sevier turned to intrigue with the Spanish. One of the objects of this intrigue aimed at securing for the Franklinites the privilege of settling lands south of the Tennessee River.[36] The refusal of Spain to accede to the wishes of the intriguers dealt a final blow to the development of Muscle Shoals in this period. Sevier also had some connection with the later projects for the development of the Shoals under the leadership of Zachariah Cox. The later organization, known as the Tennessee Company, formed one of the speculating schemes originating about 1789.

The speculative nature of the operations of land companies, as well as the lengths to which Sevier was willing

---

[35] Draper MSS, 7XX, 17-18; extract of a letter from a gentleman in the western territory "lately ceded by North Carolina" to a friend in Virginia, dated Dec., 1784; Whitaker, "The Muscle Shoals Speculation," *loc. cit.*, p. 371.

[36] *Ibid.*, pp. 382-83.

to go, appears from the plans of the South Carolina Yazoo Company, from which he received the promise of fifty thousand acres and to which he promised aid in colonization. The project aimed at the settlement of the Yazoo area, which was opened by the Bourbon County Act passed by the Georgia legislature in 1785. The basis of the claim held by the men who formed the enterprise had been obtained by one of the original company, Thomas Washington.[37] It very clearly illustrates the methods pursued by unscrupulous speculators.

John Wood, a white man who lived in the Choctaw country, and who "had been useful to them on several occasions," had received a deed of gift from four Choctaw chiefs in the form of a tract of land containing two or three million acres. Washington had obtained half of Wood's rights, although the assignment extended to the whole deed. Wood sold the other half to John Cape of Kentucky, evidently upon the promise of the latter to pay 25,000 pounds Virginia currency. Cape's attorneys, Spring and Platt, sold this half to Washington and the Company who bound themselves to give Wood "500,000 acres in continental military warrants." By a manipulation, Wood did not receive any return from the half

---

[37] *An Extract from the Minutes of the South Carolina Yazoo Company* (Charleston, 1791), Library of Congress, *Miscellaneous Pamphlets*, Vol. 254, No. 6. This document was published evidently to be used in advertising the project. There are three parts to the publication: The first gives a historical account of the acquisition and development of the scheme; the second deals with a plan for the more permanent establishment of the Company; and the third outlines a scheme for raising the value of the Company's territory. The outline of the activities of the Company given here follows closely that of the first section of the document. Other sources consulted were: C. H. Haskins, "The Yazoo Companies," *American Historical Association Papers*, V, 395-437; J. C. Parish, "The Intrigues of Doctor James O'Fallon," *Mississippi Valley Historical Review*, XVII (Sept., 1930), 230-63; and *Documents*, "The South Carolina Yazoo Company," ed. A. P. Whitaker, *Mississippi Valley Historical Review*, XVI (Dec. 1929), 382-94.

which he sold to Cape. The whole scheme appears to have been directed toward the elimination of Wood after the Company had obtained his shadowy claims. The Company wrote to him and "made him a promise in general terms of just and generous recompence," which was just another way of saying that they would give him a promise of a grant of land when they settled the area.

Washington, Alexander Moultrie, William Clay Snipes, and Isaac Huger comprised the original Company. They later took in other influential persons of Georgia and South Carolina, and Alexander McGillivray, the famous Indian chief, became a member. Attempts were made to consolidate with the Virginia Yazoo Company, composed of Patrick Henry, David Ross, and others, who planned settlements on the headwaters of the Tombigbee River just south of the Muscle Shoals, but these attempts at union came to nothing. The Company applied to the Georgia legislature for a grant in fee simple for the territory outlined. The act passed in 1789 and provided that when the Company deposited $66,964 in the treasury the governor should make them a grant. They would then be responsible for the extinguishment of the Indian rights, which they claimed had already been accomplished by the acquisition of Wood's claim.

Soon after that act was passed, the Company received a request from General Wilkinson, the arch intriguer of the West, who declared that Wood's grant was not "worth a pinch of snuff," and who also recommended himself as a proper person to act for the Company in their negotiations with the Indians. The Company promised to admit him and his friends in Kentucky, Innes, Muter, Nicholas and Sebastian, whom he had recommended. Sevier wrote to them about the same time requesting a share and promising his aid in the settlement. "His propositions were immediately acceded to."

In the meantime, the Company had engaged John Holder of Kentucky to lead a colony of four hundred families to the region and to effect a settlement. But this agent partly disposed of the goods advanced to him by the Company and failed to carry out the project. The Company then decided to send Dr. James O'Fallon to take up the work and to act as its agent-general in the West. In 1790, O'Fallon set out for the western country carrying credentials to leaders of prominence in the West, among them being Sevier, and to the Spanish officials at New Orleans.

The Company expected to be able to pay the amount due the State of Georgia in audited claims against the state. However, when these claims representing the amount were presented, the treasurer and the governor refused to accept them, and a special session of the legislature decided that the obligation must be paid in specie or in paper money. The Company found itself unable to raise the sum required. They deposited one thousand pounds sterling, and upon this they expected to gain "a firm footing in the territory."

O'Fallon proceeded toward the west, advertising his scheme in bombastic and enthusiastic terms. He engaged Sevier to act as sub-agent in the Franklin settlements. Wilkinson was similarly engaged to act in Kentucky. All were "bound to the company's interests by the strongest of all ties, views of advantage to themselves; for he made promises to them of considerable shares in the purchase, which could be of no value if the project should fail of success." Wilkinson was promised a full share in the Company. O'Fallon promised Sevier and others fifty thousand acres of land. He corresponded with the Spanish officials and even directed a letter to the President of the United States, "pointing out the commercial and other advantages which might result to the union from their intended settlement, and calculated to obtain from the supreme executive a direct or implied sanction for their measures." He claimed to have conciliated the Spanish and the Choctaws to the project and that he had three thousand men prepared to go to Natchez in November, 1790. Of these he expected Sevier to conduct one thousand men from Franklin.[38] His plans smacked too much of a military enterprise to suit even the gambling spirit of the members of the company, and they had to disapprove his plans. Their agent had overreached himself. A proclamation by President Washington against him and the leaders of the expedition which he had organized effectually brought to an end the designs of the Company for an immediate settlement.

In his last dispatch to the Company, O'Fallon complained that Sevier was jealous: "he is of great moment to our interests. Why have you not written to him?" This speculating scheme definitely placed Sevier in a company of men who were willing to seize control of vast areas of valuable lands in the Indian country upon the flimsiest pretext and to gamble upon their ability to secure legislative sanction for their pretended holdings. The project embraced the whole of the old Southwest and illustrated the imperial designs of the speculators.

In all of these attempts, Sevier showed his tendency towards land speculation. He wanted to have a part in the development of the western country, and he hoped to increase his wealth by uniting with those companies which operated with the idea of profits uppermost in the minds of their directors. Perhaps Sevier, who possessed the confidence of the people on the frontier, served as a will-

---

[38] Letter from the Gentleman in Kentucky to his Friend in Charleston, in *Augusta Chronicle and Gazette of the State*, April 16, 1791. Quoted from the *Columbian Herald*. This letter was dated September 15, 1790, and evidently was written by O'Fallon.

ing tool of these promoters in order to assure success to their schemes. He continued to hold the confidence of his friends and neighbors in spite of the nefarious operations of some of the projects with which he was more or less directly connected. He did not escape censure for underhand methods in land dealings. This, however, is a separate chapter in his life and will be treated in its proper setting.

CHAPTER V

GOVERNOR OF FRANKLIN

SEVIER served as the first and only governor of the State of Franklin. This commonwealth, created from the North Carolina counties west of the mountains, presented one of the most conspicuous examples of separatism in any frontier region.

Sectionalism formed one of the roots from which grew this attempt at self-government. The same disdain for the conventions and institutions of the older sections of the mother state which had characterized earlier days of settlement now animated the settlers in these new counties to an increasing opposition and to a growing spirit of independence. The eastern section of North Carolina met the movement with a threat of force, and this attempt appeared to the frontiersmen as an additional illustration of arrogance and haughty superiority. Speculators living in the East feared for their investments in western lands—another element in the bitterness between the sections. Jealousy and discord among the citizens of the tiny commonwealth contributed to the decline and failure of their attempt to maintain a new state, which they hoped might become a member of the Union. The disappointed leaders of this abortive government in the end attempted to retrieve their lost cause by a forlorn intrigue with officials of the Spanish Crown. Yet, in its inception, the movement gave promise of success, and at the height of its power it voiced an efficient expression of the independent spirit of the frontier.

The genesis of the movement is to be found in the policy of the Continental Congress, which advocated cession of the western lands of the states to the Union. As early as 1780 that body made reference to the disposal of such a cession in case the states agreed to it. On September 6, of that year, Congress passed a resolution declaring that if Virginia, North Carolina, and Georgia should make a cession of their portions of the West, "the territory so ceded shall be laid out in separate States at such times and in such manner as Congress shall hereafter direct."[1]

As a result of this resolution, Arthur Campbell circulated a document in the counties of southwestern Virginia and western North Carolina, probably early in 1782. This paper contained a scheme for a convention to meet later in the year "to adopt such measures as may be adjudged proper by a majority for the interest and safety of their constituents as members of the American Union."[2] No record of elections to this convention can be found, and it may be assumed that it did not meet. The project of Campbell looked toward the establishment of a state which should include those areas of the frontier of Virginia and North Carolina in which practically the same conditions existed. Since this document was published as a result of the resolution of Congress, referred to above, it is certain that the people of the western border sensed the possibilities of separate statehood. They were by no means indifferent to the action of Congress or to the policy of their own state in regard to the situation. In all probability Sevier knew of Campbell's scheme, but his attitude toward it cannot be definitely determined.

The cession of her western lands to the Union by the State of North Carolina gave ample proof of the cupidity

---

[1] S. C. Williams, *The Lost State of Franklin*, p. 5; *Journal of the Continental Congress*, XVII, 808.

[2] Williams, *op. cit.*, p. 6.

of the eastern land speculator. William Blount and Hugh Williamson, two of North Carolina's representatives in Congress, advocated the cession in 1782, in order that the state might escape the valuation of the western possessions in the distribution of war expenses among the states. North Carolina's share of the costs of the Revolution would be doubled if it included the unimproved western lands.[3] Since Congress had based the apportionment upon the value of the land possessed by each state, North Carolina, if it followed the proposal of Congress, would relieve herself of the necessity of paying a large quota to the Union. If the state retained her western territory, these lands would be counted as a part of her wealth, and her share of the national obligations would be correspondingly increased.

When John Armstrong opened the land office at Hillsborough in 1783, large quantities of western lands immediately passed into private hands.[4] Those interested in land speculation had no thought of permitting the field of their operations to pass into the control of another government. North Carolina, therefore, refused to consider such a cession before her citizens had full opportunity to appropriate the most desirable portions of the unsettled territory.[5] The Assembly did not wish to make a cession until the coffers of the state had been filled with the revenues proceeding from the sale of those lands. There would remain sufficient time, after most of the available land had been appropriated, for North Carolina to make the cession and to permit the formation of a new state, which should be required to assume its proportion of the expenses of the Revolution and to guarantee payment to North Carolina soldiers in the form of land.

[3] *Ibid.*, p. 18.   [4] See p. 64.
[5] *SRNC*, XVI, 919; Williams, *op. cit.*, p. 19.

The greater part of the land outside of the Indian territory had been claimed or included within the military reservation. Speculators who had purchased large quantities of military warrants probably would reap the greatest profits by handling the problem in this manner. It would give them time to secure their holdings under the none too scrutinizing government through which they had become accustomed to operate. It was a most mercenary scheme, undertaken without any concern either for the Union or for the state's own citizens in the West. In the wild scramble for possession of title to western lands following the opening of the land office, little attention was paid to limitations imposed by the Indian line. The territory open to the speculator included practically all of the lands within the present bounds of the State of Tennessee which had not already been taken, with the exception of the area held for North Carolina's Revolutionary soldiers and a part reserved for the Indians.[6]

The cession of her western lands to the Union by Virginia placed the whole matter in a different light. Virginia had declined for a time to cede her lands, and this delay on her part enabled North Carolina to grasp the wealth of the West. But when Virginia receded from her position and made the cession, it appeared necessary for North Carolina to consider similar action. In the Assembly of the latter state, which convened on April 19, 1784, a bill was introduced to cede the western territory. It passed on June 2, by a vote of fifty-two to forty-three, the members from the western counties being divided in their support of the bill.[7] The act provided that after the cession should be accepted by Congress, these lands should not be counted in the valuation upon which distribution of the Revolutionary debt was to be made; the

---
[6] *Ibid.*, pp. 20-21.
[7] *SRNC*, XXIV, 561-63; Williams, *op. cit.*, p. 23.

rights of the Revolutionary soldiers to lands in this territory given to them by the state should be recognized; the ceded territory should be laid out into a state or states and admitted into the Union with the provision that slavery should not be prohibited except by the Assembly of the state or states thus formed; acceptance by Congress should be acknowledged within a year. Some days later the Assembly passed a bill which declared that there should be no change in the government of the western territory until Congress adopted the cession.[8]

A group in the Assembly violently opposed the cession on the grounds that North Carolina would cede too much in comparison to the amount retained by Virginia and Georgia and that the domestic debt of the state, which had been secured by these lands, ought to be paid before her possessions were given away. They also urged that the amounts expended in the Indian wars which the state had conducted should be included as a part of the Revolutionary expenses.[9]

The passage of the cession act created the conditions out of which grew the movement for a separate state in the West. It is probable that Sevier was one of a majority in the West who favored the cession. The movement cannot be attributed to dissatisfaction with the act. The old antagonism between the sections was still present, but sectionalism cannot be assigned as the sole reason for the movement unless some irritating features accompanied the cession. Two circumstances of such a nature certainly played an important part in giving impetus to the movement.

It is not difficult to interpret the attitude of the westerners toward one of these circumstances. They well knew that Armstrong's office had recorded claims and had issued

---
[8] *SRNC*, XIX, 712; Williams, *op. cit.*, p. 24.
[9] *SRNC*, XVII, 78.

warrants for large quantities of land. They also realized that North Carolina did not intend to make any sort of settlement with the people of the frontier counties in regard to the revenues which had been collected through the sales represented by these warrants. They found themselves confronted with the problem of financing a new state, the formation of which had been contemplated in the cession act. The means of financing a new government in the West must be found in the ability to collect money from the sale of unappropriated lands, and the policy of North Carolina largely had deprived them of this source of revenue. To the leaders in the West it appeared highly important to get the new state under way as soon as possible in order to preserve what little income remained to them. Otherwise, the land speculators in the East would acquire that remainder.

The other irritating incident arose in the debate over the cession. Some of the members from the West who opposed the act pleaded with the Assembly to allow them to remain a part of the state. In reply some of the leaders in the Assembly cast epithets upon the people of the western counties, calling them the "off-scourings of the earth, fugitives from justice and we will be rid of them at any rate."[10] The westerners in that Assembly who opposed the cession later occupied places of importance in the Franklin government, and their position can be more satisfactorily explained as a reaction to this intemperate language than in any other way. The West resented the unmerited insult. It is easy to imagine with what feelings the pioneers received the news of this attitude on the part of the state's political leaders.

After the cession became known to the people of the West, plans were immediately inaugurated to call a convention to consider what should be done. The plan fol-

---

[10] Williams, *op. cit.*, p. 61.

lowed that of Campbell described above. The convention met on August 23, 1784, in Jonesboro, with John Sevier as its chairman. The Declaration of Independence was invoked as embodying a statement of the grievances of the westerners against North Carolina. The convention declared the three counties of Washington, Sullivan, and Greene independent of the State of North Carolina, and then proceeded to adopt a provisional plan of government to provide for another convention to meet the next month.[11]

Those who had opposed the cession act in the North Carolina Assembly, particularly certain members from the eastern part of the state, made it an issue in the political campaign during the summer of 1784. Hugh Williamson, delegate to Congress from North Carolina, took the lead in the matter and urged that the act be repealed. He based his changed attitude upon the ground that an immediate cession made it impossible for the state to claim credit for her Indian expeditions, one of the points urged in the Assembly in protest against the cession. Williamson was by no means disinterested and impartial in his position, for he had important interests in land grants in the West.[12] The land speculator in the East realized that it would be easier to complete titles to such lands under the authority of North Carolina, where he had influence, than to take the risk of unfavorable action by a new state in which he had no part. When the matter came up in the Assembly which met in October, 1784, an act of repeal passed by a safe majority.[13] It is impossible to say what effect the action of the Jonesboro convention had upon this move of the Assembly. It may be supposed that the news of the convention had reached Newbern before the repeal had been passed.

[11] *Ibid.*, pp. 28-33.   [12] *AHM*, I, 281; Williams, *op. cit.*, p. 35.
[13] *SRNC*, XIX, 761; Williams, *op. cit.*, p. 35.

The second convention of the three western counties called for September did not meet until December. This assembly determined to form a separate state and to draw up a temporary constitution. A report of the committee appoined to outline a plan of action described the situation in the participating counties. One of the principal reasons advanced for the formation of a new state, besides the fact of the cession, was that such action would tend "not only to keep a circulating medium in gold and silver among us, but draw it from many individuals living in other states, who claim large quantities [of land] that would lie in the bounds of the new state." The question of the currency possessed an importance which is not usually recognized, and lack of it on the frontier constituted one of the real hardships. This statement implied that the continued operation of the North Carolina land laws would draw a large portion of the currency away from the West, to the more fortunate and wealthy East. The westerner felt the effect of this drain of money to the East whenever he desired to purchase any commodity. A new state would hold a larger amount of it in the West.

The report displayed evidence that sectionalism had some part in the movement. It cited the latest taxation law passed by the North Carolina Assembly as another reason for the organization of Franklin. This act provided that western lands should be assessed at the same value as those in the East, although the land was worth only one-fourth as much.[14]

The constitution prepared by the convention closely followed that of North Carolina. It was meant to be a temporary instrument, since this body provided for another constitutional convention to meet before a year had passed and to make the constitution permanent or to

---

[14] Williams, *op. cit.*, pp. 38-39.

amend it as the people desired. The constitution also contained a Declaration of Rights and a Declaration of Independence.[15]

Sevier opposed the Franklin movement in its inception. His attention at that time centered upon the Muscle Shoals project, and he knew that any attempt to set up a new state would halt the development of the speculation for the time being at least.[16] Just after the meeting of the December convention he received word of the repeal of the cession act, through Colonel Joseph Martin, one of the members of the Muscle Shoals Company. Martin also told him that the Assembly had formed a new district in the west for which Sevier had been made brigadier general.[17] Sevier believed that this attempt on the part of the Assembly to conciliate the people of the West would be acceptable: "I conclude this step will satisfy the people with the old state, and we shall pursue no further measures as to a new state."[18] He later said that he had been "dragged with the Franklin measures by a large number of the people of this country."[19] He carried his opposition so far as to oppose elections to the first Assembly of the State of Franklin.[20]

While Sevier feared that the organization of a new government would divert the attention of the people of both East and West from the Muscle Shoals project,[21] he fully recognized the temper of the western pioneers. He found himself in a dilemma. If he carried his opposition to the new government too far, he could expect no aid from it in the development of the colony in the Bend

---

[15] *Ibid.*, Appendix, pp. 332-38. [16] See p. 72.
[17] Draper MSS, 11DD76.
[18] Sevier to Kennedy, Jan. 2, 1785, in Ramsey, *op. cit.*, p. 291.
[19] Sevier to Martin, Mar. 27, 1788, *Calendar of Virginia State Papers*, IV, 416.
[20] Williams, *op. cit.*, p. 54.
[21] Whitaker, *The Spanish-American Frontier*, p. 55.

of the Tennessee. If he accepted the cause of the West he would alienate the support of some of his friends in the East. The course which he pursued was logical and practicable. He opposed the movement until he saw that it would proceed without him and then grasped the reins of power. Thus he hoped to occupy a position in which he might be able to further the Shoals speculation and to retain the support by the frontiersmen, without which the scheme was doomed to failure.

The first General Assembly of Franklin met in March, 1785, in Jonesboro.[22] It elected Sevier as governor and Landon Carter as speaker of the Senate. William Cage served as speaker of the House. It established a judiciary, made David Campbell superior judge, and Gist and Anderson assistant judges. A number of acts were passed during the session which applied North Carolina laws to Franklin.

Early in 1785 Governor Martin of North Carolina determined to take definite action in regard to the movement. In order to ascertain the facts, he sent an emissary, Major Henderson, to the Franklin country to find out whether the movement seemed to be of a temporary nature or whether it was an attempt toward independence. The Franklin Assembly formulated a message to Governor Martin in reply to a letter which the latter had written to Governor Sevier. It recited the grievances of the western people and stated the reasons which led to the separation.[23] A new charge found expression in this communication. Certain goods which had been promised the Indians by the State of North Carolina had been delayed, and as a result the savages had taken their revenge upon the settlements, to which the state had offered no protection.

Before the adjournment, the Franklin Assembly made provision for a conference with the Cherokees. It also com-

[22] Williams, *op. cit.*, p. 55.   [23] *Ibid.*, pp. 61-63.

missioned William Cocke to present a memorial to Congress asking for admission into the Union.

When Henderson returned to North Carolina and reported upon his mission, the Governor and the council of state decided to take aggressive action. The Governor issued a manifesto and circulated it in the western counties.[24] This document was meant to spread discontent among the Franklinites and, in reality, it carried the threat of subjugation by force if they did not abandon the movement. When Sevier received a copy of the manifesto, he issued a proclamation designed to counteract that of Governor Martin.[25] Governor Martin's term expired in the spring of 1785, and he was succeeded by General Richard Caswell, a man who enjoyed the confidence of the westerners. Sevier immediately wrote to Caswell and protested against the charges in Martin's manifesto, stating in respectful but definite terms the position of the Franklin government. Caswell adopted a policy of conciliation and waited for the meeting of the Assembly.[26]

In June, 1785, Sevier and the other commissioners appointed by the Franklin Assembly negotiated a treaty with the Cherokees, the treaty of Dumplin Creek, which extinguished the Indian title to a large tract of land lying south of the French Broad River. Settlers immediately crossed that river and occupied the lands under the authority of the State of Franklin.[27]

Another session of the General Assembly of Franklin convened in August.[28] This Assembly decided to turn over to North Carolina the public money which remained in the possession of the former officers of that state who now had become citizens of Franklin. It appointed a

---

[24] *Ibid.*, pp. 67-69.   [25] *Ibid.*, pp. 70-71.   [26] *Ibid.*, pp. 71-74.
[27] For copy of treaty see Williams, *op. cit.*, pp. 75-76; *SRNC*, XXII, 649.
[28] Williams, *op. cit.*, p. 87.

commissioner to lay the Franklin case before the Assembly of North Carolina in the hope of arriving at some agreement in regard to the separation. It also issued a call for another constitutional convention to meet in November.

The convention called by the August Assembly met on November 14. A committee headed by the Reverend Samuel Houston drew up a constitution and presented it to the delegates, but immediately opposition arose to it, and it was rejected. Out of this rejection a division developed which threatened to disrupt the state, and ultimately a modified form of the North Carolina constitution was adopted, "doubtless in the form of the North Carolina Constitution under which the state was being governed at the time."[29]

It is impossible to enumerate in detail the events which took place during the years when the Franklin government exercised actual or nominal control. Many of the documents have been lost, and the actual events are not easy to determine. Some of the more prominent features of the movement deserve mention, particularly those events in which Sevier had a strong personal interest aside from his routine as an executive.

In an attempt to establish a definite and general Indian policy, agents of the United States government negotiated a treaty with the southern Indians at Hopewell in 1785.[30] Its provisions satisfied neither the East nor the West. William Blount, who represented the State of North Carolina at Hopewell and who already had become identified with the interests of the West through extensive land speculation, voiced a very serious protest against it. The United States government meant by this treaty to institute a policy of restriction against encroachments

---

[29] *Ibid.*, p. 92.
[30] *United States Statutes at Large*, VII, 18-19.

upon Indian territory, and such a policy on the part of any government whatsoever was certain to encounter dissatisfaction and resistance from the frontiersmen. The Hopewell treaty directly affected the Franklinites, for if the Indian line should be established according to its provisions a large section of their territory would be cut off and returned to the Indians.[31]

Meanwhile North Carolina adopted a policy of conciliation toward the people of Franklin. The Assembly passed an act on December 6, 1785, to pardon those who had taken part in the attempt at separation, and to provide a method by which the people in the disaffected areas might elect delegates to the North Carolina Assembly. The freemen might convene on the day set for the election and ballot for their representatives.[32] In this way it was possible that a small number might elect a delegate. The discontented groups within the State of Franklin took advantage of this opportunity to disrupt that government.

When John Tipton announced his candidacy for election to the North Carolina Senate, the opposition to the Franklin government became formidable. The open feud between Sevier and Tipton began with the latter's attempt to undermine the influence of the Franklin governor over the people of the West. It is probable that Tipton was jealous of Sevier's popularity, and the two men may have had personal difficulties previous to this time. At any rate, they became bitter enemies, and Tipton headed the movement to destroy the unity of the West.

The Franklinites met this move by providing also for an election of representatives to the North Carolina Assembly. Both elections took place on the third Friday in August.[33] As a result, two returns of the election were

---
[31] Williams, *op. cit.*, p. 96.   [32] *SRNC*, XXIII, ch. 46.
[33] Williams, *op. cit.*, p. 104.

made to the North Carolina Assembly. In October the Franklin Assembly appointed a commission to attend the sessions of the North Carolina legislature and to negotiate for a separation. But the attempt resulted in failure, for the Assembly seated the rival Tipton delegation and refused to treat with the commission from Franklin. Tipton made the most of his influence in the legislature, which aided his attempts to capture control of the western counties.

The opposition in the West to the Franklin government came to a head in contests which arose concerning the jurisdiction of the Franklin courts and of the courts which remained loyal to North Carolina. The Tipton followers, representing the latter, attempted to obtain possession of the records in the Franklin courts. Resistance led to armed struggle between Sevier as the leader of the Franklin government and Tipton, the representative of North Carolina. The government of the mother state wisely held aloof, allowing the struggle to be carried on in the western area and making no atempt to use force to bring it to an end.

The situation resolved itself into a state of civil war on the border. Early in 1787, Sevier was induced to enter into negotiations with Evan Shelby, brigadier general of the Washington District at that time, for a peaceable solution of the whole matter.[34] Nothing came of the attempt to carry out the tentative agreement reached by these two. A proposal was advanced in the Franklin Assembly in November of the same year that the Franklinites should participate in the North Carolina elections by offering their ablest men as candidates. By this maneuver they hoped to gain a hearing in the North Carolina Assembly and to arrive at some compromise. This proposal caused another division of sentiment among

---

[34] *Ibid.*, pp. 138-39.

the Franklinites, and they again resorted to a commission.[35] When attempts at compromise between the factions in the West failed, the Franklin leaders adopted the scheme of entering the elections. Some of them were chosen, and these men took their places in the North Carolina Assembly. Judge Campbell, the head of the Franklin judiciary, accepted an appointment from North Carolina as superior judge for the district of Washington. This process of disintegration, skillfully aided by the wise policy of the North Carolina administration, developed rapidly in the latter part of 1787, and, when Sevier's term of office expired on March 1, 1788, the government came to an end. After the failure of the state to maintain its existence, the struggle degenerated into a personal feud between Sevier and Tipton.

Tipton had been a candidate for the state Senate in the election of 1787, in which the Franklinites took part. However, he was not allowed to take his place because the Assembly declared his election illegal.[36] This embittered him still more against the Franklin adherents, and he opposed every move for a peaceable solution of the difficulties. As colonel of the militia in his county he gave aid to the North Carolina courts and took part in the attempts to obstruct the Franklin judiciary. His partisans organized and carried out raids in order to gain possession of the court records which Sevier protected.[37] Thus the struggle between the factions ceased to be that of two governments and became one of partisan strife with all the accompaniments of bush-whacking. Jonesboro became the center of this intermittent warfare, and Sevier and his men soon left it, retreating to Greenville.

In the early part of 1788 Sheriff Pugh of Washington

[35] *Ibid.*, pp. 145-55.
[36] *SRNC*, XX, 202, 279-80; Williams, *op. cit.*, p. 190.
[37] *Ibid.*, p. 193.

County, acting under Tipton's orders, levied upon some of Sevier's slaves. The order for this action had been given in one of Tipton's courts. Sevier determined to revenge himself upon Tipton and to recover his property. He collected about fifty men and marched to Tipton's home, where he found the latter fortified and guarded by his partisans. Sevier sent in a demand for the surrender of the place, which was refused. After some skirmishing the Sevier party settled down to a seige. During the night Tipton succeeded in dispatching messengers to his friends, who raised reinforcements and hastened to his aid. On the next day Sevier again demanded a surrender, but Tipton retorted that he would disband his men if Sevier would promise to submit to the laws of North Carolina. Information reached Sevier during the afternoon that reinforcements were coming to Tipton's aid, but the beseigers did not believe it. The reinforcements arrived, however, early the following morning and succeeded in joining Tipton. A heavy snow was falling, which aided the Tiptonites in uniting their forces. They attacked Sevier's camp almost immediately after their arrival, and the Franklinites retreated. One man was killed and Sheriff Pugh, who was wounded, died about a week later. Several others on each side received wounds, and two of Sevier's sons were captured as they returned to camp believing it still in the possession of their father.[38]

In his anger Tipton wanted to hang Sevier's sons, but Thomas Love convinced him of the rashness of such an act. The Sevier party retreated, and Tipton released his prisoners, together with the property captured in the camp. Efforts were made to patch up the differences, but no agreement could be reached. Joseph Martin succeeded General Shelby as commander of the brigade west of the mountains, and after a trip to North Carolina and con-

---

[38] This account is taken from Williams, *op. cit.*, pp. 192-204.

sultations with the officials there, he took the affairs out of the hands of Tipton for a time. Martin, who had associated with Sevier in the Muscle Shoals speculation, soon found himself the recipient of Sevier's enmity.[39]

While the fortunes of the Franklin government were on the decline, Sevier engaged in an intrigue with the Spanish government. From this source he hoped to obtain aid and commercial privileges which would retrieve the fortunes of the waning state. Don Diego de Gardoqui, the chargé d'affaires at New York, carried on this intrigue for the Spanish government, which cherished the hope of separating the western territory from the states east of the mountains.[40] James White, who lived in the Cumberland region and held the office of superintendent of Indian affairs under the authority of Congress, acted as Gardoqui's agent. White arrived in Franklin from New York about May 1, 1788.[41] The Franklin movement had collapsed, and Sevier appeared to be without any considerable following. He had taken refuge upon the frontier and was spending his time in raids against the Cherokees and in marking out land claims in the Indian territory.[42] Such was the situation when White arrived. White carried letters from Gardoqui to the leaders of Franklin assuring them that "if they wished to put themselves under the protection of Spain and favor her interests, they should be protected in their civil and political government" on condition that the inhabitants took the oath of allegiance to Spain and renounced loyalty to any other power.[43]

Sevier wrote two letters to Gardoqui, dated September

---

[39] Draper MSS. Draper's Notes, XXX, 54-63.

[40] A. P. Whitaker, "Spanish Intrigue in the Old Southwest," *loc. cit.,* XII, 155-76.

[41] *SRNC,* XXII, 691-92.

[42] *Ibid.,* 695-96.

[43] Archibald Henderson, "Spanish Conspiracy in Tennessee," *THM,* III, 232.

12, 1788,[44] which his son James carried to New York and delivered to the Spanish chargé. In the longer of these letters Sevier mentioned the relations of Franklin with North Carolina and asked for money, munitions, and the privilege of trading down the rivers: "We possess some of the most fertile lands on this continent and easy means of exportation, yet we cannot dispose of a single article of its products . . . unless we have the authority to make use of our rivers toward the ports below." If the Spanish should advance money, it would be repaid in goods. He concluded by requesting a passport to go to the Spanish ports.[45] In the briefer letter he sought aid from the Spanish government in establishing a settlement at Muscle Shoals.[46] Sevier obtained a passport to go to New Orleans,[47] which represented the entire success obtained by the intrigue with the Spanish official, as far as Sevier and the State of Franklin were concerned.[48]

To what extent Sevier would have carried out a plan to secede from North Carolina and to join the Spanish cannot be definitely ascertained from these letters. The separatistic tendencies of the frontier were by no means confined to the Franklin area. Sevier had just experienced a deep disappointment in the Franklin government, and this frustration, united with the usual attitude of the pioneer, would have carried him to almost any length to aid his cause and personal fortune. Dr. Whitaker summarizes this situation very admirably: ". . . it seems probable that his real purpose in opening a correspondence with Gardoqui was revealed in his shorter letter of September 12, in which he spoke of his intention of establishing

---

[44] Whitaker, "Spanish Intrigue in the Old Southwest," *loc. cit.*, p. 160.
[45] Henderson, *op. cit.*, pp. 234-35.
[46] Whitaker, "Spanish Intrigue in the Old Southwest," *loc. cit.*, p. 160.
[47] *Ibid.*
[48] *Ibid.*, pp. 161-62.

a colony at Muscle Shoals and requested Spanish intervention to prevent the southern Indians from attacking the colonists." "On the whole we may describe it as an attempt on the part of the frontiersmen to discover what their southern neighbors could do for them with respect to their three principal interests, commerce, land speculation, and the Indians."[49]

Some time after Sevier dispatched the letters to Gardoqui, he was arrested by Tipton. On July 29, 1788, Governor Johnston, who had succeeded Caswell, issued an order to Judge Campbell to bring about the arrest of Sevier on the charge of high treason. Judge Campbell was instructed to issue the warrant if he thought Sevier guilty of levying troops to oppose the laws of the state. After he had been apprehended, he should be removed to the Hillsborough jail for safe keeping. The Governor issued an order to the militia officers of the District to aid the sheriff in making the arrest. Campbell was reminded that the business should be carried out with secrecy and dispatch.[50]

Campbell refused to obey the order. Judge Spencer of the North Carolina bench, who was in Jonesboro, issued the warrant.[51] Tipton found Sevier near Jonesboro on October 10, and the former governor of Franklin quietly submitted to arrest.[52] Several days later, Tipton's friends started across the mountains with him for Hillsborough. On the way Sevier tried to escape because he believed that Tipton had given orders to his guards to kill him. They frustrated his attempt and completed the journey. General McDowell, a comrade of Revolutionary days, secured bail for him, and he spent the time until the trial with friends in Morgantown. When it became known that Sevier had been taken to the East for trial, some of his friends

[49] *Ibid.*, p. 173.
[51] Ramsey, *op. cit.*, p. 424.
[50] *SRNC*, XXI, 484.
[52] *SRNC*, XXII, 699-700.

planned a rescue. They arrived in Morgantown just as the trial began. While one of them questioned the judge, Sevier dashed from the building, mounted his horse, and rode away with his associates. No one tried to recapture him, and no further attempt was made to prosecute him.[53]

Sevier and Tipton maintained a hostile attitude towards each other for many years. Tipton allied himself with the Jackson forces in later years, and in 1803 he was one of the men instrumental in pushing the investigation into Sevier's connection with land frauds.[54] After the organization of the territory Governor William Blount endeavored to heal the breach between the two men. He wrote to Sevier on March 8, 1792: "On Tuesday I paid a visit to Colonel Tipton, my Reception was Kind and the Interview satisfactory—Conciliation and Public happyness were the Objects. While I was there the Petition of which you have heard was committed to the flames by the Colonel himself in the presence of Dd. Alison."[55] It is not known what the petition to which he referred contained. Willie Blount recorded in the same year that both men lived in Washington County, "where they each maintain a respectable standing & although their party distinctions are now at rest, the scenes of unpleasant kind in those struggles are still somewhat remembered though not to the disturbance of the country—a circumstance in the latter sense peculiarly gratifying to the Governor, who having done what he could before coming here to lessen the Evils which grew out of the struggles of those days & bring about a forgetfulness of those unfortunate strifes, . . . endeavors by mild even-handed justice towards both of these former parties to consult the public tranquillity and prosperity of the Country."[56]

---

[53] Ramsey, *op. cit.*, pp. 424-30.
[54] See p. 155.
[55] Draper MSS, 4XX27.
[56] Draper MSS (Blount papers), 4XX42^{10}.

CHAPTER VI

IN CONGRESS AND IN THE TERRITORY

IN a comparatively short time after the Franklin movement had failed, Sevier retrieved his position in public affairs. The North Carolina administration had no desire further to humiliate the most popular citizen in the West. Since the attempt at self-government had come to naught, men in the East wished for a return to conditions which had obtained before the organization of the new state. The land speculators realized that the western pioneers must be placated as quickly as possible, and they knew that the surest method involved preferment to Sevier. By the raids against the Indians which he had conducted just previous to his arrest and trial, he had largely regained his popularity among the frontiersmen. He became a candidate for the North Carolina Senate in 1788 and was elected. When the Assembly met on November 2, Sevier took his place as a representative of the people of his county. To complete the work of reconciliation, the Assembly passed a bill on November 30 which pardoned him for his share in the Franklin government.[1] That body then proceeded to settle the question which had arisen concerning the command of militia in Washington District. Sevier had been commissioned brigadier general of that District in 1784, when he found himself "dragged" into the Franklin movement, but under the conditions he could not accept. The Assembly now

---

[1] *SRNC*, XXI, 285-86.

decided that Sevier should assume the duties of that office under the authority of the commission which had been issued to him at the earlier date. This action disqualified General Joseph Martin, who had served as brigadier during the later stages of the disturbances in the western counties.[2] These moves indicated to the westerners that the Assembly was striving to appease those who lately had actively opposed the mother state. Sevier took the place of power in state affairs occupied a short time previously by Tipton and his followers. He quickly vaulted from a position as leader of a formidable movement for independence in the West to a seat of power in the government which he had tried to disrupt.

His reëntry into North Carolina politics occurred while the people of that state were engaged in consideration of the Constitution for the United States which had been submitted for ratification by the Philadelphia Convention. A state convention had been called to pass upon it. This body had convened in Hillsborough on July 21, 1788. It had decided to present a bill of rights and twenty-six amendments to Congress for consideration before North Carolina should ratify. This action delayed the entry of the state into the Union, and the whole question remained open pending the action of Congress.[3] The state Assembly which met in November, 1788, passed a resolution authorizing a new convention, which should meet in November, 1789, to consider the Constitution a second time.[4] This convention met during the session of the Assembly in which Sevier served as senator. Many of the members of the Assembly served also as members of the convention. Sevier represented Greene County in the convention and voted in favor of ratification of the Constitu-

---

[2] See p. 87.
[3] S. A. Ashe, *History of North Carolina*, II, 88-94; *SRNC*, XXII, 29-31.   [4] Ashe, *op. cit.*, p. 101.

tion.⁵ The Assembly adjourned while the convention considered the Constitution and the amendments submitted by Congress.⁶ The vote on ratification was taken on November 21 and resulted in a majority of 118 in favor of the Constitution.⁷

The delayed entry of North Carolina into the Union under the Constitution prevented her from having representation in the first session of the First Congress. The Assembly, therefore, passed a law providing for the election of representatives to Congress,⁸ which included a special provision for the districts of Washington and Mero in order that the election of a representative by the people west of the mountains might be facilitated. The election should be held on the second Monday and Tuesday in March, 1790. The returning officers were to meet in Jonesboro and Nashville on the first Monday after the election and to make out a statement of the vote to the clerk of the superior court of their respective districts. Within twenty days after the election the clerk of Mero District should transmit the report from Nashville to the Washington clerk, who was to receive it at the home of James White in Hawkins County. The clerk of Washington District had the authority to issue a certificate of election to the successful candidate. In this special election Sevier was chosen to represent these western districts in Congress. It cannot be determined whether any opposition to his election developed.

For many years Sevier kept a *Diary* or *Journal* in which he erratically recorded unimportant and bizarre facts and occasionally a bit of information of some value. He obviously intended it rather as a memorandum of expenses during the term which he served as a member of Congress. He began it with the following entry written

⁵ *SRNC*, XXII, 48.
⁷ *SRNC*, XXII, 48-49.
⁶ Ashe, *op. cit.*, pp. 111-12.
⁸ *Ibid.*, XXV, 1-3.

upon his departure for New York: "Left home Wednesday 19th May 1790 at 10 o'clock. Rained on us in the evening. Lodged that night at my father's. 25m."[9] He rode his horse to Philadelphia and traveled from that place to New York by stage. His route led him through the Shenandoah Valley and Maryland. He kept a record of his expenses and purchases on the way, and among these items may be found such articles as boots, jacket, breeches, wine, vitriol, and gifts. In Philadelphia he bought a beaver hat for which he paid seven dollars. He arrived in New York on June 15 and took his place in Congress the next day.[10]

Several questions of general interest agitated the public during this session of Congress. The attempt to pass an excise tax aroused the South and especially the Old Southwest. Another question was the establishment of a national bank. Both of these measures had been designed by Alexander Hamilton, the secretary of the treasury, as a part of his financial policy for the new government.

The southern people looked upon grog as a necessity. In some sections of the frontier it served as a medium of exchange where currency was lacking.[11] To place a tax upon a necessity seemed unjust and arbitrary. Some of the arguments advanced against the excise reflected the attitude of the people of the South and the West. The first session of the First Congress had passed a bill providing for the assumption of state debts by the federal government. In those sections where currency was scarce, sentiment against assumption was aroused because of the rewards which it brought to speculators. In the debates on assumption it had been stated that the income of the

---

[9] Sevier's *Diary*, in S. G. Heiskell, *op. cit.*, II, 511.

[10] *Ibid.*, pp. 511-13; *Annals of Congress, 1 Cong. 2 Ses.*, 1640.

[11] J. B. McMaster, *A History of the People of the United States*, II, 29.

government would be sufficient for all demands, but the supporters of the administration now declared an excise tax necessary to prevent a deficit. Such a tax appeared to be in imitation of the tyrannical acts of Great Britain. It was asserted that the consumption of ardent spirits in the South was so great that, should the bill pass, North Carolina alone would be required to pay ten times as much of the tax as Connecticut.[12]

There existed a feeling in the Southwest that this bill might prove to be something of a blessing to the people on the frontier. Daniel Smith wrote to Sevier after the bill had passed but before news of its passage had reached Tennessee that "The excise bill which you seem to expect to pass, if this territory can be exempt, will assuredly have a tendency to excite migrations to this country. To render our Country populous should be our first object— and on this principle I wish it may take effect."[13] If the bill should not apply to the territory which had been ceded by North Carolina, the West would favor it. If no discrimination in favor of the territory were made, it would be opposed.

Sevier opposed the excise tax. While he did not vote on the bill when it finally passed on January 27, 1791,[14] he voted against it on the second reading June 21, 1790. The bill had been defeated in this earlier vote but was submitted again later. It was stated in Congress that a universal opposition to an excise existed in North Carolina,[15] and Sevier by his vote reflected this general attitude as well as that of his constituents in the West.

The proposal to create a national bank met with the opposition of the Anti-Federalists in Congress. The capital

---

[12] *Ibid.*, pp. 25-28.
[13] Smith to Sevier, Feb. 17, 1791, Draper MSS, 11DD92.
[14] *Annals of Congress, 1 Cong. 2 Ses.*, 1884.
[15] *Ibid.*, p. 1859.

of the proposed institution was placed at ten million dollars. The government expected to subscribe two million and to require a loan of an equal sum from the bank payable in ten yearly installments. The remainder of the capital stock should be open to the public. The life of the bank should be twenty years, and the government pledged itself to incorporate no other like institution within that time.[16] Some of the arguments advanced against this kind of financial organization resembled those later used against monopolies. A bank would create a money monopoly and become an aristocratic institution. It would encourage usury and take coin out of circulation, set up false credits and unsettle all safeguards of trade.[17] The fight was long and bitter, but the bill finally passed the House on February 8, 1791, by a vote of 39 to 20.[18] The division on the bank bill indicates the sectional support given to it. Of the twenty-four members from the South, nineteen voted against it.[19] Sevier voted for the bill, but he gave no indication of his reasons for voting in favor of a measure which lacked support in his own section.

Another measure which held the attention of Congress in the early part of this session concerned the location of the capital for the Federal government. Southern votes for the assumption of state debts had been given as a result of a compromise between Hamilton and Jefferson by which the Federalists agreed that the capital might be removed to Philadelphia for a period of ten years and at the end of that time permanently located on the Potomac.[20] The matter had not been completed when Congress adjourned, and one of the first measures to face the second session was the temporary and permanent establishment of the capital. Sevier consistently voted in favor of the

---

[16] McMaster, *op. cit.*, p. 28. [17] *Ibid.*, p. 30.
[18] *Annals of Congress, 1 Cong. 2 Ses.*, 1960.
[19] McMaster, *op. cit.*, II, 32. [20] McMaster, *op. cit.*, I, 582.

compromise agreement. At least twelve votes were taken on amendments, and he voted against all of them. The division was 32 to 29.[21] In this matter he voted with his friends from the South. On July 20, 1790, John Steele, a member of Congress from North Carolina, wrote "We have fixed with uncommon difficulty the permanent seat of government on the potowmac and until the buildings are completed congress will hold their sessions in Philadelphia—this is a great point gained by the Southern delegates, and were it possible to reject the assumption project once more and disappoint these reptile speculators who are preying upon Government, I would return to my fellow citizens perfectly satisfied."[22]

While the question of the assumption of state debts had been settled in the first session, attempts were made during the second session to over-ride that decision. Jackson, an influential representative from Georgia, offered a motion to disagree with a Senate proposal in which the assumption of state debts was involved. Sevier voted in favor of this motion, which was lost by a vote of 29 to 32, the same vote by which the question of the location of the capital had passed. This close vote indicated the sharp division on the question of assumption, and Sevier's vote on the motion indicated his own opposition to the plan to assume the debts.

These votes give some idea of Sevier's attitude toward major public measures. In this early Congress party division had not materialized except along the lines of Federalism and Anti-Federalism. Sevier's son George reported to Dr. Draper that his father "was in politics in every sense of the word one of General Washington's disciples."[23] These few votes show, however, that he sup-

---
[21] *Annals of Congress, 1 Cong. 2 Ses.*, 1678-80.
[22] Steele to Winston, *Steele Papers*, II, 70-72.
[23] Draper MSS, 11D164.

ported the administration outright upon only one measure, the bank bill. The other votes were cast in the interest of the South and the West. Independence characterized his conduct in Congress. While he supported the Constitution and the type of government which it created, he was not a Federalist. It cannot be doubted that he entertained a great deal of respect for Washington and his administration during these critical years when a new system of government had to be firmly established. Partisanship did not divert his attention from the needs and desires of his constitutents. He cast his votes for his section and not for a party. It is probable that he felt a bank to be necessary for the efficient administration of government finance and that he voted for it for this reason rather than as a supporter of the administration.

Sevier retired from Congress to become an influential and important official in the government organized in the territory ceded to the United States by North Carolina, which had finally made a cession of its western lands to the Federal government in 1789. Sevier, as a member of the North Carolina Assembly at that time, voted for the cession act, which passed on December 12.[24] This cession provided that neither the inhabitants nor the lands of the territory ceded be estimated in "ascertaining the proportion of this State with the United States in the common expense occasioned by the late war." The lands reserved for the soldiers of the Revolution should not be taken by others, and if there were not sufficient lands within the bounds reserved for them, they might be allowed to locate their claims upon other lands within the territory. North Carolina reserved the right to have all claims which had been made under the provisions of her land laws perfected according to those same laws. Any entry made "agreeable to law, and within the limits hereby intended

---
[24] *SRNC*, XXI, 679.

to be ceded to the United States, shall have the same force and effect as if such cession had not been made." The territory should be formed into a state or states according to the provisions laid down by Congress in the Northwest Ordinance of 1787. The inhabitants of the territory should bear their just proportion of the debt of the United States. Congress was required to accept the cession within eighteen months, and the laws of North Carolina were to remain in force until such action should be taken.

This cession was not so favorable as that of 1784 and occasioned some bitter criticism. Patrick Henry said that "the people of Franklin are much more injured now than they were by the first cession act. I am apprehensive Sevier may be hushed by preferment so as to make no opposition."[25] This sentiment also existed among some of the leaders in the ceded territory. David Ross wrote to Sevier that the men elected to that Assembly had been "sent to Legislature and not to dismember the state. . . . The property of the unappropriated Lands is given up to Congress—so that nothing is left to the District but to labour & pay taxes and how they shall be able to pay taxes for some time to come is a mystery to me."[26]

The situation caused by the cession brought about a confusion which continued for many years. An example may be shown by the situation in Washington County. In 1791 Secretary Jefferson reported to the President that at the time of the cession all lands "susceptible to culture and cleared of Indian title" except the lands south of the French Broad and Big Pigeon rivers had been taken up and that those lands not taken up amounted to "about 300,000 acres and we are told that 300 families have already set down upon them without right or license."[27] In

---

[25] Draper MSS, 11DD87.   [26] Feb. 20, 1790, Draper MSS, 11DD86.
[27] Jefferson to Washington, transmitted to Congress Nov. 10, 1791. *ASP Public Lands*, I, 22-25.

Washington County, he stated, entries had been made for 746,362 acres, and 531,812 had not been granted. (This statement furnishes a striking illustration of a practice common upon the frontier. There existed entries for 531,812 acres of land not granted, and the holders of these warrants evidently were waiting until the Indian line should be moved westward. When that took place, they could locate their claims on more desirable soil.) By December 20, 1790, the records showed that warrants had been issued for 3,736,493 acres of land, and grants had been issued upon 1,762,660 acres of that amount. The practical application of these approximate figures given by Jefferson showed that within the bounds of the territory at that time the United States had the duty of granting 300,000 acres upon which lived 300 families of squatters with first claim to their land. The State of North Carolina reserved the right to grant, at the lowest possible estimate, 1,973,833 acres. The overlapping of jurisdiction in regard to the lands was certain to cause confusion and friction, which increased when Tennessee became a state and asserted her authority to grant lands still unappropriated.

The cession was accepted by the United States Senate on March 5,[28] and by the House of Representatives on March 29, 1790.[29] The President approved the bill April 2.[30] Washington appointed William Blount of North Carolina as governor of the new "Territory South of the River Ohio" on June 8, 1790.[31] Blount had sought the appointment to this office through the agency of John Steele.[32] He plainly stated to Steele that his speculation

---

[28] *Annals of Congress, 1 Cong. 2 Ses.* I, 952.

[29] *Annals of Congress, 1 Cong. 2 Ses.* II, 1478.

[30] *Ibid.*, pp. 2208-9.

[31] J. T. Moore and A. P. Foster, *Tennessee, the Volunteer State*, I, 148.

[32] Blount to Steele, Apr. 18, 1790, *Steele Papers*, I, 57: "The cession of Western Territory to the United States I am taught to believe is

in land in the West made it necessary for him to live there, and that the salary would prove attractive: ". . . the appointment is truly important to me more so in my opinion than any other in the Gift of the President could have been, the Salary is handsome, and my Western Lands had become so great an object to me that it had become absolutely necessary that I should go to the Western Country to secure them and perhaps my Presence might have enhanced their Value—I am sure my present appointment will."[33] The Governor immediately proceeded to organize the territory, an account of the officers appointed being given in his *Executive Journal*.[34] He was authorized to appoint all militia officers below the rank of brigadier general. For the two military districts in the territory, the President, evidently upon Blount's recommendation, sent the nominations of Sevier and James Robertson as brigadiers to the Senate on February 22, 1791. That body ratified them the next day in executive session.[35]

The Ordinance of the Northwest Territory was made applicable to the new territory with the exception of those sections in conflict with the act of cession by North Carolina. The Northwest Ordinance provided that as soon as there were five thousand free male inhabitants in the territory, an *election* should be held for representatives to a territorial legislature. This Assembly should be composed of five members *appointed* by Congress from ten nominations made by the governor.[36] After the Constitution had been adopted, Congress passed an act which gave the president the power to appoint those officers who,

---

accepted. I wish to be Governor of it and shall feel honored in your interesting yourself in my Behalf with the President or others."

[33] *Ibid.*, pp. 67-68.   [34] *AHM*, II, 213-77.
[35] *Annals of Congress, 1 Cong. 2 Ses.* II, 1763, 1765.
[36] Edw. Scott, *Laws of North Carolina and Tennessee*, I, 440-46.

under the Ordinance, had been subject to appointment by Congress.[37]

On October 19, 1793, Blount issued a call for an election of representatives to take place in December. Those chosen met at Knoxville on February 24, 1794, for the purpose of nominating ten men for the Legislative Council.[38] From these nominations, the President selected Griffith Rutherford, James Winchester, Stockley Donelson, Parmenas Taylor and John Sevier.[39] Blount, in acknowledging the receipt of the commissions for these members of the Council, said that all of them except Taylor were "considered by the people at large as a thing certain from the Moment their Nomination was generally known."[40]

The first session of the territorial legislature convened August 25, 1794. Sevier played a leading rôle in the business of this session. He served upon important committees and sponsored some of the bills passed, among which was one for the relief of such persons as "have been disabled by wounds, or rendered incapable of procuring for themselves and families subsistence, in the militia of this Territory, and providing for the widows and orphans of such as have died."[41] The Assembly remained in session until September 30. The Governor called an extra session which met on June 29, 1795, to consider steps necessary for the organization of a state government. It made provision for an enumeration of the inhabitants of the territory to ascertain if it contained sufficient population to become a state under the regulations designated by Congress. If they numbered 60,000 an election should be ordered in which the voters were to choose members to a

---

[37] *Ibid.*, p. 447.   [38] *AHM*, II, 257-62.

[39] *Journal of the Legislative Council of the Territory South of the River Ohio*, Aug. 25, 1794.

[40] Blount to the Secretary of State, July 28, 1794. *BRL* 7882.

[41] *Journal of the Legislative Council of the Territory*, p. 5.

convention for the purpose of forming a state constitution.[42] The census authorized by this act showed that 77,262 inhabitants resided in the territory, and so an election for the convention was ordered. Sevier did not participate in this convention which met January 11, 1796,[43] and prepared the constitution for the State of Tennessee.

Under the direction of the territorial government Sevier led the Etowah Indian campaign which has been described in another chapter. This was his last adventure in Indian fighting. The *Knoxville Gazette* of November 23, 1793 reported that "success has ever crowned the arms of this experienced and valuable officer."

Some attention must be given to the policies of William Blount while he served as governor of the territory. The first administration of Sevier as governor of Tennessee followed immediately after Blount's term as executive, and similar problems, in fact some of the same questions, confronted both of them for solution. No essential differences in policy existed in the conduct of the two men while in office. Each of them possessed a vital connection with land speculation, and they were close friends as well as business associates. They had the same outlook upon the West and its development. Consequently, the people expected and demanded that Sevier should carry on the policies of his predecessor. Since Sevier fell heir to some of these unsolved difficulties bequeathed to him by Blount, it becomes necessary to glance at the attitude of the latter toward western problems during this time.

One difficulty which arose in the early part of Blount's term related to the people living on the Indian lands south of the French Broad River. It was difficult to take a census

---

[42] Ramsey, *op. cit.,* p. 643.
[43] *Journal of the Constitutional Convention of Tennessee,* 1796.

of the inhabitants in that section because the "heads of families very generally were opposed to giving in their numbers—fearing a General Assembly would shortly be the consequence."[44] They probably thought that an Assembly, if elected, would force them to remove from their lands. They possessed little interest in any government unless it afforded them protection against the savages and opportunity to obtain additional territory. Blount found himself forced to accept the policy of the Federal government regarding settlements beyond the Indian line. Its program of restriction, inaugurated by the Treaty of Hopewell in 1785, required him to prevent settlements on land claimed by the Indians to which their title had been guaranteed by the central authority.[45] North Carolina persisted in issuing grants for land in this section which had been recognized as Indian property at Hopewell. This attitude on the part of the mother state greatly aggravated the difficulties of the situation by causing a conflict of authority between that state and the government at Philadelphia represented by the governor of the territory. Blount brought the matter to the attention of the governor of North Carolina and obtained a promise that no more grants would be made out for such lands. However, grants had been issued after this promise had been made. Blount then referred the affair to the secretary of state.[46] Jefferson called the attention of the governor of North Carolina to the irregularity and requested Blount to allow no new settlements to be made.[47] Finally the whole matter was left to the discretion of

---

[44] Blount to Secretary of State, Sept. 19, 1790. *BRL* 7848.

[45] Secretary of State to Daniel Smith, Dec. 24, 1791, *American Letters*, IV, 7854. *State Department Archives.*

[46] Blount to Secretary of State, Apr. 23, 1792, *BRL* 7857.

[47] Secretary of State to Blount, June 6, 1792. *BRL* 7858; Secretary of State to Governor of North Carolina, same date, *American Letters*, IV, 7859.

Blount, who did not insist upon the removal of the settlers. The final disposition of this problem had to wait until the administration of Sevier.[48]

As Blount had established his residence in the territory, he completely transferred his activities in public affairs to the West. He had always been in sympathy with the western people and in return enjoyed their confidence. His general attitude toward the problems of the frontier closely resembled that of the pioneers. He combined his western sympathy with his knowledge of governmental affairs in the East and became very popular with the frontiersmen.

The situation in the Cumberland region regarding Indian affairs became rather precarious with the threat of war in 1791. The frontiersmen expected the United States government to protect them, and hope for aid had caused many of them to favor the cession by North Carolina. Shortly after the organization of the territory, the civil and military officers of Mero District presented a memorial to President Washington in which they asked his interposition to prevent attacks by the Creeks.[49] Andrew Pickens reported to the governor of South Carolina that the people in the Cumberland region were in a "most pitiable and distressed situation almost continually harassed by the Creeks and the four lower Towns of the Cherokees on the Tennessee."[50] The frontiersmen felt that the government should protect the settlements since it restrained them from fighting the savages and prohibited further acquisition of Indian lands.

Blount's attitude toward conditions in the West differed not at all from that of the frontiersmen. His absences

---
[48] See p. 135.
[49] August 1, 1791, *BRL* 7843.
[50] Sept. 13, 1792. Bureau of Indexes and Archives (hereafter cited *BIA*), *Miscellaneous Letters*, X, 7861. *State Department Archives.*

from the territory at critical times possessed a diplomatic significance. The Nickajack and Etowah campaigns against the Indians occurred while he was engaged in governmental or private business far from the scene of the trouble.[51] The people of the territory probably appreciated his ability to find an excuse to leave the savages to their care at appropriate intervals. When he left the territory the executive duties passed into the hands of the secretary, Daniel Smith, who favored extreme measures toward the Indians. "A war," he said, "well directed against the hostile part would be a mercy, as it would check the evil before it becomes too general."[52] Blount, in his absences, could escape responsibility for the actions of the enraged frontiersmen by passing it to Smith. The latter had little to lose by accepting it. His office might have been taken from him, but such a move on the part of the president would have elevated Smith to a position of popularity surpassed by only a few in the West. Blount hoped that Wayne's army, if it forced a peace upon the tribes in the Northwest, might be moved southward and united with the militia of the territory so that "our perfidious Yellow Brethren to the South" could be chastised.[53]

Blount's attitude towards the Indians and the extension of the Indian line may be gathered from a communication to James White, the territorial delegate to Congress, in December, 1795.[54] Georgia had applied to the president for a commission to purchase land from the Creek nation. The commission had been appointed, and Blount said that this action by the administration established the method by which land might be obtained from the Indians. If Georgia obtained lands in this manner,

---
[51] See p. 36.
[52] Smith to Secretary of State, Oct. 27, 1792, *BRL* 7862.
[53] Blount to Sevier, Aug. 28, 1793. Draper MSS. 4XX33.
[54] Dec. 14, 1795. *BRL* 7891.

no reason existed to prevent the same method from applying to the lands adjacent to the territory. He advised White to ask that the same commission be empowered to purchase land from the Cherokees in order that the Tennessee River might become the line from the mouth of the Clinch River to Chilhowee Mountain. The advantages of making the river the boundary were obvious. A line marked by blazed trees presented no barrier to either man or animals, and the crossing of the line by both increased the possibilities of trouble between the settlers and the Indians. The purchase would also make the military defense of that part of the frontier much easier. "The Tennessee being a fine bold River with but few Fords between the Mouth of Clinch and Chilhowee Mountain would form a Boundary that Cattle and horses would not voluntarily pass, and the Proprietors themselves would at this Time consent to *halt at it*, and at which Government by keeping up regular troops at Tellico Blockhouse, Fort Grainger and South West Point might *stop them a long Time*, I would hope until the Cherokee Nation shall have passed away by some other Means than that of being destroyed by the arms of the United States." He said that he had no personal interest in the lands under discussion, but that he had refrained from mentioning it before this time because he "feared that it would have been supposed as I am known to be a large Landholder that it was some interest of my own which promoted me."

No essential difference can be found between his Indian policy and that later followed by Sevier. Blount's attitude may have been tempered somewhat by his knowledge of feeling in the East, but he looked upon the West as a field for speculation and upon the Indians as a hindrance to the development of the territory. The two men were kindred spirits in many ways.

This period in Sevier's life was marked by a great

amount of varied activity. He served the State of North Carolina in Congress and the territory in its legislature. He closed a military life which had been uniformly successful. It was evidently a period of activity in land speculation, for in 1795 he obtained large grants from the State of North Carolina founded upon warrants which he had received from the Washington County land office.[55] In December, 1795, his brother, evidently at his request, informed him of the price of lands in the Cumberland region, saying that tracts might be bought for about two dollars per acre.[56] He had an interest in any section which held a possibility of profit from purchase and sale of land.

Sevier had swung from one extreme to another. While governor of Franklin he had been practically a revolutionist, but during the territorial period he proved to be a valuable supporter of the government. His popularity had steadily increased, and his political power had been greatly augmented by the arrival of Blount in the territory. The friendship between the two men and their association in business and speculation drew them closer together. They mutually benefited by these relationships, and when Blount donned the senatorial toga in 1796, the governor's mantle descended to the shoulders of Sevier.

---

[55] See p. 68.
[56] Valentine Sevier to John Sevier, Dec. 13, 1795. Draper MSS, 11DD122.

CHAPTER VII

FIRST GOVERNOR OF TENNESSEE

FEW of the details concerning the first election for governor in the State of Tennessee have come to light. Sevier encountered opposition in some form during the campaign, but the exact nature of the contest has remained in doubt. Intimations of this opposition have appeared and will be noted in connection with the election of militia officers which occurred in the early part of Sevier's first administration. It cannot be determined whether an active campaign of opposition was carried out against Sevier by another candidate or whether certain persons publicly voiced their dissatisfaction at his leadership. The latter supposition probably represented the actual situation. An active opposition candidate would have been too important in the campaign for his identity to have become hidden in the obscurity of time. At any rate, Sevier received the honor of election to the executive power in the state which demanded admission into the Union.

The government of Tennessee began to function when the legislature organized on March 28, 1796. The next day the Assembly confirmed the election of Sevier as governor by a count of the returns from the counties of the Territory.[1] On March 30 Sevier was inaugurated as the first governor of Tennessee. The Assembly selected William Blount, the ex-governor of the territory, and

---

[1] *Journal of the Senate of Tennessee,* 1796, p. 8.

William Cocke to serve as United States senators, and these two men immediately left for Philadelphia.

The state encountered some difficulty in securing immediate admission into the Union in spite of the fact that the people of the territory had complied with the regulations which Congress had established for that purpose. Political considerations formed the principal reason for the reluctance of certain members of Congress to agree to the immediate entrance of Tennessee. The Federalist party realized that the electoral vote of the new state would be cast for Jefferson in the approaching presidential election, a circumstance which its leaders desired to avoid. Sometime during the first few days of July Sevier received a communication from Blount, who informed the Governor that Tennessee had been admitted but that the Senate objected to seating the senators because they had been elected before the admission of the state by Congress. Congress had accepted the state as a member of the Union on the first of June,[2] and the people of the new commonwealth had no representation in the national legislature. Sevier immediately issued a call for a special session of the Assembly to meet on the last Saturday in June to reëlect the senators and to make necessary changes in the method of electing representatives to Congress. At its first meeting the Assembly had provided for the election of two men to represent Tennessee in the House of Representatives, but Congress reduced this number to one. Consequently, the Assembly had to make a change in the plans for representation in the lower House of Congress. The extra session of the Assembly convened on July 30 and received the Governor's message two days later.[3] It reëlected Blount and Cocke as senators and made the necessary changes for the election of a representative.

---

[2] James Phelan, *History of Tennessee*, p. 189.

[3] *Journal of the Senate of Tennessee*, 1796, p. 4.

The work of this session of the legislature completed the organization of the state, and Tennessee cast aside the tutelage of Congress and accepted the responsibilities borne by the other states of the Union.

During his first series of administrations as governor, Sevier confronted the usual problems of establishing a state government in a rapidly growing frontier territory. He was reëlected in 1797,[4] and again in 1799. A study of a map of Tennessee for this period discloses the fact that probably two-thirds of the area which is now included in the state still remained under the control of the Indians in 1796.[5] Indian relations formed the basis for many of the problems with which the state had to contend. Military affairs and elections, administration of land laws, relations with the central government and with other states, internal improvements and other questions of less importance were forced upon Sevier for administration. Each of these items had a more or less direct connection with the Indians, who, under the protection of the Federal government, held possession of a large proportion of the area nominally under control of the state.

The first of these problems to face Sevier after his induction into office concerned the state militia. Military leadership presented the most certain means by which a man could win public favor with the people of the frontier. Successful officers in the militia enjoyed a prestige and a respect impossible of attainment by one who did not participate in fighting the savage. Men in the militia eagerly sought for office from the lowest to the highest in rank. In the elections for military office partisanship ran

---

[4] The Constitution provided that the first governor should hold office until the fourth Tuesday in September, 1797, and that thereafter the term should be two years.

[5] Such a map, which shows the Indian cessions, may be found in Garrett and Goodpasture, *op. cit.*, pp. 128-29.

high, and those interested employed every possible means to secure the coveted positions. No candidate overlooked a false move of his opponent or failed to take advantage of possible technicalities to attain his goal.

The legislature in 1796 established the system for election to military office.[6] The active members of the militia companies elected their own officers below the rank of major. However, the field officers, a colonel and two majors, were elected by the citizens of the county who were subject to military duty. As every free man between the ages of eighteen and fifty was subject to call, the field officers of the regiments practically depended upon the suffrage of the male citizens of the county for their election. The field officers of a military district elected their brigadier general, and the field officers of the state elected the commanding major general. The cavalry composed a separate unit in a district, and its captains and subalterns elected their field officers, a lieutenant colonel and two majors. These contests for military preference caused a general interest which even campaigns for civil office could not arouse, because military officers wielded an influence proportionately greater than civil officials. The first military elections after the organization of the state government, therefore, possessed an especial importance. The successful candidates for military office would play an important part in making popular the administration of Sevier. These considerations caused the Governor to use his influence in the races in which his political friends were involved.

The Governor issued military commissions to the officers elected in the various counties and districts. This constitutional requirement involved the Governor in disputes which arose over the military elections. It really

---

[6] Scott, *Laws of North Carolina and Tennessee*, I, 559-61.

resolved itself into a question of whether he had the right to determine when the candidate had been legally elected. The problem which arose from the disputes in these first elections proved a difficult one. If Sevier acted as a state election judge and determined whether certain candidates had been guilty or innocent of fraud in the election, he would lay himself open to charges of political favoritism which would react against him and his administration. If he refused to have anything to do with the disputes, no authority existed which had the power of immediate decision.

Contests arose in Washington,[7] Knox,[8] Sumner,[9] and Davidson[10] counties. Partisanship ran high in Mero District, especially in Davidson County. Sevier sensed the political importance of the situation and refused to make a decision in any of the contests. He said that he did not wish to decide them nor did he think it his duty to do so but would "submit all of the kind to the legislative body of the state."[11]

The contests for commissions in the Davidson County militia must have been lively, and they assumed a political significance greater than in the other counties. General Robertson wrote to Sevier on August 10 that he was happy to inform him that his "administration are very satisfactory to the people of the District, and tho you Run high in your last election I am apprehensive you would go much higher at this time."[12] He also made the statement that the struggle had become more intense because of the approaching election for brigadier general. Another correspondent informed the Governor that "The Chief of

---

[7] John Sevier, Jr., to Sevier, Aug. 5, 1796. Sevier Papers. (Hereafter cited *SP*.) These Sevier Papers are in the Tennessee State Library.
[8] George Gillespie to Sevier, Aug. 17, 1796, *SP*.
[9] Blakemore to Sevier, Oct. 19, 1796, *SP*.
[10] James Winchester to Sevier, Aug. 14, 1796, *SP*.
[11] Sevier to Thomas Buckingham, Oct. 15, 1796, *SP*. [12] *SP*.

our Elections were Intirely Conducted by parties and those parties had nothing Else in view but the Appointment of a Brig. Gen."[13]

These fights had a direct political connection with Sevier's election as governor, for he encountered opposition during the campaign in Davidson and possibly in other counties. Sevier's opponents in the gubernatorial election now concentrated their antagonism upon the candidates for military office who had previously supported him and who naturally enjoyed his favor in the military elections. It appeared that Sevier's prestige had increased with the people in Mero District—at least his supporters seemed to believe so—for William Cage informed him that the people appeared happy under his administration, "even those who were opposed to you in your election."[14] These military elections formed an important stage in the attempt by Sevier to perfect an efficient political machine for the control of the government and the perpetuation of his leadership in the state.

Sevier exerted his influence in the election of brigadier general for Mero District. Opposition to his administration indicated that it was highly desirable for a friend to receive this honor. Joel Lewis wrote to him and expressed the hope that he might come to Nashville before the election, since his presence would "prevent some very disagreeable consequences that may arise from the election of that officer."[15] The day of the election was the second Thursday in October.[16] The election for field officers of cavalry in the district had been placed upon the same day. This apparently made it impossible for the newly elected field officers of the cavalry to take part in the elec-

---

[13] Thos. Johnson to Sevier, Sept. 4, 1796, *SP*.
[14] William Cage to Sevier, Sept. 21, 1796, *SP*.
[15] Lewis to Sevier, Sept. 17, 1796, *SP*.
[16] Scott, *op. cit.*, I, 559-61.

tion of the brigadier general under whom they would have to serve. Winchester and Ford were the candidates for brigadier. The old officers of cavalry favored Winchester, while Sevier evidently wished to see Ford elected.[17] The election of field officers for units of the militia other than the cavalry had already taken place on the first Thursday of August, but their commissions had not been issued by Sevier until after the first of October, just a few days before the election of a brigadier general.[18] Lewis, in the letter referred to above, requested Sevier to send blank commissions to some one in Davidson County so that the names of the newly elected cavalry officers might be inserted on the day of their election and the commissions delivered to them. Sevier's friends expected that these new officers would then participate in the election of a brigadier. They appeared to feel confident that the new field officers of cavalry would be favorable to Ford. Robert Prince informed Sevier that the election of a brigadier depended upon the officers of cavalry. The old officers whose term ended on the day of election would vote unless this method were adopted, and they would elect Winchester. "The salvation of your warmest friends depend upon the count," Prince said; unless Sevier did as requested, the Governor's friends would be "D——d and Trod under foot by people who were your greatest enemies in *your* Election."[19] These letters from Robertson and Prince definitely establish the fact that Sevier had opposition in Davidson County in his election for governor, and that the same group now opposed his candidate, Ford, for brigadier general. Sevier sent the blank commissions to General Robertson as requested by Prince, Lewis, and others.[20]

---

[17] Prince to Sevier, Sept. 20, 1796, *SP*.
[18] Sevier to Hays, Oct. 4, 1796, *SP*.
[19] Sept. 20, 1796, *SP*. Italics are mine.
[20] Sevier to Robertson, Oct. 4, 1796, *SP*.

General Robertson, however, did not use the commissions as Sevier intended,[21] and Winchester was elected. Robertson excused himself by stating that "party Run uncommonly big. . . . I did not think myself at liberty to fill such Commissions it is Believed your excellency intended by sending and atherizing me to fill them to give general satisfaction to the District." He also said that the two lower counties favored Ford and the two upper counties preferred Winchester; the Ford supporters wanted the commisions filled out, and the Winchester party did not. This refusal on the part of Robertson to fulfill the wishes of Sevier led to criticism of the former by the Governor and threatened to cause a break between the two.[22] Naturally Sevier thought that Robertson had gone over to the opposite party. Andrew Jackson attended the election and challenged the action of the Governor,[23] and by this move he definitely aligned himself with the enemies of Sevier. It is not known whether Jackson had already announced his candidacy for the position of major general at that time. He became a candidate for the office at the head of the military system of the state in the election which took place in November, a month after the election of a brigadier. Jackson and Conway were the candidates for major general. Sevier favored the latter, who was elected.

The second important problem of Sevier's administration concerned the military land office in Nashville. In 1797 Governor Ashe of North Carolina discovered through the agency of Jackson[24] that improprieties had taken place in the conduct of the land office in Nashville. This office

---

[21] Robertson to Sevier, Oct. 14, 1796, *SP*.
[22] Isaac Roberts to Sevier, Nov. 22, 1796, *SP*.
[23] Jackson to Sevier, May 8, 1797, J. S. Bassett, *Correspondence of Andrew Jackson*, I, 32.
[24] *Ibid.*, p. 39. note.

handled the surveys for land given to the Revolutionary soldiers by the State of North Carolina. In running the lines of tracts for which the warrants had been issued, the surveyors of the office often managed to include many times the number of acres called for in the warrants. The clerk in the office at Raleigh acted as a party to the scheme, and Glasgow, the secretary of state for North Carolina, probably took a leading part in the perpetration of the frauds. Other fraudulent methods came to light in the investigation which Governor Ashe inaugurated. At first it was not thought that any fraud existed because of the confidence enjoyed by the officials involved. But the clerk of the secretary's office in Raleigh fled when the discoveries were made, and in April, 1798, Governor Ashe learned that a plot had been formed to burn the State House in Raleigh, in which the books of the secretary had been placed for safe keeping.[25]

In order to carry on the investigation into the affairs of the land office at Nashville, the Governor of North Carolina requested Sevier to seize the papers in Martin Armstrong's office and to deliver them to representatives whom he had delegated to carry them to Raleigh.[26] Sevier informed Governor Ashe that he would comply with the request, and he expressed the wish that Ashe would be able to bring to justice "the culprits who had been guilty of fraud and forgery practiced in obtaining warrants and grants for military lands."[27] Sevier requested Judge Tatum of the superior court to take charge of the affair in Nashville and to seize the papers of the office.[28] Judge Tatum did as requested[29] and held the papers in the office.

---

[25] Ashe, *op. cit.*, pp. 152-53.
[26] Sevier to the Governor of North Carolina, Dec. 31, 1797, *SP*.
[27] *Ibid.*
[28] Sevier to McNairy, Jan. 2, 1798, and Sevier to Tatum, same date, *SP*.
[29] Sevier to Tatum, Jan. 29, 1798, *SP*.

Sevier then issued orders to Martin Armstrong to deliver the papers to the commissioners appointed by the Governor of North Carolina.[30] Up to this point Sevier appears to have been entirely willing to have the papers removed from the state.

By the middle of the next month something had changed his mind in regard to the removal of the books from the office. On February 14, 1798, he asked an opinion of the attorneys-general of Tennessee whether he should allow the commissioners from North Carolina to carry the papers away.[31] Three days later they delivered their opinion. They decided that the governor of North Carolina was not legally authorized to make such a request and that it was the duty of the executive of Tennessee to regain control of the papers if they had passed into the hands of the commissioners.[32] On February 17 he wrote to the commissioners and informed them that he could not allow the books to be removed but that they would be permitted to take authenticated copies and transcripts of the records which he hoped would "be amply sufficient for the detection of any frauds alleged to have been committed."[33] He also ordered Judge Tatum to withhold the books from the commissioners and to seize the papers if they had already been delivered.[34] Sevier authorized William Maclin, secretary of state for Tennessee, to take these books into his possession.[35] In this manner Sevier obtained control of the papers of Armstrong's land office. The reasons for this move on the part of the Governor are plainly apparent. The land office operated under the direction of North Carolina, and for that reason the governor of that state

---

[30] Sevier to Martin Armstrong, Jan. 29, 1798, *SP*.
[31] Sevier to the Attorneys-General, *SP*.
[32] The Attorneys-General to Sevier, Feb. 17, 1798, *SP*.
[33] Sevier to N. C. Commissioners, Feb. 17, 1798, *SP*.
[34] Sevier to Tatum, Feb. 17, 1798, *SP*.
[35] *SP. Proclamations*, etc., p. 55.

claimed jurisdiction over it. The conduct of the office affected the citizens of Tennessee, and, if the records were removed, it would be all but impossible for any injured party in the state to obtain redress without access to the papers. Sevier also may have felt that the investigation might possibly bring out facts which would connect him with Glasgow in suspicious land dealings, a happening which later occurred. While this may have influenced him to a certain extent, the duty which he owed the citizens of Tennessee amply justified his action. He took advantage of the technicality mentioned by the attorneys-general to keep the records within the State.

The North Carolina legislature passed another resolution in December, 1798, authorizing other commissioners to receive the papers.[36] These commissioners attempted to get possession of them in the same manner as those in the previous year.[37] Sevier again refused to deliver them.[38] On October 5, 1799, he laid the whole affair before the Tennessee Assembly. This body, unfortunately, did nothing in regard to the matter,[39] and the records were removed.

No adverse criticism could be directed against Sevier for his attempt to preserve the records for the use of the citizens of his state. He offered the commissioners free access to the papers at all times, but he felt that the records should remain in Nashville. Had he been apprehensive that his own reputation would suffer by reason of their removal and examination, he would have been equally fearful of their inspection in Nashville. Unfortunately the land system so intimately affected the governments of the two states that an investigation by either of them

---

[36] W. R. Davie to Sevier, Mar. 1, 1799, *SP*.
[37] Willis and Locke to Sevier, Apr. 30, 1799, *SP*.
[38] Sevier to Armstrong, May 1, 1799, *SP*.
[39] Sevier to Daniel Smith, June 2, 1800, *SP*.

caused friction and misunderstanding. In June, 1800, the citizens of Nashville presented their grievances in regard to this matter to Sevier.[40] They pointed out that the removal of the records would make it necessary for everyone desiring a grant to produce a certificate from a clerk of a North Carolina court stating that the transfers had been proven in open court by evidence of disinterested parties. A justice of the peace of that court would have to certify that he believed in the credulity of the witnesses by whose testimony the transfers had been proven. This one provision was manifestly unfair and impracticable for the citizens of Tennessee, for they could not possibly appear in a North Carolina court. Such regulations as this made it imperative that the records remain in Tennessee.

Glasgow's trial for participation in land frauds occurred in 1800. John Haywood resigned his position as judge of the superior court of North Carolina to defend the secretary of state. The evidence proved too conclusive against Glasgow, and the court removed him from office and fined him two thousand pounds. A negro who had attempted to burn the State House at Glasgow's instigation was made the scapegoat and was executed.[41] As a result of Glasgow's trial, Jackson secured copies of letters which Sevier had written to the secretary of state of North Carolina in 1795; these letters formed the basis for an attack against Sevier in the political campaign in 1803, when Jackson charged Sevier with fraud and bribery.[42] They will be considered in connection with that campaign.

Internal improvements constituted another problem which received Sevier's consideration during these administrations, although it did not attain the prominence given to the elections or to the land office. The energy displayed

---

[40] *Memorial*, June 3, 1800.
[41] Ashe, *op. cit.*, pp. 176-77.
[42] See p. 150.

in the construction of roads illustrated his interest. He sent a message to the Assembly on April 1, 1796, in regard to the construction of a road over the mountains to North Carolina.[43] The governor of North Carolina had written to Sevier about the matter, and the latter expressed the wish that the Assembly would see the necessity for its accomplishment. Some communication had been carried on between Governor Vanderhorst of South Carolina and Governor Blount of the territory concerning the construction of a wagon road connecting those two areas. Sevier answered one of Vanderhorst's letters and informed him that pressing business of the Assembly made consideration of the project impossible. The people of Knoxville had contributed money for it, and Charles Robertson had agreed to undertake the construction. Robertson had already given bond to have it completed by October 1, 1797, so as to "enable a wagon with only four horses to travel and pass the same with fifteen hundred weight."[44] In August of the same year he brought the matter to the attention of the Assembly and said that it was expected that that body would reimburse the subscribers. Such a road would induce immigrants to come into the state and would open easy communication with seaports and trading towns in neighboring states.[45] The road was opened before October 4, 1797.[46] The same kind of project was undertaken in 1800 between Tennessee and Georgia.[47]

The Muscle Shoals venture again involved Sevier during 1797 and 1798. Zachariah Cox, who had been connected with the earlier project,[48] at this time headed a company for the development of that region. Sevier ac-

---

[43] Sevier to the Assembly, *SP*.
[44] Sevier to Vanderhorst, June 7, 1796, *SP*.
[45] Sevier to the Assembly, Aug. 2, 1796, *SP*.
[46] Sevier to the Assembly, Oct. 4, 1797. *SP*.
[47] T. P. Carnes to Sevier, Feb. 14, 1800, *SP*. [48] See p. 72 n.

quired some fifty thousand acres of land from this company.[49] The United States government became interested when it appeared that Cox meant to establish a trading post at Muscle Shoals. The Indians looked upon this move as an encroachment upon their lands.[50] Cox requested permission from Sevier to pass from East Tennessee down the river to the Shoals.[51] Colonel Butler, who commanded the Federal troops in that section, prompted an investigation by the Assembly, but the investigators came to the conclusion that Cox had not been guilty of any attempt inimical to the interests of the country.[52] Sevier evidently was intimately connected with this adventure, but he hesitated to bring on trouble by openly encouraging the expedition. He received a promise from Cox that the latter would not proceed with the attempt to go down the river with a party of settlers without his consent.[53] In September, 1798, he defended Cox in a letter to the secretary of war, saying that he could find nothing which indicated an attempt to plant a permanent settlement at Muscle Shoals. His permission had not been given for the journey down the Tennessee River, although he well knew that Cox intended to go on to Kentucky and that he did not intend to stop at the Shoals.[54] Cox transferred his activities to another quarter, and the threat of trouble with the Federal government disappeared so far as Sevier was concerned. The incident showed that Sevier had not lost his interest in western lands.

There is little available material by which to ascertain Sevier's attitude towards the Blount conspiracy and its

---

[49] *ASP, Public Lands*, I, 141, 244.
[50] Robertson to Sevier, Apr. 15, 1797, *SP*.
[51] Cox to Sevier, Aug. 31, 1797, *SP*.
[52] *Senate Journal, Second General Assembly*, Oct. 10, 1797.
[53] Sevier to Jackson, Anderson and Claiborne, Jan. 22, 1798, *SP*.
[54] Sevier to the Secretary of War, Sept. 18, 1798, *SP*.

leader's expulsion from the Senate, which occurred during Sevier's first term. It is entirely probable that he held the frontier view that Blount had done nothing reprehensible. Then, too, Sevier always had been on friendly terms with Blount and had been associated with him in business. Sevier received a letter from David Henley, an agent of the War Department, who informed him that a packet of letters had arrived at the postoffice in Knoxville addressed to Col. McKee in the handwriting of Blount. He suggested to the Governor that it might possibly contain something detrimental to the peace of the United States and requested Sevier to issue an order to the postmaster to break the seals and examine the contents.[55] Sevier issued the order directing the postmaster to open the letters. If he found anything inconsistent with the peace and interest of the United States, he should forward it to the government; if he found nothing of the kind, he should replace the seals and offer "no further interruption."[56] The incident, so far as it concerned Sevier, closed with this order.

When the threat of war between the United States and France developed in 1798 Sevier received appointment as one of the brigadiers in the provisional army. He immediately placed himself at the disposal of the Federal government. His letter to the secretary of state clearly portrayed his attitude:[57]

---

[55] Sevier to David Henley, Aug. 16, 1797, *SP*.

[56] *SP, Proclamations*, etc., Aug. 16, 1797.

[57] Draper MSS, 11DD142. Sevier also wrote to the secretary of war on May 4, 1798: "Not far from this place, and on the main river Holston I have a new and well erected set of iron works, suitable for casting almost every kind of mettle, and manufacturing of bar iron, the same shall in the shortest notice be converted to any public use that might be deemed expedient, and should be glad to be honored with any commands that might be thought necessary." *SP*.

Knoxville 25 Apl 1798

Sir

Should it be deemed necessary by the president to raise the Army contemplated in case of an eventual necessity, I shall hold myself ready to accept the appointment I had the honor of being nominated for in the provisional army, provided I may be thought adequate to such a command.

Permit me to assure you, Sir, nothing but a real desire to serve my Country in the time of imminent danger could induce me to accept such a Command, filling already the most respectable My country can confer.

I flatter myself I could be useful in the state of Tennessee and be the means of inducing a number of very active men to engage in the Army Both as officer and soldiers, and be assured the Government will have my hearty support in opposing the aggressions of any invader whatever, let my situation be what it may.

I have the honor to be Sir

Your Honors etc.,

JOHN SEVIER

SECRETARY PICKERING

Washington did not approve of the appointments of Sevier and White as brigadiers general. He wrote to Secretary Pickering and asked, "What in the name of military prudence could have induced the appointments of White and Severe as Brigadiers? The latter never was celebrated for anything (that ever came to my knowledge) except the murder of Indians. . . . To give *two* to that State (Tennessee) when more important ones furnished none . . . is to me inconceivable . . . as to Severe, as he is little known little is said abt. him yet."[58]

Indian affairs occupied a great deal of Sevier's attention during these years. The Holston Treaty, which Wil-

---

[58] Pickering Manuscripts, XXIII, 134. (in 11 Sparks 297), Washington to Pickering, September 9, 1798. Massachusetts Historical Society.

liam Blount negotiated with the Cherokees in 1791, proposed to take care of the settlers who had located beyond the Indian line and to open new lands for settlement. The line provided by this treaty had not been completed when Sevier became Governor. In 1797 President Adams appointed Colonel Hawkins, General Pickens, and General Winchester to run the line.[59] The attitude of the officials of the State of Tennessee did not differ from the usual frontier policy. The frontiersmen did not demand the survey. They knew that some of the settlers would be found beyond the line and that procrastination would give these intruders a firmer hold upon their lands. Early in 1797 Sevier wrote to Tennessee's representatives in Congress that he would be glad if the running of the boundary might be delayed until after the next session of Congress.[60] Several months later he made a formal protest to the secretary of war, saying that it might well have been "evaded and procrastinated until a time more suitable would present itself for such a purpose."[61] He offered as an excuse that the European situation made it desirable that neither the Indians nor the whites should be disturbed by running a line unsatisfactory to both. Delay had become so important to the people of Tennessee that General Winchester did not meet with the commissioners when they arrived at Tellico Blockhouse to begin their work.[62] Those interested hoped that matters would be delayed by his absence, but the commissioners set to work without him, and he later joined them. The attempt on the part of the Federal government to proceed with this task produced great uneasiness among the settlers who resided beyond the line. Sevier realized the temper of these

---

[59] Royce, *op. cit.*, pp. 165-69.
[60] Sevier to Blount, Cocke and Jackson, Jan. 29, 1797, *SP*.
[61] Sevier to McHenry, Apr. 24, 1797, *SP*.
[62] Royce, *op. cit.*, pp. 165-69.

people and feared open resistance to the work of the commission.[63] The attempt to survey the boundary brought out the sharp differences between the frontier settlers and the Indians. The commissioners began their work in the Cumberland region, and as soon as they approached the Indian towns the Cherokees protested and complained so violently that the work had to be halted temporarily.[64]

The political implications of the dispute between the settlers and the commissioners were important. Pickens and Hawkins reported to Secretary McHenry that some respectable citizens who found themselves on Indian lands had said that they had been the "dupes of a party," evidently referring to the state administration. Sevier branded this charge as false, saying that the commissioners had reported an untruth. Since the Treaty of Hopewell, the people of the frontier looked upon boundary commissioners as "inveterate enemies to this country."[65] They confidently believed that the commissioners had been appointed because their views on Indian affairs coincided with those of the administration in Philadelphia, whose policy included protection of the savages. The Governor believed that this attitude of the United States government had resulted in a movement of the whites to Spanish dominions, and, if continued, it would induce more to take the same course. In spite of his opposition the line was completed, and many citizens remained on Indian lands, from which the Federal government threatened to remove them. The whole affair offers a striking illustration of the frontier spirit. The settlers inevitably felt that they had a right to the land and that the government favored the savages by insisting upon a strict adherence to treaties. Circumstances such as these alienated the

---

[63] Sevier to Cocke and Blount, June 6, 1797, *SP*.
[64] Report of Winchester to Sevier, July 16, 1797, *SP*.
[65] Sevier to Cocke, July 6, 1797, *SP*.

frontier from the Federalist party and allied it with the Jeffersonian movement, which promised a friendlier attitude toward the westerners.

Closely allied with the question of the survey of the treaty line was that of the removal of the settlers from Indian lands. In 1797 the secretary of war ordered United States troops to remove those settlers who had possessions beyond the boundary. Sevier's son-in-law, Captain Sparks, commanded a company of Federal troops at Southwest Point and took part in the removals. This officer, together with Captain Wade, enjoyed the confidence of the settlers, and they succeeded in persuading the groups which the order affected to follow a policy of peace toward the government.[66] The acquiescence of the frontiersmen did not indicate that their feelings were allayed to any great extent. Those who lived in Powell's Valley claimed their land by reason of Henderson's Purchase[67] and viewed the removals by the United States as inhuman and unjust treatment. One of them in a letter to the Governor expressed the sentiments of the settlers in the following language: "we Bought our Lands paid deer for it Both by the Sword prosperity and money and to be turned off from our Lands and livings like a parcel of heathens will Look very inhuman and I expect will Cause a revolution."[68]

Sevier took up the matter with the United States government indirectly through the representatives in Congress and directly with the secretary of war. The affair threatened to bring on a serious disturbance along the whole of the southwestern frontier. The distress of the previous winter and the drought of the summer had caused

---

[66] *Address to the People of Powell's Valley*, etc., by Captains Sparks and Wade, Feb. 2, 1797, *Knoxville Gazette* of Feb. 6, 1797. McClung Collection, Lawson McGhee Library.

[67] *Knoxville Gazette*, Feb. 27, 1797.

[68] John Hunt to Sevier, July 17, 1797, *SP*.

a great scarcity of provisions in the affected areas. While the Governor realized the necessity of supporting the laws of the United States, humanity demanded that something be done for the relief of the settlers.[69] In October he laid the matter before the Assembly, which passed resolutions asking that the Federal government make some provision for the settlement of the question. Of course, everyone realized that the matter could be adjusted only by securing another cession of land from the Indians.

Sevier's problem consisted in preserving peace on the frontier and in securing an additional cession of land from the Cherokees. This latter could be obtained only by persuading the Federal government to negotiate a treaty for that purpose. The settlers evidently had confidence in Sevier's ability to bring about the adjustment of the problem, for, while they threatened violence, they did not openly resist removal. Sevier outlined his attitude in a communication to Jackson, Anderson, and Claiborne on November 20, 1797. He said that the settlers possessed a right to their land by reason of Henderson's claim, which North Carolina had accepted. The Federal government had not taken an acre from Kentucky and North Carolina because of the Indian boundary; Tennessee alone had suffered. A great number of people determined to go down the Mississippi into Spanish territory if the policy continued: "I fear one-half of our citizens will flock over into another government, indeed they are now doing it." This policy meant a direct check to the progress of the state.[70] By the first of February, 1798, Sevier had informed the inhabitants of Powell's Valley that the United States government would soon take measures to relieve their distress.[71] He felt that "there

---

[69] Sevier to Secretary of War, Aug. 22, 1797, *SP*.
[70] Sevier to Jackson, Anderson and Claiborne, Nov. 20, 1797, *SP*.
[71] Sevier to the Inhabitants of Powell's Valley, Feb. 1, 1798, *SP*.

never was an instance of such mistaken policy in any other government since governments had an existence."[72]

An irritating accompaniment of the policy of the government appeared in connection with the removals. Settlers had to have a permit from the colonel commanding the Federal troops before they could visit their farms. If they should be found across the line on Indian lands without it, they were subject to arrest. In order to obtain such a permit, they had to cross the line to Southwest Point, where the commander of the troops was stationed. This situation made it impracticable for them to visit their lands. Sevier proceeded to issue permits, and this action brought forth a complaint from Colonel Butler.[73] The Federal troops arrested a Tennessee judge, Campbell, and Sevier immediately protested to the president of the United States. He thought it a high-handed procedure: "I cannot admit that martial law has any right to be enforced when the civil meets no obstruction or impediment."[74] Although Sevier at a later time aided impeachment proceedings against the Judge,[75] he was entirely unwilling that a citizen of the state should be imposed upon by the Federal government. In a message to the Assembly on December 18, 1798, he placed information before them relative to arrests of citizens beyond the line. Those arrested had been taken under military guard to Nashville for trial before a Federal judge. He regarded it as an unhappy situation when every man who killed a deer or a bear "on the land falsely claimed by the Cherokees" could be punished, while the atrocities of the Indians passed unnoticed.[76]

The policies of the state and Federal governments

---

[72] Sevier to Jackson, Anderson and Claiborne, Feb. 5, 1798, *SP*.
[73] Sevier to Col. Butler, Feb. 17, 1798, *SP*.
[74] Sevier to the President, Feb. 6, 1798, *SP*.
[75] Message to the Assembly, Dec. 8, 1798, *SP*. [76] *SP*.

diametrically opposed each other in these questions which involved the Indian boundary. It is certain that the Federalist administration became fearful of the consequences if they delayed the settlement of the question by obtaining the lands desired by the citizens of the frontier. Otherwise the steps leading to a treaty would not have been taken. This whole situation showed conclusively the independent and particularistic spirit which dominated the frontiersmen.

These considerations led to the movement on the part of the Federal government to draw up a treaty with the Cherokees by which the unfortunate situation of the removed settlers might be remedied. The Federal government determined upon this course early in 1798, and it is quite possible that Senator Andrew Jackson exerted an important influence in bringing it about, for Sevier wrote to him and thanked him for his part in the affair. Sevier expressed the hope to Jackson that the commissioners would come soon as "the people are becoming uneasy and anxious to return in time to make crops."[77] The Governor issued a circular in which he stated that the commissioners named by the government were Walton, Moore, and Steele and that $25,800 had been designated as the amount to be used for the negotiation of the treaty.[78]

Before the commissioners arrived in Knoxville, Sevier requested Colonel James Ore to go on a secret errand to the Cherokee Nation.[79] Steele arrived on May 8, and Sevier informed Claiborne that the President's conduct toward Tennessee lately "had gained him much friendship" and if continued "he will become much admired by the people."[80] After the arrival of the commissioners Sevier issued instructions to Colonel Ore on May 12 con-

---

[77] Sevier to Jackson, Apr. 5, 1798, *SP*.　　[78] Apr. 23, 1798, *SP*.
[79] Sevier to Ore, Apr. 27, 1798, *SP*.
[80] Sevier to Claiborne, May 9, 1798, *SP*.

cerning his secret mission to the Indians. He should urge them to make a treaty, discover their attitude toward a cession of their land, and find out whether they were unanimous in favor of such a cession. The mission must be kept as private as possible.

The states concerned in negotiations with the Indians usually sent representatives to attend the conferences for the purpose of protecting the interests of their state. For this purpose Sevier appointed General Robertson, James Stuart, and Lachlan McIntosh as the Tennessee delegation and offered instructions for their guidance. They should endeavor to secure the communication of the Holston and Clinch with the Tennessee; the right bank of the Tennessee from the southwestern boundary of the state to its confluence with the Clinch; the incorporation of the settlements on the northern and western boundaries of the state; and the connection of Mero and Hamilton districts. They should examine the basis of the Cherokee claim as derived from the original rights, and, if necessary, question the constitutionality of any measure prior to the Holston Treaty which might have "prostrated the guaranteed rights of the whole people of the State."[81]

Sevier hoped that the discussions with the Indians would begin as soon as possible. The place of meeting was one of importance, and he offered his advice to the commissioners in which he advocated Southwest Point as the most favorable, because "soil [land] is with difficulty obtained in the rear of ground on which Indians treat, whilst they yield without much reluctance to that point."[82]

Colonel Ore reported upon his mission on May 31. He said that Dinsmore, the United States Indian agent then stationed in the Cherokee Nation, would not commit

---

[81] Sevier to Tennessee Agents, July 4, 1798, *SP*.
[82] Sevier to U. S. Commissioners, May 20, 1798, *SP*.

himself upon the place of meeting. The agent evidently acted for the treaty commissioners. The Indians complained that they received inferior goods and low prices for skins at Tellico. Ore reported that the number of the Cherokees had diminished considerably in the last few years: "It is accounted for by their Emigrations to the West of the Mississippi and it is said many more contemplate going." He advised that more attention be paid the warriors, who believed that the chiefs were more willing to sell the lands than the warriors themselves.

The commissioners evidently held aloof from the Governor; at least they did not freely give him information in regard to their plans, for Sevier, as late as June 2, did not know when they expected to hold the conference.[83] Several days later the Governor informed the Tennessee agents that the meeting would take place near Tellico Blockhouse on June 25. The delay made Sevier impatient, and it appears quite reasonable that the people also shared his uneasiness. He believed that a good treaty might be obtained "if desired by the commissioners" and that "nothing but a good treaty in my opinion will ever regain that confidence the people very short time since so fully placed in the government." He had done everything he could to quiet them, but "the enemies of government are in an indirect manner making no little use of the opportunity to sour the minds of the people."[84] A successful treaty would add to the popularity of the Governor and increase the confidence of the citizens in his administration.

The conference with the Indians must have taken place some time between July 4 and 15, for on the latter date Sevier wrote to Steele that he was sorry for the failure

---

[83] Sevier to U. S. Commissioners, *SP*.
[84] Sevier to Anderson, June 28, 1798, *SP*.

of the treaty.⁸⁵ For some reason the conference adjourned until autumn; to Sevier this meant failure. He said that this adjournment came from the inexperience of the commissioners,⁸⁶ and that "If the treaty fails the art of man could not convince the people otherways than it had been a designed diplomatic trick." The Tennessee agents, Robertson, Stuart, and McIntosh on July 19 summarized the case of the state. They had followed out Sevier's instructions, and this statement represented their investigations upon the subject, as well as what they deemed possible of achievement in the conference which was to meet later.⁸⁷

The Indians again assembled in late September. The negotiations became deadlocked by the stubborn refusal of the Indians to agree to an additional cession of land. The failure of Robertson and McIntosh to appear forced Sevier to attend, and it was due to his influence that a treaty was finally negotiated. The Indians in this treaty gave up the land demanded, and the settlers were satisfied.⁸⁸

Nothing more definitely marked Sevier a typical frontiersman than his Indian policy. As governor he faced many incidents in which the Indians and the settlers were guilty of attacks upon each other. He apparently desired to preserve an open mind in regard to these incidents. The Indians frequently made raids against isolated portions of the settlements in which they committed robbery and murder. They were especially adept at horse-stealing, and Sevier recorded in his correspondence numerous complaints of losses by the settlers on the border. Settlers were waylaid and slain from ambush by unknown

---

⁸⁵ Sevier to Steele, July 15, 1798, *SP*.
⁸⁶ Sevier to Anderson and Claiborne, July 15, 1798, *SP*.
⁸⁷ *AHM*, IV, 357.
⁸⁸ *ASP, Indian Affairs*, I, 637-38, Text of Treaty.

bands of Indians. In retaliation against these acts and because of their irritation at the protection accorded the Indians by the Federal government, the frontiersmen made it a dangerous adventure for any small band of Indians or single individuals to hunt within reach of the settlements. This intermittent strife constituted a continual annoyance. Through it all Sevier counseled peace and tried to stay the progress of strife. In his communications with the chiefs of the Cherokees from time to time, he held out the advantages of peace.[89]

The desire to encourage immigration into the state dictated his policy of peace: "The rapid emigration into our State is truly flattering, but a single hostility might be the occasioning the whole prospect wholly to vanish and cease."[90] He said that a few years of peace would be the "most legal and eligible mode" of reducing the neighboring tribe of Cherokees to reason and good order. He realized that a preponderance of numbers would overawe the Indians and cause them to settle down or to move beyond the Mississippi. Colonel Weir accurately expressed the attitude of the frontier on May 5, 1796: "There has never been a time when war could have been more ruinous to this Country than at the present crisis . . . hundreds crowding the roads every day through the Wilderness and thousands in all quarters preparing to remove to this Country and should the report of war get circulated abroad, all this promising prospect immediately ceases."[91] The idea expressed by Weir constantly recurred in Sevier's writings.

Sevier had no illusions concerning the good faith of the Indians. He believed that little dependence could be placed in the treaties which they made with the pioneers.[92]

---

[89] *SP, passim.*
[90] Sevier to the Assembly, Apr. 22, 1796, *SP*.
[91] *SP.*   [92] Sevier to Secretary of War, Aug. 15, 1796, *SP*.

Early in 1797 Indian atrocities aroused much resentment among the whites, and Sevier accused the Cherokees of violating their treaty in retaliating by bloodshed: "Our people dont want to go to war against you, tho they are not afraid, and you know they are not."[93] Sevier feared that the situation would get beyond his control and that the settlers would take matters into their own hands.[94]

The Governor ardently desired peace so that the state might make progress. He realized that increased population and expanded settlements would solve the Indian question. He continually favored a policy of expansion. Naturally this would be at the expense of the Indian hunting grounds. He held to the idea that "by the law of nations" no people were entitled to more land than they could cultivate. People would not sit and starve for want of land when a neighboring nation had much more than it needed. The Indians should learn the ways of agriculture, raise stock, and make crops of grain, which was the only method for them to become wealthy.[95] He had no thought of relinquishing any of the lands claimed by the Indians, and he overlooked no opportunity of adding to the land already in the possession of the whites. In a letter to Blount in 1796[96] he stated that he regarded the encouragement of immigration as his first care and object. A war would "flusterate the desirable object" because it would obstruct immigration. Increased population was the thing needed to "make us opulent and respected."

His attitude toward the Indian never changed. His methods were practical, and they differed with changing conditions. He chose the best and most advantageous methods of crushing the power of the savages. In the early

---
[93] Sevier to Cherokees, Feb. 10, 1797, *SP*.
[94] Sevier to Hawkins, July 8, 1797, *SP*.
[95] Sevier to Col. Ore, May 12, 1798, *SP*.   [96] Oct. 7, 1796, *SP*.

days of his life on the frontier he employed military force, but as governor he encouraged immigration as a means to the same end. He desired to obey all treaties "so far as they are not pernicious, odious nor iniquitous."[97] To the end of his life, Sevier believed the Indians were licentious and erratic and led a "vagrant, lawless, debauched and immoral life and nothing will ever deter those itinerant nations from their common desperate and rapacious practices."[98] For these reasons he justified their punishment. He believed that the savages deserved it. These statements contain the heart of Sevier's whole Indian policy.

When Sevier left the office of governor in 1801, he was immediately appointed by Governor Roane to serve as one of the Tennessee commissioners to establish the disputed boundary between Virginia and Tennessee.[99] His administrations had been as successful as they had been popular. He did not expect to retire from public life, and his followers did not wish to lose his services.

---
[97] Sevier to the Secretary of War, July 20, 1796, *SP*.
[98] *Ibid*.
[99] Henry D. Whitney, *Land Laws of Tennessee*, pp. 633-36.

CHAPTER VIII

HONESTY OR FRAUD?

THE CAMPAIGN in Tennessee for governor in 1803 became one of the bitterest which has ever taken place in the state. At the end of Sevier's third administration in 1801, he found himself barred from re-election by the constitutional provision which prohibited a man from serving consecutively in the executive office for more than three terms. Archibald Roane succeeded him. During Roane's term Sevier's position as the dominating political leader was challenged by a rising and forceful group centering in the person of Andrew Jackson. Roane became a candidate to succeed himself. Sevier attempted to regain the governor's chair in order to thwart the ambitions of the Jackson and Roane political forces. The struggle became a contest of strength between the two political leaders in the state, Sevier and Jackson. Sevier, the older of the two men, had long occupied a prominent position in the western country. Jackson had held places of influence in public affairs, and he now approached a position of prominence as a political leader. A feeling of bitterness which marred their relations had existed between the two prior to the campaign. Sevier felt a sort of contempt for the younger man, which at times he had not hesitated to express openly. It must have rankled in the breast of Jackson that the veteran Indian fighter opposed him, and words which scorned his lack of legal ability added no love to their relationship.

This personal coolness did not entirely account for the issues which developed in the campaign. Jackson and his supporters desired to capture the control of the state administration. In order to accomplish this purpose they faced the necessity of finding some issue by which they might hope to destroy the confidence which the public placed in Sevier. Jackson found the issue and quite probably started the movement which furnished it.

One of the clashes between Sevier and Jackson had occurred concerning the election in Davidson County for officers of militia in 1796.[1] General Conway had been elected through the influence of Sevier. Jackson had been the other candidate. The clash of personalities resulted from this election. General Conway died in 1801, and Sevier, ever desirous of military perferment, became a candidate for the office of major general. Jackson still desired the office and opposed Sevier. The election resulted in a tie between the two men; Governor Roane cast the deciding vote, giving the office to Jackson.

It seems probable that Jackson had prepared the way for the precipitation of a political struggle, for he gave certain papers destined to become the bone of contention in the next gubernatorial campaign into Roane's hands on the day when the Governor cast the deciding vote for major general.[2] These papers in the form of affidavits were designed to make it appear that Sevier had obtained a large tract of land by means of fraudulent warrants. It may be presumed that Jackson gave these papers to the Governor in order to influence him in the selection of a general, for they formed an excellent justification for the vote which Roane cast for Jackson.

Jackson served as United States senator from Tennessee from November, 1797, to April, 1798. While on his way to Philadelphia in 1797 Charles J. Love of Nashville in-

---

[1] See p. 124.   [2] Garrett and Goodpasture, *op. cit.*, p. 147.

formed him of land frauds which were being perpetrated in Tennessee. Jackson made this fact known to the governor of North Carolina through Senator Martin from that state. The North Carolina executive instituted an investigation which resulted in the implication of Sevier on the charge of illegal practices in obtaining grants of land from North Carolina. It gave Jackson much satisfaction, and he is reported to have said that "When you set a bear trap, you never can tell what particular bear is going to blunder into it."[3] Had Jackson been wise, he would have discriminated in the game which he sought.

The whole affair gives the impression that it was meant to be a deft political move on the part of Jackson and his supporters and that it had been well planned in advance. Jackson's group had far-reaching ambitions, and the stumbling block in the way of a realization of their aims was the popular old Indian fighter of Nolachucky. He must be removed, and they prepared the way for his retirement. Jackson did not have the state-wide popularity that would bring him to the governorship at that time, and he sought to arrive at this goal by the same path Sevier had used. He knew that no surer way into the hearts of the people of the frontier existed than through military success. Jackson had done nothing in a military way up to this time to merit election as major general.[4] He had desired military office since 1791, when his plan for the defense of the Cumberland region came into the

---

[3] A. C. Buell, *History of Andrew Jackson*, I, 136.
[4] He had been appointed judge advocate of the Davidson County Regiment by Governor Blount, Sept. 10, 1792. "Blount's Journal," *AHM*, II, 247; J. S. Bassett, *Life of Andrew Jackson*, I, 75-76, says that Jackson's rise to prominence in the militia was due to native soldierly qualities "which were early manifested." Jackson was forty-five years old before he had an opportunity to prove that he was fitted for the position to which he desired election in 1797.

hands of the secretary of war through the agency of Governor Blount.[5] The probability of an Indian campaign which might bring him the desired laurels still remained.

The union of the Jackson and Roane supporters insured the election of Jackson as a military leader, and they hoped that the same political forces would be able to reëlect Roane as governor. By this process they expected to retire Sevier involuntarily and permanently as a political leader and to grasp the reins of government in the state. The scheme was ambitious and worthy of a struggle. The prizes of the offices of governor and of major general proved too tempting to resist.

This scheme resulted in a political blunder of the first magnitude. Had Sevier been allowed to obtain the office of general, he probably would not have become a candidate for governor at the expiration of Roane's term, and the Jackson-Roane group might have retained control of the administration. Enraged at his defeat in the military election and embittered against both Jackson and Roane, Sevier announced himself as a candidate for governor in the election in 1803. Immediately the question of the land frauds became the issue in the campaign, as Jackson had intended that it should. The struggle developed a bitterness and an intensity which had not attended earlier elections. The newspaper war became vituperative, and the whispering, vindictive. It soon developed into a struggle between Sevier and Jackson rather than between the two candidates.

The papers which Jackson had deposited with Governor Roane consisted of an affidavit by John Carter, entry-taker for Washington County, together with documents which supported charges in the deposition. In the early stages of the campaign Roane wrote letters

---
[5] Blount to Robertson, Sept. 21, 1791. *AHM*, I, 193.

HONESTY OR FRAUD? 149

to certain individuals in the Cumberland region in which he said that he possessed documents which would prove that Sevier had defrauded the State of North Carolina by surreptitiously obtaining grants for vacant lands. Sevier's supporters replied vigorously that the statements were false and that the charges had been made with the intention of destroying the reputation of their leader in order to prevent his election and to build Roane's greatness upon the ruin and downfall of his rival.[6]

At this time Jackson entered the contest in defense of Roane. In July, 1803, he published a lengthy attack upon Sevier in the *Tennessee Gazette*, a Nashville newspaper. In this article he included the affidavit of Carter which had been made February 16, 1802.[7] Carter based the affidavit upon the theft or destruction of certain land records of Washington County and his subsequent discovery, in 1795, of an extra file among the papers of the office upon which Sevier's entries had been recorded. This file had been delivered to the Governor with the affidavit. Jackson charged that no one except Sevier would have desired the destruction of the books of the entry office. The file placed in the hands of Roane contained 175 locations of 640 acres each in the name of Sevier, all dated Septem-

[6] Publication by Jackson in *Tennessee Gazette*, July 27, 1803, Library of Congress.

[7] The affadavit is as follows: "I, John Carter, do solemnly swear that I have delivered all the papers belonging to the entry office of Washington County, which has been in my possession since the books belonging to said office were destroyed or stolen, unto William Maclin, a commisisoner appointed to receive them, to the best of my knowledge and belief, except one file of papers, purporting to be locations, which I have delivered to his excellency Governor Roane, which file I found amongst the papers of the said office about the year one thousand seven hundred and ninety-five, and I believe it did not originally belong to the office, but has been fraudulently put in. And I do further swear, that I do not know of any of the papers belonging to said entry office to be in the possession of any other person."

(Signed) John Carter.

ber 16, 1779. Jackson contended that these entries had been made in the handwriting of Sevier himself. He said that the records showed that lands had been granted to Sevier upon these warrants and also that this had been accomplished by a fraudulent collusion between Sevier and James Glasgow, secretary of state of North Carolina. The consideration on the face of Sevier's grant read "ten pounds" instead of "fifty shillings." He reviewed the land laws of North Carolina and asserted that the grants which bore the consideration of "fifty shillings" were made on warrants from Carter's county office and that grants issued from Armstrong's office bore the consideration of "ten pounds." A subsequent law made removals from county lands possible, "but it was never understood that law authorized the removal of fifty shilling warrants to the West of the Cumberland mountain." Sevier had the warrants located west of the mountain, and then it became necessary to have the grants changed so as to apply to these lands. Hence, he said, Sevier resorted to bribery, and to support this charge, Jackson included a letter from Sevier, copied from the files of Secretary Glasgow, which he presented as evidence that bribery had really taken place. The letter read as follows:

Jonesboro 11, Nov. 1795

DEAR SIR,

I am highly sensible of your goodness and friendship in executing my business at your office, in the manner and form which I took the liberty to request. Permit me to facilitate the completion of the small remainder of my business that remains in the hands of Mr. Gordon. Should there be no impropriety I should consider myself obliged to have ten pounds inserted in the room of fifty shillings. I have instructed Mr. Gordon to furnish unto you a plat of the amount of three 640 acres, which I considered myself indebted to you for fees, etc., which I beg you will accept, in case you consider that the three warrants will be adequate to the sum I am indebted to you.

I am with sincere and great esteem, Dear
Sir,   your most obedient and humble servant,
JOHN SEVIER

Jackson asked: "Is it possible that any man can believe John Sevier so ignorant as not to know that altering a grant agreeably to his request, so as to make it speak a lye, was a crime of the highest nature?" He went on to defend himself for saying that no honest man would vote for Sevier. The remainder of the attack contained a heated discussion of the above facts calculated to arouse resentment against Sevier because of the alleged fraud.

Roane added to these charges by stating that when Carter had deposited the documents with him, the entry-taker had said that none of the locations of the file had ever been entered upon the books of the office. Other persons had filed locations and had made regular entries on the same numbers. He also said that he possessed authenticated copies of records in the office of the North Carolina Secretary which proved that other persons had actually received grants on these numbers and that Sevier had obtained grants on them also.[8]

The extra file contained entries for which warrants had been issued to the amount of 105,600 acres.[9] The amount actually granted upon warrants from this file and from John Armstrong's office totaled 57,060 acres.[10] Therefore, Sevier was charged with stealing the latter amount of land from the State of North Carolina. This charge, if

---
[8] Publication by Governor Roane, July 21, 1803, in *Tennessee Gazette and Mero District Advertiser* (hereafter cited as *Tennessee Gazette*), Aug. 3, 1803. It was indicated in the paper that a copy of this publication had been sent to the *Knoxville Gazette*.

[9] *Journal of the House and Senate of Tennessee*, Nov. 8, 1803.

[10] See pp. 68-69.

true, was extremely damaging; if false, it was essentially a grave injury. It was no wonder that Sevier seemed unfit for public office and that Jackson appeared as an unscrupulous politician to the partisan defenders on the opposite sides in this campaign fight.

It is necessary that a careful examination be made of these charges. They have been accepted as true largely because Jackson said that they were. Sevier's side of the controversy has never been published since that day. Jackson's later career served to deflect inquiry from these earlier events in his life, and the reputation of Sevier has suffered accordingly. This was a matter of practical politics and of heated resentments brought on by the ambitions of the attackers.

Sevier published his defense in the *Tennessee Gazette* on August 3, 1803. He quoted the letter which Jackson had published and said: "If the above letter were to be perused by none but those versant in the laws of North Carolina and disposed to give that construction to the contents, no comment from me would be necessary. . . . That part which mentions 'in executing my business at your office in the manner and form which I took the liberty to request' *would have been fully explained by referring to a letter previously written by me to the secretary on the same subject,*[11] which was as accessible as the one brought forward." This earlier letter, he further stated, contained a request that the Secretary issue grants on several warrants consolidated to the amount of the respective quantities specified in the different plats and certificates, a practice which was common, and that the Secretary had acceded to his request. In regard to the request in the letter which Jackson published, that the consideration on the face of the grant be made "ten pounds" instead of "fifty shillings," which he had been informed was the "strong-

---
[11] Italics are mine.

hold" of his "calumniators," no one could discover an attempt to "seduce a man from the paths of rectitude." It was not even a request, he explained, but only a proposition made to one who had a thorough knowledge of the laws and practices of the state in order that he might judge whether it was proper or not. Even if he had requested it, there would have been no guilt attached to it. Part of the warrants sent to the office of the Secretary were Armstrong's warrants and part were county warrants. No law directed what sum should be expressed on the face of a grant; it was only required that some consideration be expressed. It was "immaterial to the state, to the grantee, and every citizen of the state whether it was ten pounds, fifty shillings, or fifty cents." The part of the letter referring to the three warrants offered to Glasgow showed that they had been presented in place of cash which was due to the Secretary for fees. The greater part of his business had been done before the letter was written, the Secretary had not received his fees for it, and the surveyor, George Gordon, "had pledged his word that the whole should be paid when he returned." Had the Secretary issued a grant on each warrant which had been sent to him, the fees and "perquisites" due him would have "amounted to much more than the value of three 640 acre warrants," not counting registration fees and governmental tax. He did not know the exact sum which he owed Glasgow, but he could not believe that it amounted to "less than the value of the three warrants." As he could not conveniently procure the cash, he sent the warrants in place of currency. He closed this explanation with a warning against other attempts to calumniate him at the last minute before election.

Jackson's friends made other attacks upon Sevier in the course of the campaign. In the same issue of the Nashville paper in which Sevier published his defense, there appeared several of these publications. One of them bore the signature of "A Citizen of Robertson County." It repeated the charges in the usual style of campaign documents. The injuries which the state had suffered from these "speculative villainous characters" would not be remedied "for ages." Sevier had not yet completed the "small remainder of those fraudulent warrants" amounting to some "50,000 other acres to be appropriated." It was no wonder that they witnessed the "most unremitted exertions to get *Chucky John* into office,—he can then have this *small remainder* completed and favor such of his *good friends* in like manner as have not forsaken him, in *good and bad report.*"

Another communication appeared over the signature of "An Elector," and its author made much of the question of the fees which Sevier owed Glasgow. He cited the act of 1782 which regulated the fees that the Secretary should have received to show that Glasgow had the legal right to a fee for each grant only and not for each warrant. As only two grants had been made, the actual fee owed to the Secretary amounted only to one dollar, that is, four shillings to the grant. Even if it be allowed that he was entitled to fees upon each warrant, the fees would have amounted only to $82.50. The warrants given to him by Sevier would amount to 1,920 acres, worth at the lowest calculation $960.00, "that is, rating the lands at ten pounds the hundred acres and allowing the same for locating and surveying." These exorbitant fees gave the writer convincing proof that Sevier had attempted to bribe Glasgow.

The campaign became heated indeed. Jackson in a letter written about election time[12] reported that he had been "much threatened at Jonesborough by the Sevierites

---

[12] Jackson to John Hutchings. Bassett, *Correspondence of Andrew Jackson*, I, 70.

whilst sick, but as soon as I got upon my legs, from the fierceness of lyons, they softned down to the Gentleness of lambs, there is no spirit amongst them." Sevier was elected by a majority of 1,663 votes. Evidently the charges of fraud had not been taken seriously by as many as Jackson had hoped.

Jackson and his supporters were not through with the question of the land frauds. Roane sent a special message to the legislature on September 23, in which he advised an investigation into the conduct of the land office. The purpose of this suggestion was to produce testimony which could be used to indict Sevier of corrupt practices and to force him out of office. If this failed, impeachment proceedings would still be possible. A joint committee to conduct the investigation was appointed by the two houses of the Assembly. While this committee was engaged in taking testimony and in examining the papers of Carter's land office, Sevier sent several requests to the legislature asking to be heard upon the subject. He sent these communications on November 2 and 3. He addressed the first to the Senate and merely requested that he be heard before the committee made its report, as "the same very materially concerns my property and that of many others, and what is still more dear to me, that of my own reputation. And as this report can not be considered in any other light than that of an indirect manner of impeaching, I humbly hope, your Honorable House of Senate will be so indulging as to permit me by Counsel, to vindicate and defend my own reputation and innocence and Show to the World, that the Charges endeavoring to be brought forward against me, are exhibited by enemies, through interested Motives, and malicious designs."[13]

The second communication attempted to bring before the Assembly through the Senate a defense of himself, as

---
[13] *SP.*

he had been informed that the committee had reported and in its report had stated that he had committed fraud in obtaining the warrants. Part of the evidence had been founded, he said, upon the oath of John Carter, "a man proven to be deeply interested in destroying the Titles obtained by your memoralist for certain lands on Obias River in the county of Jackson, and to which the pretended frauds particularly relate, and therefore would not be admitted as Witness in Any Court of Justice to establish facts connected with the Titles to Said lands." He made the charge that the framers of the report meant to create evidence which could not have been directly admitted in court to establish a fact; therefore they attempted by illegal and unconstitutional means to deprive a citizen of his property and to subject him to punishment. The legislature, on the same principle, might just as well pass a law making an act an offense after it had been done, or to punish an action which was not a crime at the time of commission. He also raised the question of the power of the committee to bring out such a report. The land laws were those of North Carolina, and it seemed doubtful if the legislature had the authority to investigate such a case when the offense was charged to be against the laws of another state. No tribunal in Tennessee could take cognizance of the subject under existing law, and the Assembly had no right to assume the power to review the case. If the Assembly did not have the power, how did its committee have that power? He demanded that, as he was affected in property and character, he should be allowed to bring forth facts in his defense.[14]

The committee made its report, and it came before the House on November 8 for action. It contained charges of fraud on the part of Sevier, as he had predicted. A motion to reject the report as a whole was denied. It was

---
[14] *Ibid.*

then moved that it be amended so as to remove all charges of fraud on the part of Sevier, but to retain a summary of the irregularities found in the land office by the committee. This motion passed, and the action removed the charges of fraud. Sevier's friends voted consistently against a report of any kind.[15]

The amendment of this report completely exonerated Sevier as to the fraud, but it still contained the implication of guilt. The legal questions raised by Sevier were important ones, and he hinted that he knew that the object on the part of the committee had been to manufacture evidence to be used in court. Some years later a citizen of North Carolina instituted an action in the Federal court at Nashville to eject the owners of one of the tracts in question from their property, on the ground that Sevier, the original proprietor of the land, had obtained his grant by fraudulent methods.[16] The case was carried to the United States Supreme Court on appeal, remanded to the district court for re-trial, carried a second time to the Supreme Court and returned for a third trial in Nashville. The attorneys attempted to use as evidence the report of this investigation by the committee of the Assembly in 1803. This action may have been started earlier than 1811, the date of the first trial of the case in Nashville. William Polk, the plaintiff, secured his grant in 1800, five years after Sevier had received the original grant for the tract. It is significant that Polk obtained his grant *after* Jackson had inspired the investigation by Governor Ashe and *before* the charges of fraud against Sevier were published.

---

[15] *Journal of the House and Senate of Tennessee.*

[16] Polk's Lessee v. Hill, Wendel and others. *Tennessee Reports*, II, 118-63; *U. S. Reports*, III, 665-70; *Tennessee Reports*, II, 433-36; *U. S. Reports*, V, 92-97; *Minutes* of the United States Circuit Court in the office of the Clerk in Nashville.

It is unknown whether Sevier obtained a hearing before the legislature when he demanded it in 1803. Evidently the Assembly realized that it trod upon dangerous legal ground and gave up hope of success by this procedure. Sevier was correct in his legal interpretation of the action of the committee in the matter of attempting to manufacture evidence to be used in a court of justice, for the report was rejected in the trial alluded to, and an opinion of the United States Supreme Court in this case upheld the decision of the trial court.[17]

The Jackson party had failed in the election. They failed in the attempt at impeachment, and the only recourse left was to be found in the courts. The feeling which had been aroused came to a head while the committee conducted its inquiry. Sevier met William Martin, a member of the committee, on the street in Knoxville during the progress of the investigation. An altercation ensued during which Jackson came up and intervened. Sevier said that his "enemies were damned cowards and dare not meet him." Sevier was armed with a cutlass and Jackson with a sword-cane, and they came nearly to blows. This altercation resulted in the challenging of Sevier to a duel by Jackson, with consequences which will be described in the next chapter.[18]

---

[17] *U. S. Reports*, III, 665-70.

[18] This account is that given in the *Tennessee Gazette*, Dec. 21, 1803. Certificate of J. Wharton, Wm. Hall and J. K. Wynne, all of them members of the Assembly and friends of Jackson. William Martin was a member of the committee of the Assembly which was investigating the land office and was a son of Joseph Martin, enemy of Sevier in earlier days. See Chapter II. This account is accepted for several reasons: It is the only one in which Jackson's friends mention the fact that Jackson was armed. It appears very likely that Martin should have been the object of an attack by Sevier. It is the only account which mentions the investigation into the land fraud question as the basis for the altercation between Sevier and Jackson. It connects the feud between these two men definitely with the land question.

Jackson had been frustrated in his ambition. The major general of the militia acted under the orders of the governor of the state, his bitterest enemy, who had the power to deprive him of any opportunity to distinguish himself in Indian fighting. His friend had failed of election to the governorship, and the land fraud charges had exploded. Jackson came as near to the governorship in this election as it was ever possible for him to attain, and a like opportunity did not come his way again. It was truly a bitter defeat and explained the reason why he was willing to risk a meeting upon the field of honor: Sevier might be removed from the stage, after all, in an honorable way.

While the outcome of the campaign may have satisfied Sevier and his friends, some phases of the land question invite attention. A comparison of Jackson's charges and Sevier's defense brings out some interesting points. If Jackson had access to both of the letters written by Sevier to Glasgow—and it is probable that he had—he published only a part of the truth. Such procedure was to be expected in a political battle such as this one proved to be. Jackson charged that the law permitting removals of warrants west of the Cumberland mountains had never been understood as applying to county warrants. However, there was no prohibition against it, and it was legal for the warrants to be removed if they had been issued prior to the cession of the western lands of North Carolina in 1789:[19] that state had the right to perfect incipient titles. Sevier was correct when he said that it made no difference, then, what consideration the face of the grant bore. This being true, the charge made by Jackson that Sevier bribed Glasgow to *change* the face of the grant falls through, and the grants were not made to "speak

---

[19] Polk's Lessee v. Hill, Wendel and others, U. S. Supreme Court, *U. S. Reports*, III, 665-70.

a lye." This does not necessarily say that the 1,920 acres were not a bribe, but that they were not a bribe for the thing which Jackson said they were. Neither does this fact clear Sevier of the charge of fraud in the acquisition of the warrants. The grants had been issued upon locations authorized by warrants from *both* offices, Armstrong's and Carter's.[20]

The letter which Sevier said that he had written to Glasgow before that of November 11 which Jackson published throws considerable light upon Sevier's side of the controversy and furnishes contemporary evidence of Sevier's land speculations at that time.

Jonesbor'h Inn 1795[21]

DEAR SIR,

Sometime in the year 1779 myself with some others under sanction of a law passed in No. Carolina, entered a considerable Quantity of land which was chiefly held by suspected persons supposed to be inimical to the common cause of liberty. Some turned out, took up arms, and others that were suspected lay Quiet. The Act alluded to was at the next session in some measure repealed. We were doubtful of supporting the entries we had made, and the peace taking place in the year 1782 seemed another embarrassment—Considering every circumstance, I choosed rather to decline any farther pursuit, or at any rate not to endeavor to hold the lands from those characters who chiefly had returned to their allegiance: for my own part I did actually consider the money with the adventure all lost, therefore, everything lay dormant for several years, and until many were obtaining titles for lands under what is called the supernumary law.

I will confess that in the business I have related, I had a view of realizing some of the paper then dead on my hands

---

[20] The 25,060 acre grant was made upon Carter's warrants alone; the 32,000 acre grant was made upon both Armstrong's and Carter's warrants. *Grant Book A*, pp. 260, 216 respectively.

[21] Draper MSS, 11DD121.

(for which I had given great part of my most valuable property) and did then intend to obtain as much land for it, as I could under the shelter of any law on that head, knowing of no mode left but the one. All the land in the Country has been so culled and picked out that little good is now to be had, nevertheless I have had several tracts surveyed, some large, tho mostly Mountainous and poor, yet it may at some future period reimburse in some degree the amazing loss I have sustained by the depreciated paper.

I have given you, sir, a candid and accurate statement of the whole transaction, and should you think that in Justice we ought to have any consideration for the monies paid for these lands, and the warrants considered supernumeries, you will then please to let patents issue agreeably to the platts of surveys made, and much oblige me by consolidating a number of the warrants together in one grant.

I am, etc
JOHN SEVIER

HONBLE JAMES GLASGOW
SECRETARY OF STATE

Sevier wrote this letter, however, about the time that the books of Carter's office were reported to have disappeared and Sevier's file introduced, and if Sevier committed the fraud at that time, this letter would represent the plan upon which he based his attempt. If the scheme were fraudulent, it was a clever one. In 1779, the year in which Tory activity flourished on the western waters, Sevier served as clerk of the county court, and Landon Carter acted as entry-taker. Sevier also acted as one of the commissioners appointed to receive the property confiscated from Tory suspects,[22] an action which aroused some of them against Sevier.[23]

---

[22] See p. 43.

[23] Draper MSS., Draper's Notes, XXX, 362-63; George W. Sevier reported that Sevier and Carter had entered for a great deal of these

It was entirely possible for the original transaction to have taken place in the manner described by Sevier. The North Carolina Assembly passed a law authorizing confiscations.[24] It is true that the court confiscated Tory land in Washington County and that Sevier served as a member of the commission which received the property.[25] The law under which the confiscations took place allowed reëntry for the land. Carter and Sevier occupied positions which enabled them to know the value of these lands and also to enter for them. If this were true, the state collected for these reëntries just as upon the original entries. Had these warrants been held, they represented just so much paper until Sevier had the tracts surveyed. By 1795 all the valuable land in the county had been granted.[26] According to the law permitting removals, he could obtain grants upon these warrants for land west of the mountains. It was but a natural action on the part of Sevier, if he had retained the warrants, to attempt to recover the value given for the entries "under the shelter of any law on that head."

His case was a sound one with the exception of the incident of the destruction of the county records in 1795. This event brought about the affidavit of Carter in 1802.

---

lands. The Tories still hovering in the community got wind of it and determined to go in a body to Carter's office and demand the privilege of examining the entry-taker's books, and if it should prove true that these entries had been made, they determined to kill Sevier and Carter. These two men concluded that it would be well if their entries were not known; so they transcribed the books, leaving the entries blank opposite the Tory confiscations. They then hid the original books in the woods. Col. Carter died, and the books were never found. However, the entries were deemed valid. This account was given years afterward and with full knowledge of the double entries, and so it cannot be given full credence.

[24] *SRNC*, XXIV, 209-14.
[25] See p. 42.
[26] Report Jefferson to President Washington, transmitted to Congress, Nov. 10, 1791. *ASP, Public Lands*, I, 22-25.

There may have been some force in Sevier's contention that Carter[27] had as much of an interest in the destruction of the records as Jackson charged that Sevier had. If the facts of this event were true as Carter reported them, the reason for the silence of this bonded entry-taker from 1795 until 1802 remained open to serious question. Why did he not make it known before it became useful as a campaign issue? This fact lends color to Sevier's charge that Carter's evidence would not be admitted in a court of law.

In relation to the fees mentioned in the letter of Sevier to Glasgow of November 11, 1795, there is still more doubt. On August 2, 1795, Sevier "Sent 150 land warrants 640 acres each By Geo. Gordon to No. Carolina to Get Titles for the same to be laid on Each Side of Cumberland near the mouth of Obias River."[28] Gordon must have tarried in Tennessee until after September 6, for there are several other entries in the *Journal* of Sevier regarding warrants for the 96,000 acres.[29] When Gordon finally went he must have carried the letter which described where Sevier obtained the warrants. On November 8 of the same year, Sevier again "furnished Mr. Gordon with Land warrants to the amt. of 40,000 acres and lent him cash 10 Dollars."[30] When Gordon went to North Carolina this time, he evidently carried the letter which presented the 1,920 acres for fees.

Land warrants at this time sold approximately at their face or par value, for Sevier settled a note with Willie Blount on August 2 for which land warrants were used in payment at the rate of $250 per thousand, or 25 cents per acre.[31] At the rate of eight shillings to the dollar,

---

[27] See pp. 148-51.   [28] Sevier's *Diary*, in Heiskell, *op. cit.*, p. 526.
[29] *Ibid.*, pp. 526-27.   [30] *Ibid.*, p. 528.
[31] *Ibid.*, p. 526. The exchange rate was placed at 8 shillings to the dollar in 1779. *SRNC*, XXIV, 256. There were 20 shillings to the pound.

the exchange rate at that time, this would amount to ten pounds per hundred, the cost of land entered in Armstrong's office. This may be taken as the value of the warrants offered to Glasgow. At that rate he offered to the Secretary $480.00 for fees. It was charged that it represented double this amount, $960.00, as $480.00 should be added for surveying the tract. Gordon surveyed most of this land and also engaged in the speculation,[32] and an estimate of the value of the surveys may be correspondingly diminished. If these warrants should have been from Carter's office, the value may be estimated at about one-fourth of the amount given above.[33]

It is not possible to make any accurate estimate of the actual amount of money which Sevier owed Secretary Glasgow for fees. The two lots of warrants mentioned above amounted to 136,000 acres. There may have been more than two hundred warrants all together, or there may have been less than that number. If Glasgow collected four shillings per warrant for his own fees and two shillings ten pence for the private secretary of the Governor,[34] one might conclude that Sevier was indebted to Glasgow something less than $200. If the Secretary should locate the warrants and obtain grants upon them, he would have to pay three pounds per grant for registration in the county.[35] This would decrease their value somewhat. But this estimate cannot be conclusive because it is not known how many warrants were sent. It must be remembered also that Sevier had obtained other grants for land in the same year,[36] and this would have increased still more the amount which he owed Glasgow. It appears

---

[32] Gordon was the surveyor who located many of Sevier's tracts of land. See Chapter IV.

[33] Fifty shillings=two pounds ten shillings, or one-fourth of ten pounds.

[34] Fee Law of 1782, *SRNC*, XXIV, 445-46.

[35] *SRNC*, XXIV, 316, Law of 1780. [36] See p. 68.

plausible that Sevier actually did not know how much he owed the Secretary and that he hoped that the three warrants would cover his indebtedness. On the other hand, it would not appear that he owed as much as the warrants were worth. Glasgow was indicted and convicted of graft in the conduct of his office,[37] and it is certain that he was not above bribery. This side of the affair cannot be cleared up. In spite of Jackson's charges, it cannot be established definitely that Sevier gave Glasgow more than was due him. Sevier knew that the Secretary was acquainted with his extensive dealing in land, and it is possible that he gave Glasgow the warrants as a sort of "hush" money rather than as a bribe for changing the face of a grant.

The argument might be advanced that the grant for 25,060 acres, which had been made August 28, 1795, on Carter's warrants alone, had been brought back to Sevier with "fifty shillings" on its face and that Sevier wished it to be changed to "ten pounds." This was the grant upon which the courts later decided.[38] In the opinion rendered by Justice Marshall of the Supreme Court in 1815,[39] it was brought out that the grant stood thus: "For and in consideration of . . . pounds . . ." The Justice in his decision stated that the consideration could have been nothing else than "ten pounds." The objection brought by the plaintiff that it must have been "fifty shillings" and that it had been torn or removed was disallowed.

These explanations are not offered in defense of Sevier. They are presented in order that a fuller understanding may be had of the whole affair. The innocence or guilt of Sevier is not possible of determination. On the one hand, the charges have all the appearance necessary to brand

---
[37] S. A. Ashe, *History of North Carolina*, II, 176-77.
[38] Polk's Lessee v. Hill, Wendel and others, *loc. cit.*
[39] *U. S. Reports*, III, 665-70.

them as campaign propaganda produced to influence the electorate. On the other hand, the disappearance of the records at an opportune time, their replacement by Sevier's file, and the character of Glasgow, combined with the connecting circumstances, produce a possibility of guilt.

If Sevier was guilty, Jackson did not succeed in convincing the friends of his opponent of that fact. If he was innocent, he was justified in believing that Jackson did not hesitate to employ unscrupulous political methods or that he was a "poor, pitiful, petty-fogging, scurrilous lawyer," as he had dubbed Jackson some years earlier.[40]

While it is impossible to determine whether Sevier was innocent or guilty, a careful study of this problem leads to the conclusion that he took advantage of the technicalities of the laws to acquire these two large tracts of land. He probably knew of the unscrupulous activities of Glasgow and offered the warrants in order to facilitate the procedure of obtaining the grants. So far as the value of the warrants offered Glasgow was concerned, a man who operated as a land speculator would be indifferent to the worth of three warrants when he used hundreds of them in his business affairs. He could afford to be liberal. A warrant represented a certain value in the depreciated currency of that time, but Sevier would not have felt the loss of three of them. Thus, when he prepared to settle his accounts with the Secretary, it appears quite plausible that he thought that three warrants would cover his debt to Glasgow, and so he sent that number with Gordon. If the fees did not amount to as much as the value of the warrants, the remainder would be acceptable to the Secretary who, in turn, would hasten the grants through the office. This attitude was characteristic of the speculator and of

---

[40] Jackson to Sevier, May 8, 1797, Bassett, *Correspondence*, I, 32.

the frontier. Sevier may have thought of the transaction as an unimportant incident of his land dealing. Further than this suggestion, no conclusion as to his guilt is possible.

CHAPTER IX

THE SEVIER-JACKSON FEUD

THE FEUD between Sevier and Jackson has been presented for the most part by those primarily interested in Jackson's participation in the affair. This has been done in spite of the fact that up to that time Sevier had enjoyed a much wider popularity in state politics than Jackson had. The struggle had a political as well as a personal background. Each of the men exerted a powerful influence over the people in his own section of the state. Jackson's ambitions ran counter to Sevier's political power. The entrance of Jackson into the political arena caused the partisans of each to rally around their leader. The natural geographic conditions had produced, prior to this time, a feeling somewhat akin to sectionalism in Tennessee, but very few evidences of it appeared until the outbreak of the difficulties between these leaders. From this time forward, the differences between the sections became more and more important in the politics of the state. Jackson represented the Cumberland region, which had experienced a separate and an almost independent growth. Sevier gradually became identified with the desires of the people in the eastern part rather than those in the whole of the state. Most of the evidence appears to lend weight to the fact that political sectionalism in Tennessee began with the break between Jackson and Sevier.

The original cause for dispute between these two men cannot be found. The accounts given by the biographers of Jackson are so confusing that one seeks in vain for a satisfactory explanation in their narratives. The letters of the two men furnish only fragmentary sources. Tradition lends no aid in locating the time and place of their first unfriendly encounter.

No attention has been paid to a possible connection between the feud and the first election for governor in Tennessee. The governor was chosen by popular election, and the Assembly conducted a count of the returns from the counties in the territory as the first item of business after its organization.[1] No hint remains in any of the histories of Tennessee or in the records of the legislature concerning the circumstances of this first election. No account of the number of votes cast can be found, and no direct indication of any contest has come to light. It has been assumed, apparently, that the people unanimously elected Sevier. Why should there be this seemingly conscious silence on the part of the leaders of that time? Solution of this phase of the problem is impracticable. The first election of Sevier in 1796 was not quite so free from opposition as the meager reports indicate.

The contests which arose in the military elections that took place in the early part of Sevier's first administration have been described in a previous chapter. Before the election Robert Prince, as we have seen, wrote to Sevier on September 20, 1796, in regard to a plan by which the Governor might aid in manipulating the election of brigadier general in Mero District by forwarding blank commissions to someone in the Cumberland region. This letter indicated that many in the western counties had opposed Sevier in his election.[2] Who their candidate for governor had been, if they had supported another, cannot be determined. What form the opposition assumed

---
[1] *Journal of the Senate of Tennessee*, Mar. 29, 1796.
[2] *SP*.

remains unsolved. Jackson opposed the use of the commissions in the election according to Prince's plan,³ and it may be taken for granted that he had some connection with Sevier's opponents and perhaps opposed the Governor's election. For this reason it seems entirely possible that Sevier's enmity toward Jackson originated in the first gubernatorial campaign in Tennessee.

This assumption would make more plausible the accounts of Jackson's biographers which mention that certain meetings between the two men during this period had not been harmonious to say the least. One account related that a meeting occurred in Jonesboro in 1795.⁴ This would place it before the election, but the biographer cited no evidence to support the circumstances. He assigned as a reason Sevier's interest in a lawsuit in which Jackson acted as the opposing attorney. The differences in the court-room resulted in recriminations afterwards, which were carried to each of them by eager newsmongers. Another biographer mentioned a meeting in the same town in 1796.⁵ This author said that, since Sevier had been elected, Jackson wished the Governor to resign the office of major general and to appoint him to the position. The Governor refused to do this, and bitterness took the place of friendship between them.

There are some difficulties in the way of accepting either of these accounts. Each had its origin in reminiscence evidently repeated long after the events took place. The scene of each was located in Jonesboro, the place where the final break occurred, and this suggests that the authors had their facts somewhat confused with later

---

³ Jackson to Sevier, May 8, 1797, Bassett, *Correspondence of Andrew Jackson*, I, 32.

⁴ Buell, *op. cit.*, pp. 134-35.

⁵ Avery's account in James Parton, *Life of Andrew Jackson*, I, 163-64.

events. In the second account, the biographer stated that Jackson sent a challenge to Sevier in 1796, which shows definitely that he had in mind the facts which developed in 1803. No break occurred in the story of the feud. The events of both years were included with no distinction in dates. Sevier held no office as major general and could not have appointed Jackson to that office had he so desired.[6] Each of these accounts may be partially discarded because of this confusion.

If the trouble originated in the election for governor in 1796, an encounter may have taken place in Jonesboro after that event and before the military elections in the same year. Such a meeting would partly account for the bitterness which both men exhibited, for the dispute which developed over the military elections contained more venom than the facts would warrant.

On the second Thursday in October, 1796, the election for brigadier general for Mero District was held in Nashville. The commissions sent by Sevier to James Robertson furnished the basis for the first definite break in the relations of the two men for which we have unquestioned and direct sources. Jackson took part in the debate concerning the use of the commissions for the cavalry officers. Joel Lewis arose and, speaking against Jackson and the party opposed to the Governor, read a letter from Sevier in support of his position. According to his own version,[7] Jackson attacked the constitutionality of the Governor's action in sending the blank commissions to Robertson for the cavalry officers. The part which Jackson took in the discussion was repeated to Sevier. In subsequent letters to

---

[6] See Scott's *Laws*.

[7] Jackson to Sevier, May 8, 1797. Bassett, *Correspondence*, I, 32. The controversy arose, not at the election of major general as stated by A. V. Goodpasture, "The Genesis of the Jackson-Sevier Feud," *AHM*, V, 115-23, but at the election of brigadier general a month earlier.

Robertson and Lewis, Sevier referred to Jackson in bitter and insulting terms, naming him a "poor, pitiful, pettyfogging, scurrilous lawyer."[8] The election of Winchester in spite of his opposition increased the Governor's resentment. Sevier's comments did not reach Jackson's ears until he returned from Philadelphia, where he served as a representative in Congress.

Jackson had desired military office for some years previous to this time, but circumstances always prevented a realization of his ambition. Now he became a candidate for major general in the election which was to be held on the second Thursday in November, 1796.[9] It is not known whether he had announced his candidacy before the election of brigadier or whether he used Sevier's interference as an excuse to oppose a man picked by Sevier and his partisans. The field officers of the three military districts cast their votes for major general in Jonesboro, Knoxville, and Nashville. Jackson and George Conway were the candidates. Conway had the support of the Governor. From Sevier's viewpoint, Jackson had done nothing which showed peculiar qualifications for the position. The Governor was not prohibited from favoring one candidate in preference to another, especially since one of them possessed no more military experience than Jackson had at that time. Conway was elected, and the chief executive of the state had won the first tilt. There can be no doubt that Sevier used his influence and power in both of these elections, and the legality of his methods in the proposed attempt to use the blank commissions[10] is open to serious question.

When Sevier visited Nashville in the spring of 1797,[11]

---

[8] *Ibid.*   [9] See Scott's *Laws.*

[10] This is discussed in Chapter VII, *passim.*

[11] Sevier's *Diary,* in Heiskell, *op. cit.,* pp. 544-45, entries for May 7 and 23, 1797.

Jackson quarreled openly with him over the matter. Some correspondence took place between them in which Jackson seemed to be on the point of challenging the Governor to a duel, but the provocation did not assume such proportions as to make him unwilling to be placated. At about the same time, Jackson engaged in a duel of words with Judge McNairy, a friend of Sevier, and in a letter to the Judge he appeared to connect McNairy's opposition with that of Sevier.[12] It was probably true. Sevier said that he looked upon Jackson at the time of the election as "my enemy."[13] Why? Something must have preceded this to arouse the Governor's ire. The explanation should rest in the first election for governor or in the results of the personal encounters mentioned, possibly in all combined.

Sevier explained in the letter of May 7, 1797, last referred to above, that "I . . . thus was not choice in my language . . . a few days after you had set out for Congress, a letter from Genl. Robertson placed the matter in a different point of view and my resentment was greatly softened; on the return of Judge Claiborne my mind was considerably relieved; from that character I received a statement of the business which I fully confided in, and which led me to conclude that altho your attack upon my public character was unmerited, I was not authorized to view you as a private enemy." Jackson graciously accepted Sevier's explanations on May 8,[14] saying that "facts may be misstated," and that "at the time . . . of the election I was neither your political nor private enemy, nor am I yet inclined to be so"; he ended by requesting a conference "upon this or any other subject." Sevier answered this in a very conciliatory tone and agreed to meet him at any time and place which Jackson should

---

[12] Jackson to McNairy, May 9, 1797, Bassett, *Correspondence*, I, 34.
[13] Sevier to Jackson, May 8, 1797, *ibid.*, p. 31.
[14] Jackson to Sevier, May 10, 1797, *ibid.*, p. 35.

name.[15] But the meeting did not take place. "Professional business" prevented Jackson from waiting longer than "half after nine" on the morning appointed.[16] Sevier wrote to him on the same day and insinuatingly said that he "did not know that your professional business would interfere, having heard you had declined practice. I will do myself the honor of waiting on you this evening if agreeable to you." Whether or not they met is uncertain. Sevier made an entry in his *Diary* for this date: "Nothing extraordinary."[17]

Sevier had defended himself in a dignified manner—without a retraction, however—which soothed the feelings of Jackson, and the incident passed over without any serious consequences. To all appearances the relations of the two men remained cordial throughout the years 1798 and 1799.[18] But Jackson followed the progress of the land investigation which he had caused by informing Senator Martin of North Carolina of the irregularities in Martin Armstrong's land office in Nashville.[19]

Sevier was reëlected to the office of governor twice and served out his last term, completing the constitutional limit of three successive terms in 1801. Archibald Roane was elected to succeed him. Jackson was elected to the United States Senate in 1797, but did not retain this office very long. He resigned and, soon after his return to Nashville, accepted an office as judge of the superior court of the state.

Major General Conway died in 1801, and an election was set for February 5, 1802, for the purpose of choosing his successor.[20] Jackson, still fired by his insatiable am-

---

[15] Sevier to Jackson, May 11, 1797, *ibid.*, p. 36.
[16] Jackson to Sevier, May 13, 1797, *AHM*, V, 121.
[17] Sevier's *Diary*, in Heiskell, *op. cit.*, p. 544.
[18] See their correspondence in Bassett, *Correspondence*, I, *passim*.
[19] See p. 147. [20] Garrett and Goodpasture, *op. cit.*, p. 141.

bition, became a candidate, and Sevier, retired governor and Indian fighter of renown, opposed him. The result was a tie between the two, each receiving seventeen votes. Three of the officers cast their votes for General Winchester, who probably entered the contest because of Sevier's opposition to him in 1796 and in order to draw support from Sevier. Certification of the results of this election was made to Governor Roane on February 16, 1802, and it became his duty to cast the deciding vote. Jackson deposited with Roane on this same day the papers relating to the land frauds which implicated Sevier.[21] The Governor cast his vote for Jackson, and this action definitely marked the date of the open alliance between the political forces of Jackson and Roane. The "poor, pitiful" lawyer had routed the veteran. Naturally Sevier resented the fact that this desirable office should have gone to his inexperienced rival from Nashville.

A letter from Jackson to Sevier presented an incident growing out of this election for major general which has often been overlooked.[22] It bore the date of March 27, 1802, and read in part, as follows: "Had I stepped forward of my own accord and offered as a candidate for Major General of the State unsolicited . . . I should have held myself at full liberty to meet you on the ground proposed and *readily agreed to the withdrawing of our names and submit to another election*[23] . . . the respect I owe to my friends and the Publick will, is a sufficient reason to acquiesce under the constituted will, and that must decide." Further on in the same letter he referred to a meeting with Sevier in Jonesboro previous to this letter but subsequent to the election. The above quotation evidently referred to a proposal by Sevier to hold another election because neither had received a majority of the

---
[21] See p. 148.   [22] Bassett, *Correspondence*, I, 61.
[23] Italics are mine.

votes cast. No reason for it was stated, but Sevier may have felt that he could secure at least two of the three votes which went to Winchester. If this were the case, Jackson appeared to be equally sure of the same thing but excused himself because of the support of his friends.

Sevier, disappointed, took the field in 1803 in the campaign for governor at the end of Roane's first administration. Jackson immediately espoused the cause of Roane,[24] who became a candidate to succeed himself. The land frauds, which were discussed in the last chapter, formed the main issue of this heated and bitter political fight. It soon developed into a test of strength between Jackson and Sevier. Sevier was elected, and Jackson received the first of a series of defeats in which the personal issue held an especial significance.

The climax of the feud occurred in Knoxville and vicinity during the first half of October, 1803, following the election of Sevier. The events from the first differences between the two men to that time had accumulated a suppressed bitterness and an animosity which made any meeting between them an occasion for a possible explosion. This explosion came shortly after Sevier took office as governor.

Jackson was holding court in Knoxville on the first day of October during the time when the investigation into the question of the land frauds occupied the attention of the whole state. Sevier met Martin, a member of the investigating committee, on the street, and an altercation ensued.[25] Various accounts were related as to what actually occurred. The account given by Wharton, Hall, and Wynne, friends of Jackson,[26] definitely connected the affair with the investigation. Sevier, bitter over the charges made by his opponents in the governor's election, berated Martin, an old enemy, for his part in the affair. Jackson

---

[24] See p. 148.   [25] See p. 158.   [26] See p. 158.

came up and intervened, when Sevier shouted that all his enemies were "damned cowards and dare not meet him." Jackson demanded an explanation. James Sevier, a son of the Governor, raised a "large stone" in his hand and ordered the Judge to stand off. Jackson's friends reported further: "Some conversation taking place between them, Governor Sevier changed his abusive language from Colonel Martin to the judge. The judge told him if he had any malice against him, a modest hint to meet him behind a grove would be sufficient, and their dispute could be easily settled, that his conduct was verging too nigh that of a blackguard, and derogatory to the character of a gentleman. The Governor continued his abuse and dared the judge to an open combat in the street; the governor was armed with a cutlass, and the judge with a sword cane and just recovering from a severe illness . . . he [the Governor] called all his enemies cowards, and repeatedly dared judge Jackson publicly to invite him to the field of honor. Col. Martin took the judge by the arm and they walked towards their lodging, the governor followed, making use of very insulting and abusive expressions."

Another narrative portrayed still more of personal animosity.[27] When Jackson mentioned to Sevier that he (Jackson) had performed some service for the state and that he did not deserve these reproaches, the following conversation took place between them:

"Services?" replied Sevier, "I know of no great service you have rendered the country except taking a trip to Natchez with another man's wife."

"Great God," cried Jackson, "do you mention *her* sacred name?"

---

[27] Parton, *op. cit.*, p. 164. The date of this is placed by Parton in 1795, but it is evidently a reference to the meeting in 1803. This inaccuracy need not impeach the correctness of the substance of the conversation, and this is borne out by the correspondence between the two men.

This immediately set fire to the tinder. Jackson charged that Sevier made "repeated darings for me to invite him to the field of honor,"[28] and that the Governor was "armed with a cutlass and I with a cain."[29] Jackson made much of the point that he was armed only with a "cain." His friends said it was a sword cane, which weapon would have made a combat on the street much more equal than if Sevier had attacked an unarmed man with a cutlass. This sword cane was a handy weapon used by Jackson in other affairs besides this one.

These accounts may be accepted as given. It is not to be thought that Jackson's friends would give information against him which would mislead the public. The source of the brawl on the street had its immediate cause in the charges of land fraud which had been aired thoroughly during the campaign. In these charges Jackson had used his opportunity to cast a strong suspicion of dishonesty upon Sevier, and in doing it he had conveniently neglected to give available information which would have taken the force from the accusations. Still the Governor's enemies were not satisfied. They goaded him with investigation and threatened him with impeachment and prosecution.[30] It is small wonder that he lost his temper or that Jackson, embittered by defeat, should have provoked an attack.

As a result of this meeting on the street of Knoxville, Jackson the next day challenged Sevier to a duel.[31] "The ungentlemanly expression and gasgonading conduct of yourself, relative to me yesterday, was in true character of yourself, and unmasked you to the world, and plainly shows that they were the ebulitions of a base mind, goaded

---

[28] Jackson's *Publication* of Sevier as a coward, in *Tennessee Gazette*, Oct. 26, 1803.

[29] Jackson to Sevier, Oct. 3, 1803, Bassett, *Correspondence*, I, 71.

[30] See Chapter VIII, *passim*.

[31] Jackson to Sevier, Oct. 2, 1803, Bassett, *Correspondence*, I, 71.

with stubborn proofs of fraud, and flowing from a source devoid of every refined sentiment or delicate sensation. But Sir the voice of the people has made you a Governor, this alone makes you worthy of my notice, or the notice of any Gentleman. For the office I have respect, and as such I only deign to notice you."

Sevier answered it on the same day.[32] He revealed a vein of mockery in this reply: "Your ungentlemanly and Gasconading conduct of yesterday, and indeed at all other times, heretofore, have unmasked yourself to me and to the world. The voice of the Assembly has made you a Judge, and this alone has made you worthy of my notice or any other gentleman; to the office I have respect, and this alone makes you worthy of my notice." Sevier further stated that he would wait on him at any time and place not within the State of Tennessee. He suggested that Georgia, Virginia, and North Carolina were near, and that it would be easy for them to repair outside the state.

Jackson replied on the following day in a letter which was somewhat clouded as to its meaning.[33] In the first place, he said that he regarded Sevier's scruples about meeting in the state as mere subterfuge, and that as Sevier gave the offense in Knoxville, the Governor should atone for it in the neighborhood of that town. He later added that "If it will obviate your squeemish fears, I will set out immediately to the nearest part of the Indian boundary line." Then he reverted to his first assertion by saying: "I am therefore compelled to be explicit; you must meet me between this and four o'clock this afternoon, or I will publish you as a coward and poltroon." Sevier acknowledged this, asserting that he would leave the set-

---

[32] Sevier to Jackson, Oct. 2, 1803, W. W. Clayton, *History of Davidson County, Tennessee*, p. 145.
[33] Jackson to Sevier, Oct. 3, 1803, Bassett, *Correspondence*, I, 71.

tlement of time and place to his second.[34]

Nothing of importance to the development of the duel took place until six days later. On the ninth of October another long and severe letter from Jackson showed that his purpose of forcing Sevier into a fight had not diminished.[35] In a memorandum attached to this letter, Jackson referred to one which had been written by Sevier in which the latter had said that business with the legislative committee would prevent the meeting until that was completed. This was the committee investigating the land frauds.

A petition was addressed to Jackson on October 5 which may have had some influence upon the progress of the feud. Jackson's friends in the legislature drew up a statement in which they requested him not to resign from his office as judge "when Party is raging in a most extraordinary manner."[36] John and Samuel Tipton, old enemies of Sevier, were among this group. Two days later Jackson received another petition on the same subject, signed by seventy-six persons. Jackson informed them on October 7 that, although he had planned to resign,[37] he would hold office two years longer.[38] These petitions were important to Jackson because they definitely showed him that he might expect support from these signers in the event of serious consequences arising from the duel.

A letter from Jackson which has not been preserved reviewed the proceedings in their relations up to the ninth of October. He threatened to advertise Sevier as a coward and poltroon in the *Knoxville Gazette* the next day, space for which he said he had already reserved.

---

[34] Sevier to Jackson, Oct. 3, 1803, Clayton, *op. cit.*, p. 143.

[35] Jackson to Sevier, Oct. 9, 1803, Bassett, *Correspondence*, I, 73.

[36] See *Petition*, Bassett, *Correspondence*, I, 72.

[37] Martin Armstrong to Jackson, Aug. 29, 1803, Bassett, *Correspondence*, I, 69.

[38] Jackson to Rutledge and Tipton, Oct. 7, 1803, Clayton, *op. cit.*, p. 147.

A letter without date may be taken as a reply to this communication.[39] Sevier hinted at collusion between Jackson and "several other poltroons" against him. Another letter, possibly on the next day, carried the charge of Sevier that Jackson had not named a place outside the limits of the state where they might meet.[40] Jackson replied on October 10: "I hasten to reply, that you have been well informed what part of the Indian boundary line, I would go to relieve you from your fears, South West Point was named . . . you may yet retrieve your character by seeing me in this neighborhood or at South West Point. If in this neighborhood, this evening or early tomorrow morning. If at South West Point tomorrow evening, or on Wednesday next any time before twelve o'clock. . . . The advertisement (is) in the press. I leave Knoxville tomorrow after breakfast. will obey a call from you between this and that time in the vicinity of this place."[41]

Sevier replied the same evening.[42] "I am again perplexed with your scurrilous and poltroon language. You now pretend you want an interview in this neighborhood. . . . I have constantly informed you I would cheerfully wait on you in any other quarter, and that you had nothing to do but name the place and you should be accommodated. I am now constrained to tell you that your conduct during the whole of your pretended bravery, shows you to be a pitiful poltroon and coward, for your propositions are such as you and every other person of common understanding do well know is out of my power to accede to, especially you a Judge!!! Therefore the whole tenor of your pretended readiness is intended for making nothing more than a cowardly evasion."

---
[39] *Ibid.*, p. 144.   [40] *Ibid.*
[41] Jackson to Sevier, Oct. 10, 1803, Bassett, *Correspondence*, I, 75.
[42] Sevier to Jackson, Oct. 10, 1803, Clayton, *op. cit.*, p. 144.

A friend told Jackson that Sevier had intimated that he would meet the Judge on the Virginia line on a farm belonging to a Mr. Robertson. Jackson accepted the place as satisfactory,[43] claimed the right of the injured party to name the hour, and set the time between Monday evening and Thursday evening. A. White carried the letter to Sevier, who absolutely refused to open it.

This ended the correspondence between the two. Jackson published his advertisement of Sevier in the *Gazette* on October 11, and the Nashville paper re-published it fifteen days later. These publications made the whole affair public to the people of the state. Whatever arrangements were agreed upon after this, if such arrangements were made, must have been through mutual friends; it is probable that this ended any communication between them.

The final scene of the affair took place on the road to Kingston. In Sevier's *Diary* he made these entries for October 15, 16, and 17, 1803:

"Sat 15 set out for So. west Point in company with And. Greer esqr. & my son Washington. Lodged at John Woods.

Sun 16 Sit out early and arrived at Kingston & arrived to breakfast after having a violent dispute with J (udge) Jackson —lodged at Jessie Birds. Had this day a salute of sixteen rounds by the garrison. Dined with Col. Meigs in the garrison.

Mon 17 Went with the agent of the Indian affairs, Majr. Macrea & others to the Council House on the south side of the Tennessee River to hold a conference with the Cherokee chiefs concerning a road and other matters. Our talks were delivered and the Indians required time to give their answer. Adj. till next day (Dined with Majr. Macrea."[44]

These entries gave the reason for Sevier's trip to Southwest Point. He went not to meet Jackson but to confer

---

[43] Jackson to Sevier, Oct. 11, 1803, *ibid.*, p. 145.
[44] Sevier's *Diary*, in Heiskell, *op. cit.*, p. 587.

with the Indians. Jackson had lingered in Knoxville presumably trying to force Sevier into a duel. The Governor evidently ignored the belligerent Judge of the Superior Court. The latter may have got wind of the proposed trip to Southwest Point and thought to forestall Sevier, and so he hastened to that place in order to be on the ground when the Governor arrived. Had Sevier gone there on any business and found Jackson absent, he could easily have claimed, on the basis of their correspondence, that Jackson dodged a meeting.

Partisans of both men published statements which purported to describe what actually took place on the road when they met on that Sunday morning, October 16. Andrew Greer made out an affidavit on October 23 which described the meeting in the manner in which Sevier preferred to have it appear. Dr. Van Dyke, the companion of Jackson, made a statement defending the action of the Judge. Several anonymous publications appeared in the newspapers of Knoxville and Nashville in November and December. These reports were rather confusing, and it is difficult to determine what really happened. Greer said[45] that he and John Hunter rode in front of the Governor and his son Washington. They met Judge Jackson and Dr. Van Dyke armed with pistols riding up the road. Jackson stopped and talked with Greer, but the doctor rode on. While they talked, Jackson suddenly threw his umbrella on the ground, drew one of his pistols, dismounted, drew the other pistol and advanced up the road. Greer looked around and saw the Governor off his horse with his pistols in his hands advancing towards Jackson. This procession continued until they stood about twenty steps apart. The two principals hurled abusive language at each other. The Governor "damned Jackson to fire away," but after a little parley they re-

---

[45] Andrew Greer's *Affidavit, AHM*, V, 208-9.

turned their pistols to the holsters. Then Jackson swore that he would cane Sevier. Sevier's horse became frightened and ran away carrying his pistols. Thereupon Jackson immediately drew his pistol and advanced toward Sevier. The latter dodged behind a tree and abused Jackson for attacking an unarmed man. Sevier's son drew his pistol and covered Jackson, and Dr. Van Dyke threatened young Sevier in the same manner.

Dr. Van Dyke reported[46] that Jackson stopped to talk with Greer and Hunter, and that he proceeded to meet Sevier and to deliver a note from the Judge. Sevier refused to accept the note, drew his pistols and dismounted. Jackson did the same and walked up the road toward the Governor. Sevier took refuge behind a tree, and Jackson remarked that, as both were armed, the former should come out from behind his protection and fire. The Governor said that he did not wish to be assassinated, as he had been informed that Jackson and Van Dyke had traveled up the road with that intention. The doctor informed Sevier that the story was false. He requested the men to deliver their pistols and to meet in a proper manner on the field of honor. Jackson readily agreed, but Sevier positively refused. Then they put up their pistols and mounted, after which "some scurrility ensued." Jackson said that he would "correct" Sevier, drew his sword cane and pistol, and rode up to his enemy. The Governor dismounted and let his horse loose. Jackson pursued him around the party several times. In other points his story agreed substantially with that of Greer. Van Dyke concluded that: "After some time, however, I prevailed on General Jackson to desist, finding that General Sevier would not defend himself."

Meetings upon the field of honor have sometimes ended grotesquely as well as tragically. The ending of this affair

---

[46] *Tennessee Gazette*, Dec. 21, 1803.

tended toward the grotesque. At least it had its humorous aspects. The spectacle of the governor of a state and a judge of the superior court hurling abusive epithets at each other, waving swords and shouting when neither could be accused of cowardice in public service and yet seeming to fear the results of a meeting certainly presented a scene which neither could boast of nor defend.

A publication appeared in the *Tennessee Gazette* of November 25, 1803, over the signature of a "Citizen of Knox County" which defended Sevier.[47] The Governor's advocate, after reviewing with reasonable accuracy the correspondence of the two men, asked: "The Judge has published the Governor a coward, and for what reason? Why, because he says so himself and that the Governor would not turn out Don Quixote like, to fight a duel at the seat of government, and in the face of the General Assembly, and for doing of which was sure to have been fined, imprisoned sixty days without bail or mainprize and deprived of his citizenship for twelve months, which would have been gratification to the judge and his party, immeasureably indeed. Now, let us ask, how many hundreds of respectable characters are in this and several other states, who have been eye witnesses of the Governor's courage; where he displayed as much as was necessary to be found in the most experienced veteran? Who is it that have fought the battles of this country, and drove from its borders its numerous and desperate enemies? Who are the people beholden to for the settlement of the same? Is he not the man, whose exertions have taken from the numerous hords the savage wilds and placed thereon a rising, growing and respectable republic . . .? Strange indeed that after so many battles and engagements the governor has encountered that such a thing as cowardice should be imputed to him!!!" He described the meeting

---
[47] *Tennessee Gazette.*

near Kingston: "... he (Jackson) met the Governor on the great road, armed with great rifle pistols in his hands, swearing by his maker that he had come on purpose to kill him, and that he would do it, why did not the judge fire...? I answered that at a time when the governor's horse had run off with his pistols in the holsters and was left without arms to return the fire, and of course the heroic judge had nothing to fear!" He evidently intended to leave the intimation that the Governor's friends prevented the assassination. The whole article attempted to make it appear that Jackson had tried to waylay Sevier and to force him to fight a duel; failing in that, he might kill the Governor and claim self-defense. Van Dyke's statement partly upheld this intimation, for Jackson made an effort to force Sevier into a duel, and, when he failed in this, pursued the Governor, who was unarmed except with his sword.

An unnamed author answered this publication in the same paper on December 21. He charged that the "Citizen of Knox County" was Sevier himself, and the publication, a tissue of lies. The author challenged this "Citizen" to make himself known. He tried to portray Sevier's actions in a ridiculous light: "... depend upon it ... if you had saw the ease with which his excellency dismounted and the good use he made of his heels after he had dismounted to prevent a caning, you would have thought him a youth of not more than 18, although his flight was somewhat impeded in tramping off the scabbard of his sword from his belt."

The attitude of Sevier towards Jackson presented some similarity to that urged upon Jackson himself by Judge Overton several years afterward: "No man, not even your worst enemies, doubt your personal courage, and you would gain much more by not noticing anything that these people may say, than otherwise. Be assured that their slander can do you no harm among your friends."[48] Sevier, by ignoring Jackson, saved his reputation, and it has been asserted with some truth that Jackson lost popularity by the whole affair.[49] Jackson had missed his opportunity to attain prominence in state affairs, and another did not present itself until the War of 1812. The personal encounters marked the collapse of the Jackson political organization. The campaign for governor had been lost; the investigation into the land frauds indicated that it would be unsuccessful in ousting Sevier from office; the Governor had publicly insulted Jackson and escaped unscathed; Sevier could not be forced into a duel; if assassination had been contemplated, even that had been frustrated. Jackson would have fought Sevier anywhere within or without the state, but Sevier had everything to lose and nothing to gain by such an encounter. He knew that Jackson had lost; so he cleverly sidestepped his opponent and left Jackson with an injured reputation. In reality it appeared that Jackson received a severe personal as well as political defeat from the old veteran of the frontier.

From this time forward nothing indicated that the relations of the two men ever became cordial. In November of the same year Jackson engaged in a tilt with William Maclin, secretary of state, over the insertion of the article by the "Citizen of Knox County" in the *Knoxville Gazette*.[50] Jackson pretended to believe that Maclin was the author of it. The affair degenerated into a duel of bricks and Jackson's ever-ready sword cane, an encounter lacking in dignity on the part of either a judge or a secretary.

In November Sevier wrote a letter to General Robertson which clearly portrayed his feeling for Jackson:

---

[48] Overton to Jackson, Sept. 12, 1806, Clayton, *op. cit.*, pp. 149-50.
[49] Bassett, *Life*, I, 60.
[50] Account of H. Tatum, Clayton, *op. cit.*, pp. 146-47.

Knoxville 8th. November 1803

DEAR GENERAL,

I make no doubt but you have heard many ill-natured things said respecting me and my conduct, of my being a rogue, a coward, and a thousand other things, but however as either the one or the other, it is for members to say. If I have been a rogue, I suppose there must come forward those that I have wronged and make it known wherein I have injured them. As to cowardice, there are thousands who have witnessed my conduct as a soldier, and it is for them to say on that point. I have to observe to you that in the whole course and experience of my life, I have never been as much insulted, and the many little practices made use of to injure and deceive, as have been made use of by Jackson to injure me, and the whole tenor of his conduct has been transacted in a manner that would greatly injure anyone, and for what is unknown to me. If he has any objections against me respecting land, he might have had as much and perhaps a great deal more against some nearer home, whose conduct would probably have had reason to have tarnished his own house, and injured and disturbed his quiet, much more than mine would have done—when I take his whole conduct into view, and call to mind the ties that are in society to bind men together, so far as right, and also common and reciprocal politeness that ought to be observed amongst mankind, I am sorry that I am bound to view him, Judge Jackson, as one of the most abandoned rascals in principle my eyes ever beheld. So far is saying you may think too much, but I am sorry that I have so much cause from the person I am writing about. I shall leave the whole subject, but will observe to you that Jackson will have full opportunity to try his bravery. There is to be a force raised immediately to march to Natchez, of five hundred men, etc. . . .[51]

The whole affair weighed heavily upon the mind of the Governor. He could not forget what he considered an

---

[51] *AHM* IV, 373-74. The reference to "some nearer home" meant Stockley Donelson, a kinsman of Jackson's wife. Donelson had a part

unprovoked attack upon his reputation and popularity. An account in his *Diary* suggested that Jackson disturbed his thoughts and haunted his dreams:

"Tues. 10. . . .

Curious dream. I dreamed my Father came descending in the air in what appeared at first like a cloud. As it came nearer it assumed the appearance of one of the finest Rigged vessels I had ever seen that the sail roaps and everything of the apparatus appeared Richer & of superior quality to anything I have ever seen. He came out of the vessel when it halted or alighted and told me that on the Friday before New Years day he had to sit out to the Great high Court, I asked him if there was any news where he had been he answered that nothing existed there but the utmost peace and friendship, that he had heard much conversation respecting the Quarrel between Judge Jackson & myself, I then asked him if it was possible that affair had reached so far? He then replied that long before he had arrived the news was there and also every other transaction that had taken place in Tennessee—I then asked him what was said? He told me that Jackson was viewed by all as a very wicked base man, and a very improper person for a judge, and said I have it in charge to intimate to you either by dream or some other mode, that you have nothing to fear provided you act a prudent part for they are all your friends—on his saying by a dream I began to think I was dreaming & immediately awaked."[52]

---

in the frauds connected with the military land office, which have been discussed in Chapter VII, *passim*.

[52] Sevier's *Diary*, in Heiskell, *op. cit.*, p. 588.

CHAPTER X

GOVERNOR AND "WAR HAWK"

SEVIER'S second series of administrations as governor began amid the bitterness of the struggle with Jackson. Investigations into the alleged frauds of Sevier and the culmination of the feud occupied the first few weeks. The occasion for Sevier's journey[1] to Southwest Point when he met Jackson was furnished by the negotiations then being conducted by the United States government with the Cherokees for the purpose of opening a road from Tennessee to Georgia. It had been reported that a meeting with the chiefs would take place on October 15, and Sevier wrote to Colonel Meigs, the Indian agent, that he would "very willingly attend a day or two on the occasion."[2] Meigs informed Sevier that his presence at such a gathering would add much to the hope for success. Meigs believed that with Sevier, the governor of Tennessee, present he would encounter no difficulty in obtaining the concessions desired.[3]

Sevier's policies in the following six years did not differ from those in his first series of administrations. Several incidents arose which distracted his attention from the major policies concerning land and Indian affairs, but as a rule he followed the same ideas that had guided his first three executive terms.

During the summer of 1803 Sevier received a com-

---
[1] See p. 182.   [2] Sevier to Meigs, Oct. 7, 1803, *SP*.
[3] Meigs to Sevier, Oct. 10, 1803, *SP*.

munication from the secretary of war telling him that certain information led the government to believe that the Spanish officials at New Orleans might refuse to allow the United States to take possession of Louisiana according to the treaty of purchase. This report doubtless had been received from Daniel Clark, unofficial United States counsel in New Orleans, who reported in July that Laussat, the French prefect, had attempted to stir up trouble in the province.[4] The secretary requested Sevier to muster into service a regiment of five hundred mounted militia, to equip them, and to order them to hasten with all possible speed to Natchez, where they should place themselves under the command of General Wilkinson. Sevier requested William Maclin to go to Mero District and, with the aid of General Winchester, to recruit the greater part of the men from that region. The emergency demanded that he use all the means in his power to get the men into service in the least possible time.[5] The Governor issued the necessary orders to the various officers of the militia in that part of the state, directing them to aid the enterprise.

Sevier's conduct in this situation provides for us the earliest intimations of sectionalism in Tennessee. In all probability his action resulted from the violent quarrel in which he was engaged at the time with the Jackson forces. Sevier selected Colonel George Doherty, of Jefferson County in East Tennessee, to command the regiment.[6] The implications in the complaints suggested that Sevier exhibited a general preference for officers from the eastern part of the state to command this expedition. East Tennessee officers commanding West Tennessee militia

---

[4] Clark to Madison, July 21, 1803, *American Historical Review*, XXXIII, 345-46.

[5] Sevier to Maclin, Nov. 6, 1803, *Military Order Book*, p. 13, *SP*.

[6] Sevier to Doherty, Nov. 23, 1803, *ibid.*, p. 29.

caused a reaction in Mero District against the proposed expedition and threatened to defeat the plan for sending the troops under any circumstances. Criticism became so acrid that Sevier published a circular sometime in November, 1803, defending his action. In his defense against the criticisms directed toward his appointments, he declared, "It is well known to the executive that no act he can do will give a certain party satisfaction, and the better he may do, the greater will be their disquietude."[7] It was obvious that he referred to the Jackson party, which was strongest in the western part of the state. It was equally obvious that he did not consult with Jackson, the major general, in regard to the appointments.

The Federal government requisitioned Tennessee for fifteen hundred additional troops to be mustered into service and held in readiness to proceed to Louisiana in the event that their presence became necessary. Sevier ordered them placed under the command of General White. There appeared to have been some general complaint at the action of the United States government regarding the demands upon Tennessee. Sevier's opponents capitalized these complaints and criticized him for the action of the national government. To these attacks he replied that those who cast adverse criticism upon him on account of the action of Congress or of the president were actuated by nothing except partisan spirit and insincerity.[8] The tone of these rejoinders indicated that Sevier was influenced by the bitterness of the struggles through which he had passed. He stated that he had determined to act for the interest of Tennessee and the people of the western country and that the acquisition of Louisiana was one of the "greatest ends in completing their political happiness."

---

[7] *Circular*, Nov. 1803, *SP*. No day is given.
[8] Sevier to McMinn, Dec. 20, 1803, *Military Order Book*, p. 34, *SP*.

These critics carried their attack to great length. Complaints reached the president concerning the appointment of officers. In Mero District desperate attempts were made to undermine the whole undertaking. Sevier rather exultantly claimed that they "neither did them any credit nor myself any damage."[9] They were very effective in Mero District, however, despite Sevier's assertion to the contrary. Sevier said that it was necessary to enroll at least four times as many men as were needed for the expedition. Men would enlist and then find some excuse for not going. These withdrawals resulted from "insinuations and false reports of designing and malicious persons, who were constantly fabricating everything in their power to defeat the march of the mounted infantry."[10] Maclin went to Mero and personally supervised the recruiting of the troops. It was due to his endeavors that the expedition finally made its way to Natchez. By the end of January they had returned to Mero District, and Sevier gave orders for disbanding both them and the reserve brigade, which did not leave the state.[11]

The whole matter appears to have provoked much bitterness on Sevier's part. In his report to the secretary of war regarding the expedition he complained of the great difficulties encountered and of the criticism directed against him. He left the impression that the movement was unpopular because of the opposition exhibited by his political enemies. His detractors "were in March, 1803, running mad to flock down and take possession of Orleans at all events[12] and complaining against Government for not suffering it to be done—I mention this to

[9] Sevier to Doherty, Jan. 22, 1804, *SP*.
[10] Sevier to Cocke, Anderson, Rhea and Campbell, Feb. 1, 1804, *SP*.
[11] Sevier to Maclin, Feb. 2, 1804; same to Doherty, Feb. 6, 1804; same to Generals White, Rutledge and Winchester, Feb. 2, 1804, *SP*.
[12] This clamor in the West was caused by the order of the Spanish Intendant of Louisiana on October 16, 1802, which took from the

show how uniformly those friends of order and regularity go together."[13]

As long as the whole of Tennessee remained a part of the frontier, no traces of violent sectionalism can be found. After East Tennessee became thoroughly organized and thickly populated, the people of that section showed a tendency to forget, in part, the poignant problems of the frontier which had moved westward. Yet this did not produce as much sectional controversy as had existed between East Tennessee and North Carolina in the earlier days. Indeed, it is difficult to find traces of anything approaching bitterness between the sections prior to the controversy between Sevier and Jackson. As a result of their quarrel, Sevier favored East Tennessee in the appointment of officers to lead the troops to Natchez. This action on the part of the Governor produced a reaction in West Tennessee against him. It gave evidence that sectional animosities resulted from personal bitterness between the two prominent leaders.

The question of the purchase of Louisiana called forth a hearty endorsement from Sevier. "Through the extraordinary Wisdom and political conduct of the Executive of our General Government, there is an immense and almost boundless acquisition of Territory obtained, the value of which is incalculable and on which acquirement the Western Country has now secured to them and their latest posterity every natural and commercial advantage that we could ever hope or wish for."[14]

Sevier's attitude upon another public issue represented that of the state which he governed. The indignation which swept the country when the details of the Chesapeake

---

Americans the right of deposit at New Orleans, *ASP, Foreign Relations*, II, 470.

[13] Sevier to Secretary of War Dearborn, Feb. 8, 1804, *SP*.

[14] Sevier to the Brigadiers-General of Tennessee, Feb. 2, 1804, *SP*.

affair became known found expression in his message to the legislature in which he described it in indignant language.¹⁵ It was expected that the militia of the state would be ordered into service. But the legislature apparently forgot that this demanded some action on its part. Near the time for the adjournment Sevier reminded that body that the state did not possess a pound of powder and ball nor a single musket with which to defend the country. He asked how Tennessee's troops were to be furnished and equipped in case they were called out by the president.¹⁶

Another of the problems which confronted Sevier in these administrations, as in the earlier ones, dealt with the land situation. The circumstances surrounding the distribution of the public lands in Tennessee prepared the way for friction and dissatisfaction with North Carolina on the part of the young state. It is impossible to enter into a discussion of the various acts and projects which the Assembly offered as a solution of this thorny question. The people of Tennessee felt that they ought to have the right to dispose of the lands yet remaining under the control of the state, as well as of those lands still under Indian control but which were expected soon to become the public property of the commonwealth. If Tennessee possessed the rights and privileges of statehood, it should exert the sovereignty necessary to manage its own affairs. The people of the West retained their suspicion of the mother state and believed that they were capable of regulating the disposal of the lands which lay within the jurisdiction of their government. Some method should be evolved by which warrants issued by North Carolina might be honored, but the machinery for perfecting those titles

---

[15] Sevier to the Assembly, Sept. 24, 1807, *Journal of the Senate of Tennessee.*

[16] *Journal of the Senate of Tennessee,* Dec. 2, 1807.

should be put into operation by the Assembly of Tennessee.

In 1803 the Tennessee legislature appointed John Overton as an agent for the purpose of settling the differences with North Carolina over this troublesome land question.[17] An agreement was reached and accepted by Congress.[18] Tennessee agreed to allow Congress to dispose of all the lands west of the Tennessee River and within an area east of that stream between Duck River and the southern boundary of the state. The United States ceded to Tennessee under certain conditions the lands east and north of this Congressional reservation. Tennessee agreed to satisfy all North Carolina land claims and to appropriate a certain amount of land for educational purposes.[19]

Even after this agreement, North Carolina attempted to hinder its execution. Sevier appointed Thomas Buckingham as commissioner to go to North Carolina and to receive the books and papers which Overton had transcribed. He reported to Sevier that the governor of North Carolina would not allow them to be taken from the State.[20] The reasons for this action on the part of Governor Alexander, as stated by Buckingham, consisted in a doubt of the propriety of the act of Congress. He also mentioned certain technicalities in regard to bond for the commissioner and lack of notification on the part of the secretary of state concerning the passage of the act by Congress. The governor of North Carolina may have

[17] Garrett and Goodpasture, *op. cit.*, p. 152.

[18] *Annals of Congress, 9 Cong. 1. Ses.*, pp. 1262-65.

[19] One hundred thousand acres in one tract in East Tennessee was set aside for the use of two colleges, one in East Tennessee and one in West Tennessee; 100,000 acres in one tract should be used for the benefit of academies, of which there should be one in each county; 640 acres, one section, should be appropriated in each county for the use of schools and colleges and should not be sold for less than two dollars an acre.

[20] *Journal of the Senate of Tennessee*, August 5, 1806.

attempted a small amount of retaliation for Sevier's action in dealing with the records of the land office in Nashville.[21] It is not known how this controversy ended except that the act of Congress went into effect and that the land records finally were delivered to the State of Tennessee.

In his relations with the Indians, Sevier followed the same general lines of procedure which marked his earlier policy. He constantly directed his efforts toward the acquisition of additional Indian lands by the state. He could not allow the progress of the state to be hindered by savage tribes who roamed over large areas and refused to adopt agricultural methods and habits of life. The danger of an Indian war diminished as new areas were added to the state and as immigration increased the number of inhabitants. These factors caused a gradual movement of the Cherokees from territory east of the Mississippi, and it appeared to be then only a question of time until the whole nation should have emigrated beyond that river. As this process continued, there appeared no good reason for allowing the relations between the whites and Indians to become strained and to lead to war. These features of his Indian policy were portrayed in several incidents which occurred during these administrations.

At the conference at Southwest Point, which has been mentioned, Sevier addressed a "talk" to the Indian chiefs in which he pointed out the many advantages both to the whites and to the Indians of a road from Tennessee to Georgia which would facilitate trade and intercourse between the tribes and these states.[22] The Indians requested some time for deliberation, and on October 19 they gave their consent to the project.[23]

[21] See p. 126.   [22] Sevier to Cherokee Chiefs, Oct. 17, 1803, *SP*.
[23] Sevier's *Diary, in* Heiskell, *op. cit.*, p. 588.

This period marked the acquisition of the greater part of the Cherokee lands in Tennessee. By the treaty of Tellico in 1805,[24] the United States purchased the lands between East Tennessee and the Cumberland region. In 1806 Dearborn's Treaty at Washington added another large cession in the southern part of the state.[25] The activities of Sevier in these acquisitions cannot be determined. The administration in Washington, however, favored the aspirations of the westerners, and Sevier, as much as any other person in the state, encouraged this attitude.

Sevier, in 1809, requested the Assembly to give him blanket authority to carry on proceedings at the expense of the state for the purpose of obtaining an additional cession of land. In 1807[26] the Assembly had appropriated $20,000 for the purpose of making treaties with the Indians, but evidently Sevier felt that the amount would not cover the expenses involved in secret negotiations. He reported that some of the citizens who were engaged in trade with the Cherokees desired that no treaty be made at that time, and, if his plans became known, these traders would defeat his efforts.[27] The records contain no indication that he received the desired appropriation.

Other attempts to negotiate treaties with the Indians in which Sevier aided resulted in failure. Colonel Meigs received an appointment from the secretary of war to act in conjunction with commissioners appointed by Tennessee. They were to negotiate for additional purchases of territory during Sevier's last administration.[28] Sevier appointed General Robertson as one of the com-

---

[24] Whitney, *The Land Laws of Tennessee*, pp. 23-25.

[25] *Ibid.*, pp. 25-27.

[26] Scott, *Laws*, pp. 1034-35. The law was passed Dec. 3, 1807.

[27] Sevier to the Assembly, Apr. 8, 1809, *Journal of the Senate of Tennessee*.

[28] Royce, *op. cit.*, pp. 201-2.

missioners, and evidently it was understood that Sevier would be appointed as the other commissioner by the governor who should be elected in 1809. He requested Colonel Meigs to call a conference to meet on August 20 of that year.[29] The commissioners made arrangements to provide for goods to carry out such preparations as were necessary for the success of the undertaking.[30] The time for the conference, however, had to be postponed until after Sevier's term of office expired. He had no objection to a postponement of the meeting except that it would interfere with his duties as state senator, to which office he had been elected.[31] His reasons for favoring a delay agreed entirely with his usual Indian policy; "I have been constantly of the opinion that the longer the Treaty could be put off the better, for the Indians are becoming more and more attached to the West side of the Mississippi and are constantly going off to that Country and of course less attached to their own."[32] A little delay would result in a reduced price for the cession. The conference was finally postponed until December 1, at which time he hoped that they should be "rid of a number of troublesome and jealous pated fellows who will be out hunting."[33] When the conference finally met, it failed to obtain its object because the Cherokees were not in a mood to sell any more land.[34]

An interesting sidelight regarding Sevier's attitude toward a public question of national interest is shown by a part of his message to the Assembly on April 3, 1809.[35] He called attention to a section of an act establishing a college in East Tennessee, which he said should be re-

[29] Sevier to Robertson, June 23, 1809, *SP*.
[30] Same to same, July 16, 1809, *SP*.   [31] See p. 200.
[32] Sevier to Robertson, Aug. 6, 1809, *SP*.
[33] Sevier to Meigs, Sept. 2, 1809, *SP*.
[34] Royce, *op. cit.*, pp. 201-2.
[35] *Journal of the Senate of Tennessee.*

pealed. The reason he gave indicated that he had experienced a change of heart in regard to banks. It will be recalled that he voted in favor of a National Bank while he served as a member of the First Congress. The act establishing the college provided that the commissioners might use funds which came into their hands to purchase stock or shares in some respectable bank. He suggested that it would be better if such money were placed in the state treasury and kept at the disposal of the trustees of the college. In this manner, currency would be held within the state, and the money of the college would not be entrusted to an unstable institution.

Sevier's last term as governor expired in 1809. It has been incorrectly stated that he became a candidate for the United States Senate in that year.[36] He received a petition from a body of citizens in Sevier County asking him to announce his candidacy for a seat in the House of Representatives. He refused it on the ground that his duties to the state would prevent him from making the campaign.[37] On May 6 the editor of the *Knoxville Gazette* stated that he was authorized to announce that Sevier would be a candidate for the state Senate representing Knox County. The election took place on August 4, 1809, and Sevier was chosen without opposition by a vote of 1,118.[38]

In his last message to the Assembly, he reported upon the foreign situation and observed that "time can only unfold what may be the result" of the conditions of that period.[39] A brief mention of the effect of the Embargo disclosed the fact that this measure was unpopular in the state. He said that "the want of a regular market has of

---

[36] Moore and Foster, *op. cit.*, p. 334.
[37] Wilson's *Knoxville Gazette*, Apr. 22, 1809.
[38] *Ibid.*, August 5, 1809.
[39] *Journal of the Senate of Tennessee*, Sept. 19, 1809.

course reduced the quantity of circulating specie, a circumstance generally complained of." He took leave of his duties as chief executive of the state in these words: "Permit me . . . to express a hope that a benign providence will ever guard, cherish and promote the well-being and happiness of my fellow citizens of the state of Tennessee."[40] Willie Blount became governor on September 20, and on the same day Sevier entered the state Senate. He took a prominent part in the deliberations of that body throughout the session. He immediately received appointments to the land committee and to a committee on militia law.

His interest in the development of the western country found another chance for expression in the activities of a joint committee which this legislature appointed to examine a map of the territory drained by the rivers that flowed into Mobile Bay.[41] This committee on October 19, 1809,[42] reported upon the navigability of the different streams. It advocated that the Assembly pass a resolution demanding that the United States attempt to extinguish the Indian title to those lands between the Tennessee River and the rivers flowing into Mobile Bay. This action would secure the free navigation of those streams. The Assembly adopted the report and resolution.

Shortly after Sevier entered the Senate, the Assembly addressed a message to him which summarized his service to the state in a very generous manner. It is pertinent as an indication of his popularity while he served in these important offices: "The long and uninterrupted continuance of that confidence and the undiminished affection of a grateful people, are proofs of your merit to which we are sensible our testimony can add but little weight. In whatever situation you may be placed here-

---
[40] *Ibid.*
[42] *Ibid.*
[41] *Ibid.*, Sept. 27, 1809.

after, we doubt not that you will continue still to merit the esteem and affection of the freemen of Tennessee. Accept, Sir, our warmest wishes for your future welfare and happiness."[43]

His service in the state Senate ended Sevier's connection with the Tennessee government. Henceforth he was to be identified with national politics by representing his district in the House of Representatives from the beginning of the Twelfth Congress in 1811 until his death in 1815. It is possible that Sevier chose to run for election to Congress because he saw that the political alignments were changing in such a way that it would be difficult for him to regain his position of executive power for a third series of terms. The increase in population continually added to the political importance of the people in the western part of Tennessee. Sevier had never enjoyed the popularity in that section which came to him from the eastern counties. He felt sure that he could retain the esteem of his friends and neighbors in East Tennessee and represent them in the national legislature as long as he desired that position. However, there is no evidence that Sevier wished to be returned to the office of governor after the election of Blount in 1809. Any statement of that desire on his part must be based upon supposition. Although he entered Congress and came into intimate touch with national problems, Sevier remained a provincial in his attitude and regarded the office of governor as the highest in the power of the people to bestow.

The Twelfth Congress met in a mood which boded ill for coöperative work. The election showed that a different spirt had developed from that which dominated the legislative department in previous sessions under the control of the Jeffersonian Republicans. A reaction

[43] *Ibid.*, Sept. 23, 1809.

against the principles of Jefferson and Madison manifested itself in this Congress.[44] The Federalist party united more closely upon definite principles than did the Republicans, even though they were greatly reduced in numbers by the election. The sectionalism of the period as expressed in the membership of Congress showed a division in two ways. The old feeling of antagonism between the East and the West was accentuated by the war spirit of the frontier. Bitterness and distrust also existed between the ideals of New England Federalism and those of the South. The danger to the administration lay in the possibility that the war program which the West strongly supported would be endangered by the sectional feeling between the North and the South.[45] Even the frontier felt something of the division between the commercial East and the agricultural South. Sevier entered Congress to reflect the ideals and aims of the West and to support the policies of the administration. There appears no indication that he felt especially bitter toward the Federalist party; yet he uniformly extended his support to the administration when its measures coincided with the demands of his section. He ardently favored the war party, and by his support of the administration and the program of the West he may be classed as one of the "War Hawks."

It would be impossible to enter into a detailed account of Sevier's attitude toward the measures which confronted him during these years when he represented his district in Congress. There is no record in the documents of that body that he ever said a word upon the floor of the House of Representatives. No speech is recorded, and no letters or documents are available which would indicate that he took part in a single debate. Practically nothing exists

---
[44] Henry Adams, *History of the United States*, V, 316-18.
[45] J. W. Pratt, *The Expansionists of 1812*, pp. 126-52.

which would give his attitude upon the public questions confronting the government except a record of his votes in the *Annals of Congress*. Only a few letters supplement the record. Therefore, a brief discussion of some of the more important measures will serve to place him definitely in his proper relation to national politics. These are given as examples and are not meant to be comprehensive.

He did not receive appointment to any important committee posts during his terms in Congress. However, the records are not complete, and it is quite possible that he received nomination to some committees whose membership is not given. Ramsey stated that he was placed upon the Committee of Military Affairs and rendered "essential and important services on subjects referred to his committee."[46] Shortly after he entered the House, he received an appointment to a committee to which was referred that part of the president's message relating to Indian affairs.[47] Several other committee appointments came to him during the course of his services, but he did not have a leading part in determining the policies of his party through work on committees.

One of the first important bills which came to a vote concerned the reapportionment based upon the third census. The discussions quickly assumed a sectional aspect. The House placed representation upon a basis of one member for every 37,000 of the population. This bill passed after an attempt had been made to set the figure at 40,000.[48] The Senate reduced this number to 35,000, and the amended bill came before the House, which refused to agree to the change. The Senate would not recede, and finally the House of Representatives consented to the demand of the upper body.[49] The sectional differences

---

[46] Ramsey, *op. cit.*, p. 712.
[47] *Annals of Congress*, 12 *Cong.* 1 *Ses.* I, 343.
[48] *Ibid.*, p. 343.
[49] *Ibid.*, p. 558.

that arose over this bill were based upon the fractional populations resulting in both North and South which would have no representation. The 37,000 figure would prevent any state from losing a member, while the 35,000 figure resulted in a gain to the North of nine and to the southern states of only two representatives. It meant that the North would have the advantage in the presidential election. Only two of the representatives from the South voted in favor of yielding to the Senate. Sevier voted consistently for the number first determined upon in the House.

Sevier's attitude in regard to war measures found expression in his vote upon two bills for the purpose of creating a fighting force. The administration asked that provision be made for an army of ten thousand men who should be enlisted for a term of three years. In order to embarrass the government, Giles, of Virginia, sponsored a bill providing for twenty-five thousand men, which he thought would drain the treasury and discredit the government. Clay, in the House, proposed an amendment which would provide for a gradual increase of the army up to the number set by the Senate and for its organization as rapidly as recruits came in. This would take away the financial drain upon the treasury and would provide the men necessary to bring the war to a swift conclusion. In the end, the House gave way to the Senate. Sevier held out for Clay's amendment.[50] The proposal to recruit fifty thousand volunteers raised the question of the president's authority to order this body of troops to go beyond the limits of the United States. The number of volunteers remained unchanged, and nothing was said in the bill regarding the constitutional question. Sevier favored the bill, but there is no indication of what

---

[50] *Ibid.*, p. 716.

views he held concerning the president's control over the troops enlisted under its provisions.[51]

When the bill providing war taxes came before the House, Sevier at first differed with the administration upon certain sections of the measure. The war party proposed to place a tax of twenty cents a bushel upon salt, a measure which would affect the western people, who possessed a majority of the salt-works of the country. Party lines split, and the proposal failed by a vote of 57 to 60. Sevier cast his vote against the tax.[52] The leaders of the war party then exerted all possible pressure to change the attitude of those who had voted against this tax. They argued that the whole system of taxation would fall to the ground if the West refused to assume its just proportion of the war expenses. Three days later the House reopened the discussion and accepted the tax at the rate proposed by the administration. Sevier changed his vote upon this question, a desertion of his western principles in order that the administration program might not be endangered.[53] Two days after this change of front, he gained revenge by voting to provide a tax upon carriages of pleasure and upon bank notes. These provisions affected the East and the North.[54] He neglected to have his vote recorded upon a proposal to tax the capacity of stills. It is probable that he did not wish to explain his desertion of the West upon more than one measure[55] or that he did not wish to offend the administration.

The declaration of war with Great Britain passed the House on June 4, 1812, by a vote of 79 to 45. Sevier voted for the declaration with the majority of the representatives from the South and the West.[56]

It is unnecessary to go further into detail concerning

---

[51] *Ibid.,* pp. 800-1.
[53] *Ibid.,* p. 1127.
[55] *Ibid.*
[52] *Ibid.,* p. 1115.
[54] *Ibid.,* p. 1150.
[56] *Ibid.,* p. 1637.

his votes upon the measures which came before the body in which he served. He supported the administration consistently in its conduct of the war, and to all appearances he proved to be a staunch party man. One might say that he consistently supported the interests of his section, and in this manner his support of the administration upon war measures was a foregone conclusion, for a sectional party controlled the policies of the government. Sevier owed allegiance to the Jeffersonian party, which stood for the things his constituency in Tennessee desired.

In a letter written to Governor Blount shortly after the declaration of war, Sevier expressed his attitude toward affairs in Congress. This communication appeared in the *Knoxville Gazette* on July 13, 1812, and bore the marks of careful composition. Since it is one of the few sources exhibiting his views, extracts from it will describe his position in a more comprehensive manner than the record of his votes in Congress. "I have for some time past been entirely silent as to the great and important measures that have for so long a time engaged the serious consideration of both Houses of Congress. I was well assured of the course the House of Representatives would take, but was doubtful as to the other branch of the Legislature, and was unwilling to hazard or conjecture anything on such an important subject. I knew the Senators were writing you and had no doubt put you in possession of what was on the carpet. We have at length passed the Rubicon. War is finally declared against Britain and her dependencies, and every act, necessarily depending on a state of warfare will be passed in the course of the ensuing week." He mentioned the disorders in England: ". . . many of the principal manufactures with their immense apparatus and machinery are burned and destroyed by the mobs in various quarters of the nation.

Percival, the Prime Minister and Chancellor of the exchequer, was very lately shot dead in the Parliament house, and on the arrestation of the assassin, a very daring attempt was made by the mob for the purpose of rescuing." In regard to Indian affairs he stated that he was "... doubtful much is to be apprehended from the Creeks, tho Mr. Hawkins writes the Chiefs are making great exertions to have the late perpetrators punished, but this your excellency know, is the *old story*. Fire and sword must be carried into that country before those wretches will be reduced to reason or become peaceable neighbors, there can be no reliance or trust placed in them. No doubt British emisaries are among them." He expressed his desire for expansion by hoping that "measures will be taken to secure the Floridas which will cut off the supplies of that nation [the Creeks] and also open other great and important advantages and benefits to the southern and western states."

Sevier's war spirit did not diminish in the two years following the outbreak of the war. Lack of unity within the nation caused him to write to Governor Shelby of Kentucky that he hoped both of them should live to see the day "when the insidious machinations of the old and inviterate enemy, together with our domestic foes (which are not few) with their perfidious schisms will a second time be confounded . . . when I frequently hear what I deem toryism, treason and insurrection preached up in the sacred walls of our National legislature, it is so grating to my ears and feelings, that I can scarcely contain myself within the bounds of moderation & reason . . . should the enemy be as successful in Europe as is reported, we may expect to have the second battle to fight over again for our Independence."[57]

---

[57] Sevier to Shelby, Draper MSS, 1VV109.

His colleagues in Congress must have regarded him with a great deal of respect, for he was honored by selection as pallbearer at the funerals of two vice presidents, Clinton and Gerry. While he did not share in the bitter Congressional debates, there is no doubt that he enjoyed a pleasing popularity in the social and political life of the capital. Quite frequently a member of Congress exerts a powerful influence by reason of his knowledge of the intimate details of government and politics. Sevier had prepared himself for such a rôle through years of training in state affairs. The silence of the records makes it impossible for us to arrive at any definite conclusion as to his importance and influence.

His *Diary* for the period which he spent in Congress presents some interesting sidelights upon his activities in Washington.[58] He was a frequent guest of President Madison and other officials of the government. Such sentences as the following are examples of his method of recording his social activities: "Sat 21, (1811) Dined with President Madison"; "Wed. 1 (January, 1812) This day I went to the Presidents Levee"; "Wed. 15 (January, 1812) In the evening attended Mrs. Madison's levee." He evidently enjoyed these functions, for he gave much space to mentioning the evenings spent with the president, government officials, and foreign diplomats. The theatre also held an attraction for him, and a rope dancer enticed him from his lodgings several times in the course of one week. Life in the capital did not lack for pleasure, and the cares of government could not draw him away from the habits of a lifetime. Sherry and Madeira wines and whiskey, mingled with social gambling, enlivened the winter evenings after the day's work in the House. He must have been a card player of some ability, for he recorded his gains at different times—per-

---

[58] Heiskell, *op. cit.*, pp. 592-614.

haps he mentioned only his fortunate days. One evening he won eighty dollars from the editor of the *Intelligencer*, a Washington newspaper, in bets upon a card game, and he recorded that the money had not yet been paid. He won sixteen dollars at a faro bank, but the most of his winnings at card playing or gambling represented small amounts.

These facts present an incomplete and unsatisfactory story of his life as a member of Congress. It is impossible to assert with any degree of confidence that he exerted any influence upon the policies of his party. It may be assumed, however, that by reason of his long experience in dealing with the savages, his advice upon Indian affairs would be valuable to the administration.[59] Probably no member of Congress had a more intimate knowledge of questions concerning the militia. Certainly no one more thoroughly understood the West.[60] These considerations lead to the belief that his influence must have been of some importance and that these last few years in Congress brought to him some compensation in pleasure and in honor. He satisfied his friends in Tennessee that he stood as a protector of their interests. This constituted his dearest hope.

---

[59] *ASP, Indian Affairs*, I, 826.
[60] Ramsey, *op. cit.*, p. 712.

CHAPTER XI

PIONEERING PAST

SEVIER'S career as a public servant came to a close in 1815. As his life began, so it ended, upon the frontier which he had helped to push westward. He had come into the Old Southwest hard upon the heels of the first settlers. Little was known then concerning the vast areas which stretched westward to the Mississippi and south of the Ohio River. Hordes of savages roamed at will over the fertile plains and more fertile river valleys. The bolder war parties of the Cherokees and other lesser tribes invaded the white settlements on the outskirts of civilization leaving a trail of blood and devastation. The people in the colonies lived at ease, secure behind the ramparts which these western pioneers created by their constant pressure upon the savages. With little opportunity for acquiring wealth in the settled areas left to them, the pioneers were forced by economic necessity to drive the Indians from the tribal hunting grounds and to appropriate the lands. By the time of Sevier's birth this process had pushed the frontier back into the valley areas between the Blue Ridge and the Alleghenies. Within a few years after his death the last portion of the territory comprising the Old Southwest had been admitted into the Union as a state. His life spanned the period of settlement from the Alleghenies to the Mississippi.

In this constant drive toward the west, Sevier had played a part the importance of which has never been fully appreciated. It is not surprising that the historical facts concerning this hero of the western border have not been collected. Frontiersmen had a happy disregard for records. Those which they kept were fragmentary. Many which they preserved suffered from the ravages of time and ill-treatment. But most important was the fact that another and apparently a more romantic character flashed across the horizon of Tennessee history in the closing years of Sevier's glory. One writer[1] said that Tennessee has had "no real state hero since pioneer days. The list began with John Sevier and ended with Andrew Jackson." Sevier's fame has been dimmed by the light of Jackson's personality. Jackson became a national character, while Sevier always remained a state figure. Interest in frontier heroes has tended to center in the person of Jackson, who became the representative of the West in the eyes of the nation.

Jackson reflected the ideals and aspirations of the West after its civilization had become firmly established. Sevier was the true representative of the old West, the ideal of the man who struggled and fought for the acquisition of the soil. Jackson came upon the scene after Sevier and other pioneer leaders had prepared the way for the establishment of a commonwealth. Jackson's brilliance as a frontier military leader resulted from his campaigns against the savages in their last stand east of the Mississippi. His victories created opportunities for Tennesseans to migrate *from* the state to the new lands opened for settlement. Sevier led the pioneers *into* the state, helped to develop the possibilities through which Tennessee became an independent commonwealth, and served as its chief executive and representative in the formative period of its development. He remained a provincial to

---

[1] E. E. Miller, "Tennessee," in *These United States* (ed. Ernest Gruening), p. 146.

the end of his days. He cared little about ideas of nationality. His interests centered in the West. National popularity did not attract him. In the services which each rendered to the State of Tennessee, it is difficult to understand in what particular Jackson, or any other man, contributed as important and lasting benefits as its first governor.

Little except tradition remains concerning the personal characteristics of this magnetic leader of frontiersmen. He must have possessed those traits of character which appealed to the rough and often cruel life on the border. Writers of the period mentioned his tact and diplomacy as prominent attributes. Jovial, carefree, careless of danger yet not reckless, a willing participant in the rough sports of the frontier, hospitable to his friends and generous to his foes, this character rapidly won his way into the hearts of his fellows.

In his home he was a loving and kind parent of a large family of children. Little is known of his family life. In the size of his family he was typically the pioneer— he was the father of eighteen children. His first wife, Sarah Hawkins, was the mother of ten, and Catherine Sherrill his second wife, of eight. Some of them were born before his departure from the Shenandoah Valley. The sturdy sons in this family engaged in the wars with the savages with the same zest and strength which characterized their father.[2] He was a real patriarch of a clan whose members rendered unfaltering loyalty to their chief.

Sevier never displayed any inclination toward religion. His son George wrote, "My father never made a profession of religion—in his younger days he seems to have

---

[2] The children by his first wife were Joseph, James, John, Valentine, Richard, Betsy, Sally, Mary Ann, Nancy and Rebecca; those by his second wife, Ruth, Catherine, George Washington, Joanna Goade, Samuel, Robert, Polly and Eliza. Draper MSS, 11DD164.

been more attached to the Baptist church (to whom he gave 3 acres of land to build a church in the town of New Market, Rockingham County, Va.)."[3]

Even though he showed no religious preferences, his intense interest in his fellow man was manifested in many ways. Some of his ideas may have appeared impracticable; yet we see in the present time a practical application of an idea which his fertile, mechanical mind conceived. In 1800, when the plague raged in the city of Philadelphia, he wrote a long letter to Doctor Rush of that city, in which he proposed something similar to modern systems of ventilation. He had observed that the disease appeared gradually to abate with the approach of cool autumn weather: "Believing this to be the case in this as in all epidemical diseases, have thought that could some substitute, as nearly in effect as possible be constructed, it would be the most sure and likely means to help cure and eradicate the disorder—I now beg leave to suppose for a moment erecting what we call in Tennessee a Water blast, such as we now blow our Furnaces and Forges with. . . . A machine of this kind I am induced to believe would sufficiently ventilate the largest hospital. . . . The air could be easily by tubes conducted and diffused throughout every Apartment in such quantities as might be thought or found necessary. I mention the Water blast from an opinion that the Air arriving immediately off that element (*particularly a fresh and cool stream*) would be more salubrious and efficacious than the common Air. A small stream affording ten to fifteen feet fall . . . would furnish Air amply sufficient for a large building. . . . It may be objected that this kind of air would not be sufficiently cool to answer the desired purpose . . . but could not the defect in a great measure be remedied

---

[3] Draper MSS, 11DD164.

by fixing in the tubes Ice from your Ice houses Letting the Air pass through a Quantity sufficient to impregnate it with a purity (?) and cool Quality?"[4]

As a politician, Sevier combined the blunt and direct methods common in a new country with the wily intrigue of a diplomat. He did not refrain from taking advantage of an opponent in any way which he could make appear legitimate. This made him a dangerous political enemy. He displayed no outstanding qualities of national statesmanship, but he knew what was needed in his state, and he knew the methods by which these objects might be realized. The practicability of his aims and methods sometimes obscured his statesmanship which, among Tennesseans, attained a high position. He was willing to carry war into the heart of the enemy's country when that appeared to be the only method of forcing the savages from the desired territory. When he saw that the Indians might be driven from their possessions by the pressure of immigration and increased population, he became firmly opposed to further bloodshed. Yet his objective remained the same, and he would brook no unreasonable delay in the success of that movement. He remained until his last days an ardent expansionist, believing that the Indians should be conceded no right to control vast areas of uncultivated lands. His distrust of the savages followed the sentiment of the pioneer. He believed in and interpreted the desires of the men who knew the West.

Strangely enough, he exerted his last efforts in carrying out the provisions of the treaty which Jackson forced the Creek Indians to sign at Fort Jackson at the close of the Creek war.[5] On the last day of its third session, the Thirteenth Congress passed a bill which authorized the president to appoint commissioners to run and survey

---

[4] Draper MSS, 16DD36.   [5] *ASPIA*, I, 826.

the boundary provided by this treaty. Sevier received an appointment as one of the three commissioners. He recorded in his *Diary* that he attended a meeting of the commissioners in Washington on March 11.[6]

On June 10, 1815, he rode away from his home and family on the first day of a journey which was destined to be his last. He engaged in work on the Indian line during the greater part of the summer. Aside from his regular routine, of which he mentioned little, his *Diary* exhibited evidence that during these last days his thoughts turned toward two of the major factors in his whole career, Andrew Jackson and land. An undated memorandum stated that a certain man named Pope of the "Contractors department" presented a letter from General Jackson to the Department of War which described in favorable terms the great services that Pope had rendered Jackson's army in the Creek campaign. The auditor refused to pass the account, but the secretary of war accepted it. As a result "he (Pope) was allowed at least $40,000 more than he ought to have received."[7] This represented Sevier's last stroke at Jackson, even though he did it privately. As for land, his record abounded in references to the value of the areas through which he passed.[8] Even so late in life he thought of the possibilities of gain through acquisition of lands in the Indian country. It was only natural that he should show characteristics of the speculator at this time, for this trait constituted the fundamental motive in his whole life.

He made the last entry in his *Diary* some days before his death: "Sat 9 (September) Dicky Brown very sick— We started late & traveled   miles to   there is some tolerable land of Cullaba (?) Creek & about Hawkins

---

[6] Heiskell, *op. cit.*, p. 610.
[7] *Ibid.*, p. 612.   [8] *Ibid.*, pp. 611-14.

old place, but between that & other see (?) the land is sandy, poor, & the growth long leaf pine."[9]

The life of the old Indian fighter and pioneer ended in a tent on the Creek boundary on September 24, 1815.[10] He had been reëlected to Congress from his district during his absence in this service of the government. His friends and neighbors had lost their truest representative, for he knew their ideals and their life as few men knew them. The man of the frontier had passed the boundary. Tennessee had lost her first great hero. He was buried with honors of war by the troops under the command of Captain Walker of the United States Army on the east bank of the Tallapoosa River near Fort Decatur in Alabama. Through neglect of her great citizen, Tennessee allowed this grave to remain practically unknown until 1887. In that year his dust was reinterred in Knoxville. Over the grave a monument bears testimony that the passing years have but added to his fame:

> "John Sevier, Pioneer, soldier, statesman, and one of the founders of the Republic; Governor of the State of Franklin; six times Governor of Tennessee; four times elected to Congress; a typical pioneer, who conquered the wilderness and fashioned the State; a projector and hero of King's Mountain; fought thirty-five battles, won thirty-five victories; his Indian war cry 'Here they are! Come on boys!' "

---

[9] *Ibid.*, p. 614.   [10] Ramsey, *op. cit.*, p. 712.

BIBLIOGRAPHY

A. PRIMARY SOURCES

I. MANUSCRIPTS

Blount Papers. Library of the State of Tennessee.
Bureau of Indexes and Archives, U. S. Department of Archives.
Bureau of Rolls and Library, State Department Archives.
Draper Collection of Manuscripts. Wisconsin Historical Society.
    This is the most complete single source of manuscripts for the Old Southwest. From the fifty different divisions of these manuscripts, extended use was made of the following sets of papers:
- N. Frontier Wars MSS. 23 vols. Such volumes were used as are cited in the notes.
- P. Draper's Biographical Sketches. 3 vols.
- Q. Draper's Historical Miscellanies. 8 vols.
- S. Draper's Notes. 33 vols. Such volumes were used as are cited in the notes.
- DD. King's Mountain MSS. 18 vols. Of special value in this division are the Sevier Papers and the Shelby Papers.
- VV. Sumter MSS. 23 vols.
- XX. Tennessee Papers. 7 vols. This is a very valuable source.

House of Representatives Collection, No. 6. Manuscript Division, Library of Congress. This contains most of the documents which were used in the discussion of the Muscle Shoals project.
Manuscripts relating to land in which Sevier was interested. Manuscript Division, Library of Congress. See also House of Representatives Collection, No. 6, listed above.

Military Order Book. Library of the State of Tennessee.
Minutes of the United States Circuit Court, Nashville, Tennessee.
North Carolina Grant Books. Tennessee State Archives.

>These books contain official copies of the grants for lands in Tennessee. They were copied from the North Carolina Records.

Proclamations, Warrants, etc. Library of the State of Tennessee.
Roane Papers. Library of the State of Tennessee.
Sevier Papers. Library of the State of Tennessee.

>These papers consist of the Official Letter Book in which Sevier's official communications are included, as well as a file from which the Official Letter Book was copied; in this file there are many letters addressed to Sevier which are not included in the Official Letter Book.

Sevier Papers. Tennessee Historical Library.

>A few of Sevier's letters are in the possession of the Historical Society.

Territorial Papers. U. S. Department of Archives.

>These papers include much of the correspondence between the State Department and the officials of the Territory of the United States south of the Ohio, from 1791 to 1798.

II. PRINTED SOURCES OTHER THAN NEWSPAPERS

American State Papers: Foreign Relations, I-IV; *Indian Affairs,* I-II; *Finance,* I-III; *Claims; Public Lands,* I-III; *Miscellaneous,* I-II.

Annals of Congress. Debates and Proceedings: First Congress; Twelfth Congress; Thirteenth Congress.

Bassett, J. S. *Correspondence of Andrew Jackson.* Vols. I and II. Washington, 1926.

Calendar of Virginia State Papers. Richmond, 1883.

Colonial and State Records of North Carolina. 26 vols. Referred to in text as *SRNC.* This is the most valuable printed source.

"Diary," or Journal, of John Sevier, in S. G. Heiskel, *Andrew Jackson and Early Tennessee History*, Vol. II. Nashville, 1920.

"Diary," of Allaire, in L. C. Draper, *King's Mountain and Its Heroes*. Cincinnati, 1881.

Haywood, John. *Civil and Political History of the State of Tennessee*. Exact reprint of 1823 ed. Nashville, 1891. A contemporary work.

Journal of the Constitutional Convention of Tennessee, 1796. Knoxville, 1796.

Journal of the Continental Congress, XVII.

Journal of the Legislative Council of the Territory South of the River Ohio. Knoxville, 1796.

Journals of the Virginia House of Burgesses.

Land Laws of Tennessee, edited by Henry D. Whitney. Chattanooga, 1891.

Laws, Statutes, etc. Public Acts of the General Assembly of North Carolina and Tennessee, 1715-1813.

Laws of the United States, Resolutions, Treaties, etc. Relating to Public Lands, edited by Ed. de Krafft. Washington, 1817.

Legislative Journals: Journals of the House of Representatives of Tennessee, 1796-1810.

"Moravian Diaries," *Virginia Magazine of History and Biography*, 1904, pp. 144-47.

Ramsey, J. G. M. *Annals of Tennessee*. Philadelphia, 1860.

This is included among the printed sources because the author lived in direct contact with many of the men of Sevier's time; he also corrected Haywood by the use of sources later destroyed.

"Records of Washington County, Tennessee," *American Historical Magazine*, V.

Report of the American Historical Association, I (1896). "Public Documents of Early Congresses."

Tarleton, Lt.-Col. *A History of the Campaigns in the Southern Provinces*. Dublin, 1787.

Tennessee Reports, II.

United States Reports, III, V.

United States Statutes at Large, VII.
Waddell, J. A. *Annals of Augusta County, Virginia.*

III. NEWSPAPERS

Knoxville Gazette, 1791-95. State Historical Library, Nashville.
Knoxville Gazette, 1796-97. Lawson McGhee Library, Knoxville.
Tennessee Gazette and Mero District Advertiser (Nashville), 1799-1803. Library of Congress.
Wilson's Knoxville Gazette, 1809-15. Lawson McGhee Library, Knoxville.

B. SELECTED SECONDARY SOURCES

Adams, Henry. *History of the United States of America.* Vols. V-VIII. N. Y., 1891.
Alden, G. H. "The State of Franklin," *American Historical Review,* VIII, 271-89.
Allan, G. W. *Our Naval War with France.* Boston, 1809.
Allison, John. *Dropped Stitches in Tennessee History.* Nashville, 1897.
———. *Notable Men of Tennessee.* Atlanta, 1905.
Alvord, C. W. *The Mississippi Valley in British Politics.* 2 vols. Cleveland, 1917.
Ashe, S. A. *History of North Carolina.* 2 vols. Raleigh, 1925.
Bassett, J. S. *The Federalist System.* "American Nation Series," Vol. VII. N. Y., 1906.
———. *Life of Andrew Jackson.* Vol. I. N. Y., 1911.
Bemis, S. F. (ed.) *The American Secretaries of State.* 2 vols. N. Y., 1927.
———. *Pinckney's Treaty.* Baltimore, 1926.
———. *Jay's Treaty.* N. Y., 1923.
Bond, O. Z. *Old Tales Retold and Adventures of Tennessee.* Nashville, 1907.
Buell, A. C. *History of Andrew Jackson.* Vols. I and II. N. Y., 1904.
Bullock, C. J. *The Monetary History of the United States.* N. Y., 1900.

BIBLIOGRAPHY 223

Caldwell, J. W. *Studies in Constitutional History of Tennessee.* Cincinnati, 1895.

Carpenter, W. H. *History of Tennessee.* Philadelphia, 1856, 1868.

Carr, John. *Early Times in Tennessee.* Nashville, 1857.

Chambers, Henry E. *Mississippi Valley Beginnings. An Outline of Early History of the West.* N. Y., 1922.

Channing, E. *History of the United States.* Vols. III-IV. N. Y., 1917.

Claiborne, J. F. H. *Territory and State.* Jackson, Miss., 1880.

Clayton, W. W. *History of Davidson County, Tennessee.* Philadelphia, 1880.

Collins, Lewis. *History of Kentucky.* 2 vols. Louisville, 1924.

Colyar, A. S. *Life and Times of Andrew Jackson.* Nashville, 1904.

Cotterill, R. S. "The Natchez Trace," *Tennessee Historical Magazine,* VII, 29-35.

Cox, I. F. *The West Florida Controversy.* Baltimore, 1918.

Cross, Nathaniel. "The Admission of Tennessee into the Union," *American Historical Magazine,* V, 241-47.

DeWitt, John H. (ed.) "Journal of John Sevier," *Tennessee Historical Magazine,* V, 156-94, 232-64.

Draper, L. C. *King's Mountain and Its Heroes.* Cincinnati, 1881.

Emerson, F. V. "Geographic Influences in the Mississippi Valley," *Mississippi Valley Historical Association Proceedings,* VIII, 289-96.

Farrand, Max. "The Indian Boundary Line." *American Historical Review,* X, 782-92.

Fortescue, J. W. *History of the British Army.* Vol. III. N. Y., 1902.

Garrett, W. R., and Goodpasture, A. V. *History of Tennessee.* Nashville, 1900.

Gilmore, J. R. *John Sevier as a Commonwealth-Builder.* N. Y., 1894.

———. *The Rearguard of the Revolution.* N. Y., 1897.

Goodpasture, A. V. "The Watauga Association," *American Historical Magazine,* III, 103-20.

———. "William Blount and the Old Southwest Territory," *American Historical Magazine,* VIII, 1-13.

———. "Dr. James White, Pioneer, Politician, Lawyer," *Tennessee Historical Magazine,* I, 282-91.

———. "The Genesis of the Jackson-Sevier Feud," *American Historical Magazine,* V, 115-23.

———. "Indian Wars and Warriors of the Old Southwest, 1730-1807," *Tennessee Historical Magazine,* IV, 3-49, 106-45, 161-210.

Greene, F. V. *The Revolutionary War.* N. Y., 1911.

Hale, W. T., and Merritt, D. L. *History of Tennessee and Tennesseans.* Chicago and N. Y., 1913.

Hamilton, Peter J. *Colonial Mobile.* Boston, 1897.

Haskins, C. H. "The Yazoo Land Companies," *American Historical Association Papers,* Vol. V.

Heiskell, S. G. *Andrew Jackson and Early Tennessee History.* Nashville, 1920.

Henderson, A. "Creative Forces in Westward Expansion," *American Historical Review,* XX, 86-107.

———. *Conquest of the Old Southwest,* N. Y., 1920.

———. "The Spanish Conspiracy in Tennessee," *Tennessee Historical Magazine,* III, 229-43.

Holt, A. C. "The Economic and Social Beginnings of Tennessee," *Tennessee Historical Magazine,* VII, 194-230, 252-313.

Kercheval, Samuel. *History of the Valley of Virginia.* Woodstock, 1902. Reprint of edition of 1833.

McMaster, J. B. *History of the People of the United States.* Vol. II. N. Y., 1833.

"Militia Companies in Augusta County, in 1742," *Virginia Magazine of History and Biography,* VIII, 278-83.

Moore, J. T., and Foster, A. P. *Tennessee, the Volunteer State.* Vols. I-III. Chicago and Nashville, 1923.

Parton, James. *Life of Andrew Jackson.* Vols. I-III. N. Y., 1860.

Paxson, F. L. *History of the American Frontier.* N. Y., 1924.

Phelan, James. *History of Tennessee.* Boston and N. Y., 1888.

Pratt, W. W. *Expansionists of 1812.* N. Y., 1925.
Putnam, A. W. *History of Middle Tennessee.* Nashville, 1859.
Roosevelt, Theodore. *The Winning of the West.* N. Y., 1895.
Royce, C. C. "The Cherokee Nation of Indians," *Fifth Annual Report of the Bureau of Ethnology.*
Semple, Ellen. *American History and its Geographic Conditions.* N. Y., 1903.
Sioussat, St. G. L. "The North Carolina Cession of 1784 in its Federal Aspects," *Mississippi Valley Historical Association Proceedings,* Vol. II, 35-62.
Skinner, C. L. *Pioneers of the Old Southwest.* "Chronicles of America Series." New Haven, 1919.
Thwaites, R. G. *Daniel Boone.* N. Y., 1902.
Treat, P. J. *Our National Land System.* Baltimore, 1917.
Turner, F. J. *The Frontier in American History.* N. Y., 1920.
———. "Significance of the Mississippi Valley in American History," *Mississippi Valley Historical Association Proceedings,* III, 159-84.
———. "Western State Making in the Revolutionary Era," *American Historical Review,* I, 70-87.
Turner, F. M. *General John Sevier.* N. Y., 1910.
Wayland, John. *History of Rockingham County, Virginia.* Dayton, Virginia, 1912.
Weeks, S. B. "General Joseph Martin and the War of the Revolution in the West," *American Historical Association Papers,* III, 403-77.
Whitaker, A. P. *The Spanish-American Frontier: 1783-1795.* Boston and N. Y., 1927.
———. "The Muscle Shoals Speculation," *Mississippi Valley Historical Review,* XIII, 365-86.
———. "Spanish Intrigue in the Old Southwest," *Mississippi Valley Historical Review,* XII, 155-76.
Williams, S. C. *History of the Lost State of Franklin.* Johnson City, Tenn., 1924.
Wright, J. W. "The Rifle in the American Revolution," *American Historical Review,* XXIX, 293-99.

INDEX

Adams, John, appointed commissioners to run Holston treaty line, 133
American Volunteers, commanded by Ferguson, 49
Anderson, Judge, assistant judge of Franklin, 88
Armstrong, John, land office of at Hillsborough, 64; activity after opening of office, 81; granted land to Sevier, 151
Armstrong, Martin, in charge of land office, 64; papers ordered seized, 125
Ashe, Samuel, discovered land frauds, 124; investigated land office, 125; learned of plot to burn State House, 125; requested seizure of land records, 125

Baptists, presented land by Sevier, 7
Battles (Revolutionary), Monk's Corner, 28; Charleston, 44; Rugeley's Mill, 45; Ramsour's Mill, 47; Cheraw Hill, 47; Camden, 47-8; Cedar Spring, 50; Musgrove's Mill, 50; King's Mountain, 54-7
Battles (Indian), Watauga Fort, 19; Long Creek, 24; Boyd's Creek, 25; War Ford, 27; Indian Creek, 27; Middle Settlements, 27; Etowah, 36
Beard, Captain, killed Indians, 35
Bellew, Bennett, attempted to lease land, 29-30; persuaded Indians not to attend conferences, 30
Bird, Jessie, Sevier lodged with, 182
Blickerstaff's Plantation, court-martial trial of Tories at, 57
Blount, William, governor of territory, 33; faced by problem of settlers on Indian lands, 35; interested in land, 61; headed Muscle Shoals Company, 70; resigned seat in Congress, 70; communication to Georgia legislature, 70; advocated western cession, 81; protested Hopewell treaty, 90; attempted to reconcile Sevier and Tipton, 98; appointed governor of territory, 108; moved to west, 109; organized territory, 109; called extra session of legislature, 110; policies as governor, 111-14; diplomatic absences from territory, 114; instructions to White, 115; attitude towards Indians, 115; United States Senator, 116, 117; report to Sevier from Congress, 118; reëlected senator, 118; communication concerning road, 129; conspiracy, and expulsion from Senate, 130-31; appointed Jackson judge-advocate, 147n.; submitted Jackson's plan of defense, 148
Blount, Willie, appraisal of Sevier and Tipton, 98; Sevier settled note with, 163; governor of Tennessee, 201; Sevier's letter to, 207-08
Boyd's Creek, battle of, 25
Bradley (a Tory), killed, 42-3
Brindletown, Ferguson at, 53
British, thought by settlers to incite Indians, 16; hated by settlers, 18, 41; defeated by pioneers at King's Mountain, 23; westerners felt no interest in government of, 40
Brown, Jacob, purchase of land by, 12, 40
Buckingham, Thomas, appointed

228 INDEX

to receive papers concerning land, 196
Buller, Isaac, delivered to continental officer, 42
Butler, Colonel, prompted investigation of Zachariah Cox, 130; protested permits to settlers, 137

Cage, William, speaker of Franklin assembly, 88; commended Sevier's administrations, 122
Camden, American defeat at, 47-8; caused desertions, 53
Campaign (Gubernatorial, of 1796), details of, 117; opposition encountered by Sevier, 117, 123; Sevier elected, 117; possible genesis of Sevier-Jackson feud, 169
Campaign (Gubernatorial, of 1803), candidates Sevier and Roane, 145; contest between Sevier and Jackson, 145, 148; reasons for enmity of Sevier and Jackson, 146-47; union of Jackson and Roane forces, 148; Jackson's blunder in, 148; land frauds in, 148-49; charges in accepted on Jackson's word, 152; Sevier elected, 155
Campaigns (Indian), methods used in, 37-8; against Cherokees (1776-77), 19; against Overhill Towns, 20; against Chickamaugas, 21; against Cherokees, (1780), 24-7; against Cherokees, (1781), 27; against towns on the Coosa and Estenaula rivers, 28; Hiwasse, 28; against Cherokees (1788), 29-32; Etowah, 33-6, 111, 114; Nickajack, 114.
Campbell, Arthur, indignant at British inciting Indians, 17; led troops from Virginia, 25; arrived after battle of Boyd's Creek, 26; led militia against Tories, 43; circulated call for convention in west, 80; hoped to establish state, 80; plan followed in Franklin, 85
Campbell, David, superior judge of Franklin, 88; superior judge of Washington district, 93; ordered to arrest Sevier, 97; arrested by troops, 137
Campbell, General William, joined expedition against Ferguson, 51; suggested as superior officer, 53; position of regiment at King's Mountain, 54; number of troops, 56
Cape, John, bought land from Wood, 74
Carter, family in Watauga fort, 19
Carter, John, Colonel of Washington County regiment, 20; affidavit concerning Sevier's land speculation, 148-49; had interest in destruction of records, 163
Carter, Landon, filed claims for Tory lands, 43; associated with Sevier in land holdings, 69-70; speaker of senate of Franklin, 88; entry-taker of Washington County, 161
Caswell, Richard, description of situation in colonies, 46; associated with Sevier in land grant, 67; member of Muscle Shoals Company, 70; adopted policy of conciliation toward Franklinites, 89
Catawba, Colonel Cleveland at, 56
Charleston, base of British operation, 44
Cheraw Hill, mutiny at, 47
Cherokees, Robertson's lease from, 12; dissatisfied with treaty at Long Island, 20; turned against Holston settlements, 21; Sevier ordered campaign against, 24; defeated at Boyd's Creek, 25; devastation of towns, 27; Middle Settlements destroyed, 27; Indian Creek towns destroyed, 27; Sevier's method of conquest against, 37; Sevier the nemesis of, 38; Franklin assembly provided for conference with, 88; treaty with, 89; harassed settlements, 113; Blount's attitude toward, 115; protested against running of Holston line, 134; Federal government to make treaty with, 138; Ore sent on mission to,

138-40; Sevier favored peace with, 142; negotiations with to open road, 190
Chesapeake affair, denounced by Sevier, 195
Chickamaugas, ranging band, 21; organized by Dragging Canoe, 21; campaign against, 21; stronghold desolated, 27
Chilhowee Mountains, part of Indian line, 115
Chota Town, abandoned by Indians, 26; base of campaign, 27
Christian, Colonel William, led army from Virginia, 18; led expedition against Overhill Towns, 20
'Chucky Jack, Indian name for Sevier, 23; Cherokee nemesis, 38
Claiborne, William C. C., Sevier's attitude on Indian affairs expressed to, 136; Sevier to on President Adams's policy, 138; in Sevier-Jackson feud, 173
Clark, Daniel, reported French prefect stirred up trouble, 191
Clark, George Rogers, success at Vincennes, 21; captured Governor Hamilton, 21
Clarke, Colonel Elijah, exerted pressure on Loyalists, 48; attack on Augusta, 50; joined by Shelby, 50; victory at Musgrove's Mill, 50; joined by McDowell, 50
Clay, Henry, proposed amendment to army bill, 205
Cleveland, Colonel, joined forces with militia, 52, 56; forces at King's Mountain, 54; number of troops, 56; instructions to men, 56
Clinch River, part of Indian line, 115
Clinton, George, Sevier pallbearer at funeral of, 209
Clinton, Sir Henry, activities in South, 44; plan of campaign with Cornwallis, 44-5; return to New York, 44; Cornwallis's dispatch to, 45-6; sent Leslie to Chesapeake, 48
Cocke, William, presented memorial to Congress, 89; elected United States senator, 118; re-elected senator, 118
Colleges, land set aside for, 196n
Companies, Light Horse, duties of, 42
Congress, Sevier elected to, 101; attempted to pass excise tax, 102-03; question of national bank in, 102, 103-04; location of capital discussed in, 104; accepted cession from North Carolina, 108
Conway, General, elected major-general, 124, 146; death of, 146; supported by governor in military election, 172
Coosa, campaign against Indians on, 28
Cornwallis, Lord, Greene asked aid against, 27; Tories meant to join, 42; left in command in South, 44; General Buford defeated by, 45; arrived at Camden, 45; despatch to Clinton, 45-46; opposition encountered, 47; sickness in army of, 48; at Charlotte, 48; sent Ferguson to back country, 49; advanced to Gilbert Town, 51; retreated to Winnsboro, 58; foresaw difficulties, 58n; effect of King's Mountain on, 59; marched into Virginia, 60.
Cowpens, Whig forces at, 54; Colonel Williams at, 56
Cox, Zachariah, interested in Muscle Shoals, 73; headed company to develop Shoals region, 129-30; defended by Sevier, 130; transferred activities, 130
Crawford, Moses, imprisoned, and estate confiscated, 41; released, 42
Creeks, proposed expedition against, 73; memorial to Washington to prevent attacks of, 113; treaty with at Fort Jackson, 215

Davidson County, military elections contested in, 121; Sevier encountered opposition in, 121
Dearborn's Treaty, added land in Tennessee, 198

230 INDEX

De Kalb, Baron, advice disregarded by Gates, 48
De Peyster, Captain, surrendered at King's Mountain, 56
D'Estaing, Admiral, defeated at Savannah, 44
Dinsmore, Silas, would not commit self on place of conference with Cherokees, 140
Doherty, George, commanded regiment, 191
Donelson, John, interested in Muscle Shoals Company, 70; purchased land from Indians, 70
Donelson, Stockley, land joined by Sevier's, 68; member of Blount's council, 110; connected with land frauds, 188-89n
Dragging Canoe, absent from treaty of Long Island, 20; communicated with Governor Hamilton, 21; organized band of Chickamaugas, 21
Dumplin Creek, treaty of, 89
Dunmore, Lord, commissioned Sevier captain, 7

Elizabethton, Sevier settled near, 10
Estenaula River, campaign against Indians on, 28
Etowah, campaign of, 33-6; 111, 114
Excise tax, opposed by South and West, 102; passed, 103

Federalists, Sevier not of party, 106; opposed to seating Tennessee senators, 118; frontier alienated from, 134-35; closely united on principles, 203
Ferguson, Major, threatened to devastate back country, 39; sent to back country, 49; invented rifle, 49; duties in back country, 49; at Cedar Spring, 50; paroled prisoners, 51; at Brindletown, 53; asked for reënforcements, 53; stationed army on King's Mountain, 53; position revealed by Tories, 54; mistakes at King's Mountain, 55-6, 58; killed in battle, 56; number of troops, 57

Ford, Colonel, candidate for brigadier, 123; preferred by lower counties, 124
Fort Anderson, captured, 50
Fort Decatur, Sevier buried near, 217
Fort Grainger, garrison at, 115
Fort Jackson, treaty with Creeks at, 215
Franklin (State of), cause of, 28; Sevier's activities in movement for, 72-3; relation to Muscle Shoals project, 73; example of separatism, 79; genesis of movement, 80-4; convention for forming state, 85; second convention of, 86; temporary constitution prepared, 86-7; meeting of first general assembly, 88; election of officials, 88; grievances of western people recited, 88; assembly of provided for conference with Cherokees, 88; Governor Martin's manifesto against, 89; Governor Caswell conciliatory toward, 89; second assembly of, 89; constitutional convention of, 90; disruption of government, 91; jurisdiction of courts contested, 92; assembly of 1787 of, 92-3; further disruptions, 93; end of government of, 93
Fraud, opportunities for under land system, 65-6; Sevier accused of 148-52
Frontiersmen, movement towards King's Mountain, 51; feared threat of Ferguson, 51-2; method of fighting, 55; opposed to excise tax, 102-03; entries made for ungranted land by, 108; claimed had right to land, 134

Gardoqui, Don Diego de, carried on intrigue for Spanish government, 95; letters from Sevier to, 95-6
Gates, General Horatio, people not allowed to mention defeat of, 47; effect of presence on people, 47n; commander in South, 48; leaders of militia asked for commander, 52

Georgia Legislature, formed Houston County at Great Bend, 70-1; passed act regarding Yazoo Company, 75
Gerry, Elbridge, Sevier pallbearer at funeral of, 209
Gilbert Town, Cornwallis at, 51; militia encamped near, 52
Glasgow, James, in land frauds, 125, 127; tried for frauds, 128, 165; collusion with Sevier charged by Jackson, 150; letter of Sevier to, 150-51; earlier letter of Sevier to, 160-61; value of warrants offered by Sevier to, 164; Sevier's indebtedness to, 164-65
Goade, Joanna (mother of John Sevier), married Valentine Sevier, 5; signed deed, 10
Gordon, George, carried Sevier's land warrants, 163; surveyed land, 164
Grants (land to Sevier), on island in French Broad, 67; in Greene County, 68; in Middle District, 68; in Sumner County, 68
Great Bend of Tennessee, strategic location of, 70; doubt as to ownership, 70; effect of Franklin movement on, 87
Green River, Whig forces at, 53
Greene County, Sevier's land holdings in, 67-8; represented by Sevier, 100-01
Greene, General Nathaniel, asked for aid, 27; strategy in North Carolina, 60
Greer, Andrew, family in Watauga fort, 19; with Sevier at South West Point, 182; account of Sevier-Jackson encounter at Kingston, 183-84

Haile, John, delegate to provincial congress of North Carolina, 14
Hall, William, account of meeting of Sevier and Jackson, 158n; 176-77
Halifax Congress, met November 1776, 14; promoted Sevier to lieutenant-colonel, 15; Sevier represented western settlements at, 20

Hamilton, Alexander, financial policy of, 102
Hamilton, Henry, in communication with Dragging Canoe, 21; captured by Clark, 21
Hawkins, Benjamin, appointed to run Holston treaty line, 133; report to Secretary McHenry, 134
Hawkins, Sarah, married John Sevier, 7; children of named, 213n
Haywood, John, estimate of Sevier, 14, 31; cites instances of Tory activity, 42; resigned as judge, 128
Henderson, Richard, purchased land for Transylvania Company, 12; legality of purchase, 13; purchase of opened Kentucky, 40; settlers claimed land by reason of purchase, 135
Henley, David, in Blount conspiracy, 131
Henry, Patrick, received complaint of Martin, 30; member of Virginia Yazoo Company, 75; criticized cession of 1789, 107
Hillsborough, land office opened at, 64; state convention called at, 100
Hiwasse, campaign against, 28
Holder, John, planned to lead colony to Yazoo, 76
Holston, settlements on, 10; Robertson leased land on, 12; comparative quiet from Indians until 1776, 16; Sevier departed from, 23
Holsinger, David, bought land from Valentine Sevier, 10
Holsinger, Michael, bought land from Valentine Sevier, 10
Houston, Reverend Samuel, head of Franklin constitutional committee, 90
Huger, Isaac, member of original Yazoo Company, 75
Hunter, John, with Sevier on Kingston road, 183

Indians, supposed allies of British, 16-7; depended on secrecy, 18; state government punished, 18; towns destroyed

232   INDEX

by Shelby, 21; North Carolina attempted to placate, 28-9; atrocities by, 29; whites encroached on, 29; Sevier's campaigns against, 29-39; taught settlers mode of warfare, 55, 58; Sevier's attitude toward, 38, 141-44; relation to Muscle Shoals project, 130

Indian agents, settlers thought emissaries of British, 16; had not attempted to instigate Indian attacks, 17; attempted to force settlers from Indian lands, 40; settlers regarded as enemies, 41

Indian boundary, a temporary affair, 66; settlers pushed across, 66-7, 82, 108, 112

Indian Creek, Indians defeated at, 27

Internal improvements, problem of Sevier's administrations, 128-29

Jackson, Andrew, allied with Tipton, 98; challenged action of governor, 124; candidate for major-general, 124, 146; informed Ashe of irregularities in land office, 124; secured copies of Sevier's letters, 128; influenced treaty with Cherokees, 138; challenged political dominance of Sevier, 145; gave affidavits to Roane, 146; United States senator, 146; informed Senator Martin of land frauds, 147; judge advocate of Davidson, 147n; military experience, 147; union with Roane forces, 148-49; blunder in plans, 148; attacks on Sevier, 149-54; threatened by Sevierites, 154-55; failed in election, 158; altercation with Sevier, 158; ambition frustrated, 159; represented Cumberland section, 168, 212; feud with Sevier, 169-86; loss of popularity, 187; tilt with Maclin, 187; letter by Sevier concerning duel with, 188; in Sevier's dream, 189; forced treaty on Creeks, 215; Sevier's last stroke at, 216

Jefferson, Thomas, report on North Carolina cession, 107-08; protested against settlements on Indian lands, 112

Johnston, Samuel, protest to, 32; ordered arrest of Sevier, 97

Jonesboro, scene of trouble between Sevier and Tipton, 93; Jackson threatened by Sevierites at, 154-55; meeting of Sevier and Jackson at, 170; vote for major-general cast at, 172

Jonesboro Convention, adopted provisional government for Franklin, 85; second meeting of, 86

Kentucky, opened for settlement, 12, 40; General Wilkinson agent for Yazoo Company in, 76

Keywood settlement, Seviers settled in, 10

King's Mountain, increased Sevier's popularity, 24, 60; Ferguson stationed force on, 53; topography of, 53, 55; plan of battle of, 54; battle of, 54-7; results of battle of, 57-60; numbers engaged in battle of, 56; numbers lost in battle of, 57

Knox, Henry, report of campaign against Cherokees to, 29

Knox County, contest in military election in, 121

Knoxville, contributed money to road, 129; vote for major-general cast in, 172; Sevier-Jackson feud at, 176; Sevier buried at, 217

Knoxville Gazette, Jackson's publication of Sevier in, 182; Sevier's candidacy for state senate announced in, 200; Sevier's letter to Blount in, 207-08

Land, fundamental consideration of western movement, 3, 10; located during Indian campaigns, 37; pioneers speculators in, 61; state laws concerning, 63; grants obtained without title to, 63; as remuneration for soldiers, 64; office opened in

Nashville, 64; unsettled areas of opened, 63-4; cession of in 1789, 65; indiscriminate dealings in, 66; Sevier's holdings in, 67-70; companies, 70-7; distribution of public, 195-97

Leslie, General Alexander, ordered to Virginia, 44; Cornwallis to unite with, 45; sent to Chesapeake, 48; ordered to sail south, 59

Lewis, Joel, urged Sevier to come to Nashville, 122; requested blank commissions, 123; defended Sevier, 171

Lochabar treaty, modified proclamation line, 40

Long Creek, battle of, 24

Louisiana Purchase, endorsed by Sevier, 194

Love, Charles J., informed Jackson of land frauds, 147

Love, Thomas, saved Sevier's sons, 94

McBury, Colonel, mobilized force in Georgia, 18

McDowell, Charles, protested against Sevier as brigadier, 33; gave warning of Ferguson's approach, 49-50; joined by Shelby and Clarke, 50; army broken up, 51; united with militia against Ferguson, 52; ranking officer in march against Ferguson, 53; position of in battle of King's Mountain, 54; number of troops under, 56; secured bail for Sevier, 97

McHenry, James, report to of commissioners on Holston line, 134

McIntosh, Lachlan, representative to Cherokee conference, 139; failed to attend second conference, 141

McKee, Colonel John, letters from Blount to, 131

Maclin, William, ordered to take entry books, 126; Jackson's tilt with, 187; sent to Mero to recruit men, 191, 193

McNairy, John, dispute with Jackson, 173

MacRae, Major, at conference with Cherokees, 182

Madison, James, Sevier the guest of, 209

Marion, Francis, exerted pressure on Loyalists, 48

Marshall, John, decision on land case, 65, 65n., 157, 159

Martin, Alexander, instruction to Cherokee commissioners, 66; manifesto to Franklinites, 88-9

Martin, Joseph, adherents of criticized Sevier, 25; attempted to dissuade from Indian attacks, 29; complaint to Henry, 30; affairs investigated, 32; member of Muscle Shoals Company, 70, 87; purchased land from Indians, 70; carried news of repeal of cession to Sevier, 87; succeeded Shelby as commander, 94; disqualified, 100.

Martin, William, altercation with Sevier, 158; berated by Sevier, 176-77

Meigs, Return J., with garrison at Kingston, 182; requested Sevier's presence at Cherokee conference, 190; called conference with Cherokees, 199

Mero District, election of representatives from, 101; memorial to Washington from, 113; military elections in, 121-24, 169; reaction against East Tennessee officers in, 192-93

Middle Settlements, devastated, 27

Military land office, Governor Ashe informed of irregularities in, 124; fraudulent methods in, 125; struggle for possession of papers of, 125-27

Military warrants, bought by speculators, 82

Militia, leadership in sought, 119; election to office in, 120, 122-23; disputed elections in, 121-24; political significance of disputes about, 122; election for field officers in, 122-24; clash between Sevier and Jackson because of, 146; probable connection with Sevier-Jackson feud, 169-72

Millerstown, Sevier moved to, 7

Moore, Patrick, Tory leader, 50

Morgantown, Sevier's trial at, 98
Moultrie, Alexander, member of original Yazoo Company, 75
Muscle Shoals, Sevier interested in, 33, 70; company of formed, 70; activities of company at, 71; project abandoned, 72; depositions concerning lands at, 71-2n; checked by Georgia, 73; relation of to Spanish intrigue, 73; later companies, 73; Cox headed company of, 129-30; Sevier received land at, 130

Nash, Abner, letter from Caswell to, 46
Nashville, land office at, 64; improprieties in conduct of land office at, 124-28; citizens of presented grievances to Sevier, 128; vote for major-general at, 172; quarrel of Sevier and Jackson at, 172-73
National bank, opposed by antifederalists, 103; arguments against, 104; opposed by West, 104; bill for passed, 104
New Market, founded by John Sevier, 7
Nickajack, campaign of, 114
Nolachucky, Brown's lease on, 12; Sevier moved to, 23
North Carolina, state convention called at Hillsborough, 100; action on constitution of United States, 100; assembly met, 100; ratification of constitution by, 101; not represented in first Congress, 101; final cession of land by, 106; Sevier member of assembly of, 1789, 106; provisions of cession act of, 106-07; reserved right to grant land, 108
North Carolina Assembly, laws for disposition of lands by, 63; prohibited entries beyond Indian boundary, 63; closed land office, 63; set aside reservation for soldiers, 64; reopened western lands, 64; modified land laws, 64-5; cession of lands to Congress by, 80, 82; provisions of cession by, 82-3; cession by opposed, 83; act of repeal, 85; attempted to conciliate west, 87, 91; pardoned Sevier, 99; elected Sevier brigadier, 100; authorized confiscation of Tory property, 162
North Carolina Cession Act (1789), provisions of, 106-07; confusion caused by, 107-08

O'Fallon, James, agent of Yazoo Company, 76; promises to agents, 76; claimed conciliation of Spanish and Choctaws, 77; complained of Sevier, 77
Ordnance of 1787, applicable to Southwest, 109
Ore, James, on errand to Cherokees, 138-39; report on mission, 140
Overhill Towns, campaign against, 20
Overton, John, advice to Jackson, 186-87; to settle differences over land, 196

Panton, William, Spanish instigator of Indians, 35
Phillips, Samuel, paroled by Ferguson, 51
Pickering, Timothy, letter of Sevier to, 132; letter of Washington to, 132
Pickens, Andrew, report on Cumberland region, 113; appointed to run Holston line, 133; report to McHenry, 134
Plum Grove, home of Sevier, 23
Polk's Lessee v. Hill, Wendel, et. al., decision on by Marshall, 65; case of, 157; relation to Sevier's land speculation, 159
Powell's Valley, settlers removed from, 135; relief promised to settlers in, 136
Preston, Colonel, led militia against Tories, 43
Prince, Robert, interest in military elections, 123, 169
Proclamation of 1763, leases in violation of, 12; settlers felt restriction of, 39-40
Pugh, Jonathan, sheriff of Wash-

INDEX   235

ington County, 93; ordered to levy on Sevier's slaves, 94

Ramsour's Mill, battle of, 47
Rawdon, Lord, effect of Ferguson's defeat discussed, 58n
Revolution, favored by frontier, 39; Tory activity in west during, 41-3
Roads, construction of, 128-29
Roane, Archibald, appointed Sevier commissioner, 144; succeeded Sevier as governor, 145; candidate to succeed self, 145, 176; cast vote for Jackson in military election, 146, 175; papers deposited with by Jackson, 146, 148, 175; charged Sevier with fraud, 148-49, 151; defended by Jackson, 149, 176; advised investigation into land office, 155
Robertson, Charles, leased land from Cherokees, 12; delegate to provincial congress of North Carolina, 14; undertook construction of road, 129
Robertson, James, in fort at Watauga, 19; nominated brigadier by Blount, 109; member of Blount's council, 110; praised Sevier's administrations, 121; blank commissions sent to, 123, 171; failed to use commissions, 124; appointed to attend Cherokee conference, 139; failed to attend second conference, 141; letters to from Sevier regarding Jackson, 173, 188; commissioner to Indians, 198-99
Ross, David, member of Virginia Yazoo Company, 75; protested against cession of 1789, 107
Roosevelt, Theodore, conclusions of, 37-8; estimate of Sevier's services, 37-8n
Rugeley's Mill, defeat of Buford at, 45
Rush, Benjamin, Sevier's letter to, 214-15
Rutherford, Griffith, led troops from North Carolina, 18; interested in Muscle Shoals, 70; member of Blount's council, 110

Sectionalism, State of Franklin example of, 79, 83, 86; in Tennessee prior to Sevier-Jackson feud, 168, 194; shown in raising troops, 191
Sevier, George (son of John), account of removal to Holston, 11; father's politics, 105; father's religion, 213-14; father entered for Tory land, 161-62n
Sevier, James (son of John), account of arrival on Holston, 11; father in North Carolina legislature, 21n; father's residences in Tennessee, 23n; asked Congress to locate lands, 71n; carried letters to Gardoqui, 96; at Sevier-Jackson encounter at Knoxville, 177
Sevier, Major John (son of John), report to Dr. Draper, 22n
Sevier, John, fascinated by the West, 1-2; typical pioneer, 4; ancestry of, 4-5; birth of, 6; education of, 6; saved from drowning, 7; partner in Father's business, 7; married Sarah Hawkins, 7; founded New Market, 7; captain's commission, 7; moved to Millerstown, 7; occupations, 8; children born in Virginia, 8; bought land from father, 9; mortgaged land, 9; visited Watauga, 10; moved to Holston, 10; commissioner of Watauga association, 10; member of court, 10; at treaty with Indians, 11-12; obtained land from Robertson's lease, 12; signed Watauga petition to North Carolina, 13; delegate to provincial congress of North Carolina, 14; entry into state politics, 15; lieutenant-colonel of Washington District, 15; beginning of career as Indian fighter, 16; in fort at Watauga, 19; scout against Indians, 22; watched Tory activity, 22; departed from Holston, 223; built homestead, 23; clerk of Washington County, 23; Indian campaigns, 25-30, 33-6; raised men to aid Greene, 27-8; arrest

ordered, 32; elected to state senate, 32; position in militia questioned, 32-3; activities against Tories, 41-3; filed claims for Tory estates, 43; informed of Ferguson's campaign, 50-1; raised troops, 51; lead from mine used, 52; troops of captured Tory scouts, 54; in battle of King's Mountain, 54-6; opposed execution of Tories, 57; influence of King's Mountain on, 60; speculations in land, 61-2; charged with sharp land practices, 65, 77-8; land granted to prior to 1800, 67-70; interested in Muscle Shoals Company, 70; commissioner for county of Houston, 71; activities in Shoals Company, 71; relations to Franklin movement, 72-3; 87-8; turned to Spanish intrigue, 73, 95-6; interest in Yazoo Company, 74-5; engaged by O'Fallon, 76; governor of Franklin, 79-98; treaty with Cherokees, 89; feud with John Tipton, 91, 93-5, 98; arrest of, 97; escape of, 98; elected to North Carolina senate, 99; pardoned for share in Franklin movement, 99; assumed duties of brigadier, 100; member of ratification convention, 100; voted for convention, 100-01; in Congress, 101; diary record of experiences, 101-92, 182, 209, 216; opposed excise tax, 103; voted for bank bill, 104; voted on location of national capital, 104-95; opposed assumption of debts, 105; conduct in Congress, 106; voted for cession of 1789, 106; nominated brigadier by Blount, 109; member of Blount's council, 110; activities during territorial period, 116; first governor of Tennessee, 116-17; opposition encountered in election, 117; called special session of assembly, 118; problems as governor, 119; disputes in military elections, 120-24; action challenged by Jackson, 124; action concerning military land office, 124-27; copies of letters to Glasgow secured by Jackson, 128; promoted internal improvements, 128-29; interested in Muscle Shoals project, 129-30; defended Cox, 130; attitude toward Blount conspiracy, 130-31; appointed brigadier in provisional army (1798), 131-32; favored delay in running Holston line, 133; opposed Federal Indian policy, 134-37; sent Ore on mission to Cherokees, 138-39; appointed representatives to Indian conference, 139; negotiated treaty, 141; Indian policy as governor, 141-44; ended terms as governor, 144; commissioner to establish Virginia-Tennessee line, 144; in gubernatorial election of 1803, 145, 148; opposed by Jackson forces, 145-46; charged with illegal practices, 147; Jackson hoped to retire politically, 148; accused of fraud by Roane, 148-49; accusation of Jackson, 149-52; defense of, 152-53; elected governor, 155; attempt of Roane to force from office, 155; requested opportunity to defend self, 155-56; fraud charged by assembly committee, 156; charges against removed, 157; altercation with William Martin, 158; intervention of Jackson, 158; feud with Jackson, 169-86; letter to Robertson, 188; second series of administrations, 190; policies similar to those of first administrations, 190; criticism against in appointment of officers, 192-93; favored purchase of Louisiana, 194; settlement of land question, 195-97; relations with Indians, 197-99; disapproved of national bank, 200; retired as governor, 200; elected state senator, 200-01; appointed on committees, 201; elected to House of Representatives, 202; appointed on committees, 204; on reapportionment bill, 205; favored increase of army, 205-06; against tax on salt, 206;

INDEX 237

changed vote, 206; favored tax on carriages and bank notes, 206; favored war, 206; supported administration, 207; letter to Blount on affairs, 207-08; letter to Shelby, 208; respect of colleagues, 209; in Washington life, 209-10; personal appearance of, 213; family life of, 213; children of, 213n; religion of, 213-14; proposed cure for plague, 214-15; methods as politician, 215; appointed on Indian boundary commission, 215-16; last stroke at Jackson, 216; reëlected to Congress, 217; death of, 217; burial of in Alabama, 217; reinterment at Knoxville, 217

Sevier-Jackson feud, presented by Jackson's friends, 168; original cause of dispute unknown, 168; probable connection with first gubernatorial campaign, 169; early meetings of opponents, 170; possible confusions of accounts about, 170-71; quarrel in Nashville over military elections, 172-73; proposed meeting, 174; cordiality restored, 174; rivals for election as major-general, 175; open break, 175; meeting in Knoxville, 176-78; challenge to duel, 178; correspondence concerning duel, 178-82; Jackson's publication of Sevier, 182; meeting near Kingston, 182-84; publication by a Citizen of Knox County, 185-86; publication by an unnamed author, 186; friendly feelings never restored, 187

Sevier, Valentine (father of John), came to America, 5; settled in Shenandoah Valley, 5; married, 5; occupations, 5; interested in land, 6; member of militia, 6; gambler and drinker, 6; sold land to son, 9; made deed to Holsingers, 10; John lodged with, 102; death of, 189

Sevier, Valentine (brother of John), settled on Holston, 10

Sevier, Washington (son of John), with father at South West Point, 182; at encounter with Jackson, 183-84

Sevier, William (uncle of John), came to America, 5

Shelby, Evan, expedition against Cherokees, 21; joined army to aid Greene, 28; aid of requested against Ferguson, 50; joined McDowell, 50; joined Clarke's forces, 50; at Cedar Spring, 50; victory at Musgrove's Mill, 50; raised troops to meet Ferguson, 51; probably originated move to displace McDowell, 53; suggested tactics adopted at King's Mountain, 54; position of regiment at battle, 54; number of troops of, 56; opposed execution of Tories, 57; brigadier of Washington District, 92; Sevier appealed to, 92; succeeded by Martin, 95; letter from Sevier to, 208

Shenandoah Valley, Sevier settled in, 5; Indian outrages in, 5; a part of the frontier, 8; Sevier visited on way to New York, 102

Sherrill, Catherine, rescued from Indians, 19; second wife of John Sevier, 19; children of named, 213n

Smith, Daniel, secretary of territory, 34; attitude toward excise tax, 103; favored extreme measures against Indians, 114

Snipes, William Clay, member of original Yazoo Company, 75

South West Point, troops stationed at, 115; settlers obtained permits at, 137; meeting place with Cherokees, 139

Sparks, Richard, removes settlers from Indian lands, 135

Speculations, Sevier's in land, 67, 116; Sevier associated with Landon Carter in, 69-70; Muscle Shoals, 70-3; Yazoo, 73-7

Speculators, all frontiersmen were, 61; different types of, 61-2; Sevier a combination of types, 62; system of land grants favored, 65-6; cupidity of eastern, 80-1; opposed to cession of valuable lands, 81

Spencer, Judge, issued warrant for Sevier's arrest, 97
State debts, assumption of by United States, 102, 104-05
Steele, John, member of Congress from North Carolina, 105; agent of Blount, 108, 108-09n; member of commission for Cherokee treaty, 138
Stuart, James, representative at Cherokee conference, 139
Stuart, John, hated by settlers, 17; letters to British sympathisers, 17
Sullivan County, funds provided by entry-taker, 52
Sumner County, Sevier's land holdings in, 68; contest in military election in, 121
Sumter, Thomas, surprised by Tarleton, 48
Supernumeraries, issued by J. Armstrong, 64; Sevier and Carter located warrants as, 69-70
Sycamore Flats, rendezvous of militia at, 52; troops at, 56

Tarleton, General Banastre, surprised Sumter, 48; accepted report of Ferguson, 57; opinion on King's Mountain, 57-8, 57-8n
Tatum, Howell, seized papers in M. Armstrong's office, 125; ordered to withhold books from commissioners, 126
Taylor, Parmenas, member of Blount's council, 110
Tellico Blockhouse, troops at, 115; commissioners for Holston line met at, 133; Indians received inferior goods at, 140; conference with Cherokees held at, 140
Tellico Treaty, purchase of land by, 198
Tennessee, overlapping of jurisdiction with North Carolina, 108; constitutional convention called for, 111; details of first gubernatorial campaign, 117; organization of government of, 117-18; difficulties of securing admission into Union, 118; problems facing, 119; system of military election in, 120; disputes concerning military elections in, 121-24
Tennessee Assembly, question of land office papers before, 127; message to North Carolina concerning road, 129; expected to reimburse subscribers to road, 129; exonerated Cox, 130; petition to Federal government concerning removal of settlers, 136; committee appointed to investigate land office, 155; report of committee, 156-57; settled land question with North Carolina, 196-97; money from for Indian cessions, 198; message of appreciation to Sevier, 201-02
Tennessee Company, Cox and, 73
Tennessee *Gazette*, published Jackson's attack on Sevier, 149; published Sevier's defense, 152; published other articles, 154; published articles defending Sevier, 185-86; published answer, 186
Tennessee River Towns, campaign against, 27
Territory South of Ohio, Blount appointed governor of, 108; organized, 109-10; work of first legislature of, 110; extra session of legislature called, 110-11; remuneration of inhabitants in, 111; called state constitutional convention, 111
Tipton, John, candidate for North Carolina senate, 91; enmity toward Sevier, 91; seated in assembly, 92; refused seat in senate, 93; feud with Sevier, 93-5, 98; arrested Sevier, 97; allied with Jackson forces, 98; on petition to Jackson, 180
Tipton, Jonathan, in battle of Boyd's Creek, 26
Tipton, Samuel, on petition to Jackson, 180
Tories, fomented trouble on frontier, 22; activities in Washington County, 41; land of seized, 43; activities in other states, 43; bands in North and

INDEX 239

South Carolina, 46-7; flanking parties sent to rally, 49; bravery of at King's Mountain, 55; court-martial trials of, 57; discouraged by Ferguson's defeat, 58; Sevier appointed to receive property of, 161
Transylvania Company, Henderson's purchase for, 12
Treaties of Dewitt's Corner, 19; Long Island, 19, 20; Hard Labor, 40; Lochabar, 40; Dumplin Creek, 89; Hopewell, 90, 134; Holston, 132-33; Fort Jackson, 215

Van Dyke, Doctor, statement of meeting of Sevier and Jackson at Kingston, 183-84

Walker, Captain, commander of troops at Fort Decatur, 217
Walton, Jesse, in battle of Boyd's Creek, 26
Ward, Nancy, gave information to traders, 18
War of 1812, vote for, 206; favored by South and West, 206
Warrants, value of, 163
Washington County, created by North Carolina, 14; regiment of organized, 20; Sevier state senator from, 32; Tory activity in, 41-3; squatters in, 67; Campbell superior judge of, 93; special permission to elect representatives from, 101; confusion in caused by cession of 1789, 107; contest in military election in, 121
Washington, George, proclamation against Yazoo Company, 77; Sevier a disciple of, 105; appointed Blount governor of Territory South of the Ohio, 108; disapproved of appointments of Sevier and White as brigadiers, 132
Washington, Tom, member of original Yazoo Company, 74; basis of his claims, 74-5
Watauga, settlers thought they were in Virginia, 9; visited by Seviers, 10; John Sevier moved to, 10; Charles Robertson leased land on, 12; settlers on troubled by Indians, 16; settlers on angry at British for using Indian allies, 17; families in fort at, 19
Watauga Association, constitution for drawn up, 10; Charles Robertson leased land for, 12; asked to be incorporated in North Carolina, 13; request granted, and Washington County created, 14
Watts, John, leader of Cherokees, 28
Weir, Samuel, attitude toward Indians, 142
Wharton, J., account of meeting of Sevier and Jackson, 176-77
Whigs, opposed to Tories, 46; flanking parties sent to disperse, 49; forces at Green River, 53; marched to Cowpens, 54
Whitaker, A. P., summary of Spanish intrigue, 96-7
White, A., carried letter from Jackson to Sevier, 182
White, Doctor James, Gardoqui's agent, 95
White, General James, to receive report of election, 101; Blount's attitude toward Indians expressed to, 114; instructions of Blount to for Cherokee purchase, 115; Washington opposed to appointment as brigadier, 132; commanded requisitioned troops, 192
Wilkinson, James, in Yazoo speculation, 75-6; to command regiment at Natchez, 191
Williams, Colonel, forces of at King's Mountain, 54, 56
Williamson, Hugh, advocated cession of North Carolina lands (1782), 81; urged repeal of cession (1784), 85
Williamson, Colonel Andrew, led forces from South Carolina, 18
Winchester, James, candidate for brigadier, 123; elected, 124; appointed to run line of Holston treaty, 133; delayed meeting with commissioners, 133; election opposed by Sevier, 172; votes

in 1802 for, 175; raised troops in Mero, 191

Winn, Richard, Indian superintendent, 29; reports to Secretary Knox, 29-30; report of Indian campaigns, 31

Winston, Colonel, joined forces with militia, 52

Wood, John, received deed of gift from Choctaws, 74; no return from land sold to J. Cape, 75

Woodstock, called Millerstown, 7

Wynne, J. K., account of meeting of Sevier and Jackson, 158, 176-77

Xavier, family name of Sevier, 4

Xavier, Francis, probable relationship of Seviers to, 4n

Yazoo Company, Sevier interested in, 74; purpose of, 74; attempt of to consolidate with Virginia Company, 75; Wilkinson interested in, 75; John Holder to lead colony for, 76; O'Fallon agent for, 76; Sevier sub-agent for, 76

www.ingramcontent.com/pod-product-compliance
Lightning Source LLC
Chambersburg PA
CBHW021359290426
44108CB00010B/315